LLEWELLYN'S

COMPLETE DICTIONARY OF

DREAMS

ABOUT THE AUTHOR

Dr. Michael Lennox (Los Angeles, CA) is a practicing psychologist and one of the most respected and sought-after dream interpreters in the U.S. He has appeared on SyFy, MTV, NBC, and many radio shows, and has published articles in *Today's Woman*, *TV Guide*, *Star*, and other magazines. Visit him online at www.michaellennox.com.

COMPLETE DICTIONARY OF
DREAMS

**OVER 1,000 DREAM SYMBOLS AND
THEIR UNIVERSAL MEANINGS**

DR. MICHAEL LENNOX

Llewellyn Publications
Woodbury, Minnesota

FIRST EDITION
First Printing, 2015

Book design and format by Donna Burch-Brown
Cover design by Kevin R. Brown
Cover images: iStockphoto.com/27442703/©blueringmedia, iStockphoto.com/19573355/©RaStudio,
iStockphoto.com/6132056/©N_design, iStockphoto.com/22187717/©nahariyani,
iStockphoto.com/19803441/©payaercan, iStockphoto.com/22306566/©Justin Horrocks,
iStockphoto.com/24428852/©Yevgen_Lyashko, iStockphoto.com/10573601/©alexandercreative,
iStockphoto.com/18685926/©Electric_Crayon, iStockphoto.com/16502363/©LPETTET,
iStockphoto.com/9521111/©cyfrogclone

Dream Sight: A Dictionary and Guide for Interpreting Any Dream by Dr. Michael Lennox © 2011 Llewellyn Worldwide Ltd. 2143 Wooddale Drive, Woodbury, MN 55125. All rights reserved, used by permission.

Llewellyn Publications is a registered trademark of Llewellyn Worldwide Ltd.

Library of Congress Cataloging-in-Publication Data
Lennox, Michael, 1963–
  Llewellyn's complete dictionary of dreams : over 1,000 dream symbols and their universal meanings / by Dr. Michael Lennox.—first edition.
    pages cm
  Includes index.
  ISBN 978-0-7387-4146-8
  1. Dream interpretation—Dictionaries. 2. Dreams—Dictionaries. I. Title.
  BF1091.L528 2015
  154.6'303—dc23
                      2014047876

Llewellyn Worldwide Ltd. does not participate in, endorse, or have any authority or responsibility concerning private business transactions between our authors and the public.
  All mail addressed to the author is forwarded but the publisher cannot, unless specifically instructed by the author, give out an address or phone number.
  Any Internet references contained in this work are current at publication time, but the publisher cannot guarantee that a specific location will continue to be maintained. Please refer to the publisher's website for links to authors' websites and other sources.

Llewellyn Publications
A Division of Llewellyn Worldwide Ltd.
2143 Wooddale Drive
Woodbury, MN 55125-2989
www.llewellyn.com

Printed in the United States of America

OTHER BOOKS BY DR. MICHAEL LENNOX

Dream Sight: A Dictionary and Guide for Interpreting Any Dream
(Llewellyn Publications, 2011)

CONTENTS

INTRODUCTION

Dreams have been an important part of the human race since the beginning of civilization. When our predecessors sat around the fire and talked about the dream world, there emerged another dimension of reality, one that was peopled with animals and ancestors, evidence of what was later to be understood as the collective unconscious through which all humankind is connected. Even as science reveals more of the technical aspects of what happens in the brain during REM sleep, the sensation of the power of dreams to reveal more of the soul to the dreamer is unmistakable.

Though we are more disconnected from this soulful realm than ever before, through the dream world we find a profound connection to the self and therefore to all of humanity. On a personal level, anyone who has gazed into the mystery of a dream with a bit of reverence knows the value of such exploration. By understanding your dreams better, you gain a deeper understanding of yourself and the world around you.

Dreams are stories told in a language of symbols. To understand that language, you must go to the heart of the image itself. The universal meaning of any symbol is held within its use, its essence, its purpose, or its inherent qualities. Once you understand this relatively simple concept, every dream interpretation is simply a story about the story that the dream is telling. This dream dictionary is a comprehensive tool to assist you in this process. It can deepen your experience of knowledge and self-awareness by helping you understand what your dreams are trying to tell you.

I was first drawn to dreams as a very young boy. In fact, I can still remember a dream I had when I was just three years old. In a strange and empty landscape, I was aware that above me there was a realm that seemed impossibly large while I was simultaneously able to perceive a place that was infinitesimally smaller than the middle ground I inhabited. The greater part was the size of the universe itself and the smaller part was at the molecular level, though my very young mind could not really conceive of such constructs. As an adult, I now recognize this as a dream of infinity and have actually heard this exact same dream described by others. At the time, however, it was simply a captivating image that both exhilarated and terrified me. But more than that, I was acutely aware that this fantastically terrible place existed inside me, within the bounds of my own imagination.

As a teenager and by complete happenstance, I came upon a copy of Freud's seminal work *The Interpretation of Dreams*. Though it was a bit beyond my fifteen-year-old sensibilities, I was able to glean from his writing that dreams could indeed offer insights and hidden perspectives if they were explored. Social gatherings as a teenager gave me my first opportunities to give this notion a try. When friends would gleefully exclaim that they'd had a crazy dream, I would simply ask to hear the dream and then offer my intuitive response. Wide eyes and exclamations of fascination would follow. I kept doing this—thousands of times, in fact—over many years and developed what was ultimately an innate gift, which eventually led me to formal study and a doctorate in psychology.

The gift, however, is not what it seems, even if you ever have the chance to witness me interpreting a dream and you declare it to be something of note. Anyone can do what I do, and this book can assist you greatly in realizing your own abilities. My gift is not that I know such things, for we all have access to this knowledge through our humanity and the connection to the collective unconscious. My gift is that I can do this very, very fast.

My first book, *Dream Sight: A Dictionary and Guide for Interpreting Any Dream*, outlines this process in great detail and is more of a teaching tool designed to familiarize you with how to connect to the hidden knowledge of universal meaning. You may be interested in referencing this book for a more comprehensive dream interpretation experience, but all of the detailed terms from that book can be found in a simpler format within these pages as well, in addition to many more! *Llewellyn's Complete Dictionary of Dreams* contains more than 1,000 interpretations for various symbols that you are likely to encounter in your dreams. It is your go-to reference guide to help you decipher any dream by virtue of working with the symbols that it contains.

There are a few tenets of dream interpretation that you will need to know in order to use this dictionary effectively. The primary one is that there is no wrong way to interpret a dream. The meaning of a dream is deeply personal, and much depends on the dreamer and the sensation of the dream. Over time, the insight that a dream has to offer can even change and evolve. Most important to remember is that the dream itself has a consciousness of its own. Like an excited child discovering a new activity, it just wants to be seen and acknowledged. Simply thinking about a dream is enough to stimulate the unconscious mind to offer you more information to help you understand yourself better. The true value behind interpreting a dream for yourself is not in the final meaning you give to it but in the process of investigating it.

The second principle to be considered is embodied in how to approach the landscape of the dream world itself. Although dreams can mirror many aspects of your waking life, the most powerful way of working with them is to consider every element of the dream as a reflection of your own consciousness. In this way, every setting and activity that appears in a dream is a part of you, the dreamer. You can consider that your own consciousness is made up of many facets, and a dream is a symbolic glimpse into your inner world.

This approach comes right out of the work done in the late nineteenth century by noted psychologist Carl Jung, who is considered the father of modern dream work. It was Jung, a contemporary of Freud, who postulated the existence of the collective unconscious, a realm that connects all human beings to the same archetypal information no matter what culture or geography might separate them. In his travels, Jung discovered that his upper-class patients in Switzerland were having the same exact dreams as the natives in Africa he visited. Of course, the Swiss businessmen were more likely to be chased by bankers than tigers, but the themes were the same.

According to Jungian philosophy, the people in your dreams represent various aspects of yourself. I refer to these as "character aspects," where the waking-life qualities exhibited by the people represent those qualities as they live in you, the dreamer. This is reflected in many of the terms that you will find within these pages when the object of the term in question relates to a person or individual. This is referred to in different ways in various disciplines of dream work, but here you will find the term "character aspect." Every person who shows up in the dream world represents an aspect of your char-

acter and should be interpreted as such. As complex human beings, we often understand ourselves in this fractured way, as evidenced by the common phrase "part of me feels this way or that way." It is much like this in dreams, where distilled elements of your essential nature are best represented on a symbolic level by a particular person who may be known or unknown to you in your waking life.

You can practice this technique immediately by simply considering people you know and assigning them three adjectives that describe their personality. Perhaps your best friend is "warm," "gregarious," and "funny," or your boss is "controlling," "demanding," and "rigid." This is best done in a spontaneous manner, without thinking too much. The same approach would be applied to a dream. If your dream includes someone you know, use this three-adjective technique to describe the person and you will immediately have a sense of what this individual is representing as part of your dream landscape.

Here is an example of how this might work from an actual dream. A woman had a dream that her high school English teacher was floating above her in some strange setting; it was a disturbing experience and so the dream demanded her attention. When asked for three adjectives to describe the English teacher, the dreamer said "negative," "harsh," and "demanding." When asked about current stresses in her life, this dreamer told of an upcoming presentation she was required to do as part of her work, and given that she is uncomfortable with public speaking, she was quite worried about the upcoming task. It was easy for her to understand and even express to me how nervous she was, but it was by examining her teacher as a character aspect of herself that she was able to relieve some of her anxiety by understanding that she is her own worst critic.

The better you know someone from your life, the harder it may be to envision the person as operating as a part of your own personality. In these cases, it's best to attempt to stay very detached in your thinking. You might consider how someone else might describe such a person in order to reach a more objective sense of the individual as a character aspect of yourself.

Of course, the dream world is populated with many people you have never met before. When this is the case, use whatever information you have from the dream and any details you can remember about the person in it. The less stuff offered by the dream, the more work you will have to do to discover what character aspect might be represented by a stranger. Often, a stranger in a dream represents parts of your own psyche that you have yet to understand.

Sometimes this is not at all easy to do, especially if a character aspect represents elements of your personality that you don't readily relate to. I ran into this with a client who so resisted this idea that it took every ounce of my patience to guide her through the process. She was a woman in her late twenties who had a dream about an older female boss she had worked for many years prior to when she had the dream. When picking the three adjectives to describe this boss, she came up with "aggressive," "powerful," and "unethical." It was clear to me that the merciless boss-lady from the dream was a character aspect of the part of the dreamer that was also capable of being ruthless and unconcerned with the moral constructs of right and wrong.

In her waking life, this young woman certainly does her best to do the right thing in every situation and would hardly be considered ruthless. Ironically, while railing against the idea I was asking her to consider, she became quite ruthless in her defensiveness. She finally relented and understood what I was trying to convey when I explained to her that all things live inside of us, the good as well as the seemingly bad.

This does not mean that dreams do not also reflect the relationships you are engaged in with your family, friends, and acquaintances; they do. However, I work from the perspective that the best value to be gained from doing dream work is an investigation of the self. In this regard, working with every aspect of the dreaming landscape as a reflection of your own consciousness will reveal more of you to you. This does not negate the influence of your outer relationships impacting your dreaming life, but this dream dictionary is predicated upon working only from the perspective of what I call the "inner circle of interpretation," where everyone you find in your dream is a reflection of you.

The third element of dream work you need to be familiar with is what is known as the "shadow." The shadow is a term also coined by Jung, who recognized that there were many aspects of consciousness that people readily resisted. He described the shadow as a section of the unconscious mind. And as its name implies, it is home to all the elements of your personal humanity that are dark and frightening. It is where we hide the parts of ourselves that are distasteful, hated, rejected, disowned, and unacceptable. By burying these ideas deep within the hidden recesses of our minds, we are able to remain blind to them in our conscious awareness.

The basic idea behind this is that contained within everybody are all the potential expressions of the human condition. For example, murderous rage lives in us all. For the most part, not too many of us are actually going to ever act on those impulses. But by virtue of being human, every quality that can be expressed lives inside our psyches. And those qualities that are dangerous, shameful, and otherwise objectionable are housed in an area of the mind that keeps them safely out of view. That area is aptly named the shadow.

For the average person, an endless variety of dark, socially unacceptable emotions remain safely tucked away and never see the light of day outside of our dreams. By allowing them to reside in the shadow, we can be fully human but still function properly within society. However, in order to grow and expand in wisdom and consciousness, we must continually explore these dark, hidden realms in order to discover more of who we are. Dreams are perhaps the most important way in which this is done throughout life.

Nightmares and disturbing dreams are most likely emanating from the shadow. Those that take place at night or in dark landscapes are also likely to be shadow dreams. Anything in a dream that runs contrary to your nature or being, such as skin and hair color as well as gender, is also an indication that the shadow is being expressed. If a section of a dream features a dangerous, frightening, or mysterious occurrence, this too is likely to be a moment of the shadow calling to you.

Things that are within your conscious awareness have no difficulty being integrated into your sense of who you are. You discover something new and take it in, and your identity is expanded. When something is coming from the shadow, however, the process is confounded by fear and resistance. The material itself is made up of elements of your personality that you disown, and they are, therefore, more difficult to reconcile. Dreams are the best way to help release the grip of fear that can often hold you back in life. This happens by virtue of illuminating the places in your consciousness where that fear lives. The process is irrational and mysterious, but spending some quality time with your dreams can actually relieve some of the bondage that fear and inhibition can cause.

All dreams are valuable, but those that are dark and scary offer a particular opportunity. It is even possible that nightmares are scary so that they will be remembered more easily. The shadow in dreams points to the very place in the recesses of the unconscious that needs to be released in order for expansion and growth to occur. Once the fearful place has been identified, it is no longer in the shadow, and light fills the space that was once dark. This is how wisdom grows throughout life.

There are a few terms that are used throughout these pages that will be helpful for you to understand in order to put this dictionary to its best use. An "archetype" is a pattern of energy that comes together to form a single idea that is then represented by similar images. Consider the warrior as an archetype of power and aggression. The various forms the warrior archetype might take in our modern world include athletes and certain male movie stars. The same can be said of the archetype of love or compassion, mostly typified by female characters we find expressed over and over again in various media. These are just two simplistic examples of what an archetype is, and many of the terms in this book will refer to this concept. When an archetypal image is present in a dream, that dream is reflecting some of the foundational principles of consciousness that make up the human experience.

The two previous examples also illuminate another concept you will find repeated in the following pages. The idea of the "feminine principle" and "masculine principle" refers to the notion that almost all aspects of behavior and experience fall into one of two categories. This is not to be confused with male and female; this is not about gender or sexuality. The masculine principle refers to the concept of doing, taking action, and being decisive, while the feminine principle embodies the idea of being, creativity, nurturance, and receptivity. When the two are combined and in balance, we experience a sense of integration and wholeness. It is simplistic but not inaccurate to say that the entire point of doing dream work is to pursue this sense of integration and wholeness in our sense of self. Dreams, in fact, often emerge within our psyches to help us find and evolve toward this state. It is helpful then to understand that many images relate more definitively to one or the other of these two fundamental constructs, and you will find these terms throughout these pages.

Welcome to a new commitment to working with your dreams in a deeper and more meaningful way. While there truly is no one correct approach to interpreting your dreams, life has a way of pulling in the right and perfect guidance just when you need it. If you have been drawn to this particular dream dictionary, then it is the right one for you. If a dream is a story, then an interpretation is a story about the story. Use the terms within these pages to guide you and let your dreams speak powerfully as you tell yourself the story of you.

The Dream Dictionary

Abandonment: This is a dream that is reflecting your fears around self-worth. The fear of being left alone is primitive in nature and has its roots in infancy. If the loss resonates deeply enough, the emotional reaction taps into a deep reservoir of historical injuries and we experience it as a painful abandonment. Dreaming of a circumstance in which this is a primary theme is likely to be compensating for something in your waking life that is triggering thoughts of abandonment, whether consciously or unconsciously. By processing these feelings in the dream state, we are better prepared to face the world when we wake. Pay close attention to who is abandoning you in the dream, as this will factor powerfully into your interpretation.

Abdomen: This is the part of the body associated with your emotions and gut feelings about things. When this is featured in a dream, it is pointing to some sort of issue with trusting the guidance you get from your own instincts. If your abdomen is compromised in your dream, it could also be related to repressing or ignoring your gut feelings. The abdomen is also the part of the body associated with digestion and the taking in of nutrients and sustenance. As such, a dream focused on the abdomen may be a commentary on how well you are engaged in acts of self-care and feeling as if you are being well fed by your life.

Abortion: A fetus is a symbol for an idea, project, new direction, or creative impulse that has the potential to be born into form, but is still in gestation. An abortion is a choice to eradicate that possibility in order to make room for something new. This is a topic that has great charge in our world, so how you interpret this in a dream should reflect your personal viewpoint on the subject. However, from a purely symbolic perspective, the nature of an abortion relates to choosing to eliminate a course of action that you are not prepared to take responsibility for. (See *Fetus.*)

Abscess: The implication of an abscess is that there is an underlying problem that has not been attended to. Where on your body the abscess of your dream is appearing will give you clues as to where to look for the hidden issue. An abscess is an indication that something needs to be opened up so that the toxic emotions can be cleared out and the healing can begin.

Abyss: An abyss is created when the structure of a particular area is so out of reach, there is no immediate discernible sense of measurable boundaries. This fills us with anything from terror and dread to an excited desire for exploration. The bottomless pit of an abyss is a great symbol for the risks we must take in order to grow. When faced with an abyss in your dream, you have come to the edge of your known reality and are being asked to confront the unknown in a courageous way. The abyss is a symbol of the depths of your unconscious, which often inspires fear or avoidance.

Academy Awards: Any dream that involves celebrities or the milieu of the rich and famous connects you to that part of your consciousness that aspires to higher expression of your humanity. The world of films relates to your creative impulses, and the Academy Awards in a dream reveals a powerful desire to be recognized for your gifts and talents in a very public way. This may be an over-inflation of

self-worth to make up for feelings of inadequacy or a very real need to make yourself more visible in your world.

Accelerator: The accelerator in a car or other mechanism is the structure that is engineered to increase your speed and therefore get you to your desired goal that much faster. If one is featured in a dream, you may need to increase your efforts around a particular project. If the accelerator is broken or malfunctioning, you will need to do some more investigation to see why you are experiencing a block. Too much acceleration may indicate a need to slow down or back off the pressure to move too fast in some area of your life.

Accident: Remember the ubiquitous phrase "There are no accidents." An accident is an unintended and immediate course correction. When we are involved in an accident, the path we are on is instantaneously stopped and we are forced to consider new directions. There is often a good deal of damage control that needs to be done, and often the shift we are being asked to make is not of our own making. Remember, too, that the frustration and disappointment we often feel when an accident occurs is based on our added judgment that the accident was a bad thing or should not have happened. An accident in your dream could be a warning that where you are headed needs to be considered differently.

Acid: Acid causes corrosion by virtue of its ability to eat through many substances, causing chemical reactions that eradicate the structural integrity of the material being affected by it. In dreams, this is connected to the notion of certain feelings "eating away" at you, such as rage, envy, or hatred, or any deep feelings that are destructive if not kept in check. These feelings can burn when projected onto another individual.

Acorn: One of the most powerful symbols for potential, the acorn is a seed that can eventually grow into a mighty oak tree. In this way, it represents the ability to take a small idea and generate something great from it.

Acrobat: The acrobat can move gracefully through the air, which means this image is most associated with mental processes. Your ability to be agile with your thoughts, feelings, and movement through life is being highlighted, but especially your thoughts. Adobe Acrobat is also a well-known design program software, and therefore this dream image may be a pun on how you are taking charge of designing your life to suit your desires.

Actor: An actor can take on many personas and inhabit something that is not real as if it were true. You may be taking on different roles in your life and are dealing with being different people in different circumstances. This dream may also suggest a need to be more authentic and integrated.

Acupuncture: This ancient healing modality takes into consideration the grid of energy channels, known as meridians, that run throughout the physical body. This image in a dream indicates that some sort of healing is either occurring or is needed.

Addict: This is a character aspect of your personality that is aligned with escapism and being out of control. The state of the addict in your dream will determine how serious this impulse is and what damage it may be doing.

Affair: See *Infidelity*.

Age: Dreams often return us to our past. In some cases we are witnessing a past setting from our current life perspective, while other dreams of this type may find us transformed back into the person we were at the time and in the specific surroundings we are visiting. No matter what the actual structure of the dream, anytime we return to earlier moments in life, we are exploring who we are today as a result of our past. The age of someone who appears in a dream may also relate to the amount of time that particular consciousness has been alive in you. For example, a five-year-old child may represent something that emerged into your awareness five years before you had the dream.

Air Conditioning: Temperature is symbolic of mood and the escalation or decreasing of emotional intensity. Hot weather is synonymous with hot tempers and the prevalence of passion. The desire to cool the air by artificial means is symbolic of your ability to regulate such elements of life at your own whim. The larger the air-conditioning unit, the greater the sense of control that is being expressed. In this way, a window unit is reflecting a modicum of control, whereas central air relates to a more comprehensive desire to rein in your passions. If the air conditioning is broken, such a dream relates to the inability to keep cool under pressure.

Airplane: This dream means that you are experiencing some sort of transition in your life that is happening very fast. Any means of transportation in a dream is synonymous with the way we move through our lives. Because of the dramatic way an airplane leaves the ground and speeds you to your destination, it is connected with any sudden transition in life. In a dream, changes of this nature can connect either to something that is taking place in your life at the moment or to one that is needed or wished for. What happens to the plane offers more distinctions to add to your interpretation: Missing your plane could indicate a sense that something is passing you by and may illuminate a need to take stock of how aware you are of the opportunities in your current situation. Being stuck on a plane might connect to feelings of impatience and the need to accept external limitations. A plane crash indicates that something in process may not have been working properly and will have to start over. Take a look at the areas in your life that are stagnant or erupting—you may need to fasten your seat belt and take off.

Alarm Clock: This mechanism for timing your wakefulness relates to control and preparedness. Since there is often a great deal of anxiety around being on time for important events, this object in a dream may point to a desire to make absolutely sure you are ready for the things that need your attention.

Alcohol: See *Drinks/Drinking*.

Alien: Everyone in your dream is a part of your own consciousness, and an alien is a character aspect that is utterly foreign to you. This may connect to a higher, more spiritual side of you, but it could also be something that is new and different and therefore threatening. Your personal associations with outer space and aliens must feature in the interpretation you make of such a dream. Abduction by aliens might be revealing fears about unfamiliar territory or new environments in which you may be finding yourself. The more fear you feel in the dream, the more frightened you may be of the changes that are occurring. On the other side of this equation, feeling an affinity toward an alien and actually wanting to make a connection may indicate a desire to break out of a constricting mold of sameness.

Alligator: All reptiles connect with a primitive orientation toward survival and other basic instincts. Since alligators are water dwellers, their meaning and power are associated with emotional territory. They have a level of ferocity, so they also connect with scary and dangerous feelings that live just below the surface of consciousness. When dreaming of alligators, you are connecting with the power to protect yourself by lying in wait. The flip side to this is being vulnerable to your own reactivity when matters of emotional vulnerability are present. Alligators relate to precision and control in all states. Alligators and crocodiles are often confused, but the symbolic meaning is essentially the same for both.

Alternate Universe: The landscape of your dream world has a consciousness all its own, and it is not uncommon for individuals to dream frequently of alternate universes. In fact, dreams by definition take us to an alternate-universe consciousness. This is one of those enigmatic dream symbols where the universal meaning is literal. The landscape of any dream is an alternate universe of sorts. If you have the sense that your dream is taking place in some other reality than the one you reside in, the first consideration will be to take in the theme and interpretation you are assigning the entire dream as a whole. If the dream has a positive and uplifting feeling to it, the alternate universe may simply be a function of your unconscious being creative and expansive. However, there may be an element of wish fulfillment or denial being expressed. Creating an alternative universe might be a simplistic and convenient way of escaping the challenges that are present in the universe you call home.

Aluminum Foil: We use aluminum foil to wrap a perishable item and preserve it, so a dream with this object in it relates to that which you may be keeping wrapped up inside your consciousness. This may or may not be of value to you; wrapping something precious will keep it preserved for a longer period of time, while keeping something under wraps may indicate that some idea or feeling may be better off if it were unwrapped. Aluminum foil is also used to increase heat around food for efficiency in the cooking process. In this way, it represents the enhancement of your ability to take in nurturance and sustenance and engage in self-care.

Ambulance: The ambulance is a vehicle and as such relates to how you are moving through your life. Since it specifically connects to injury and illness as a rapid transport toward healing, it has this sense of rescue at the heart of it as a symbol. Given that there is a siren associated with an ambulance, in a dream it may also operate as evidence that something has occurred in your inner landscape that reflects danger or breakdown, the details of which may be unknown to you at the time.

Amethyst: Amethyst has a violet color, which associates it with the seventh chakra of higher consciousness. In the world of crystals, it has properties thought to be associated with healing, protection, and wisdom. (See *Stones, Boulders/Rocks*.)

Amputations/Missing Limbs: This is a dream about diminished capacity or ability. Our limbs are what give us mobility and the dexterity with which to create, both of which are impacted in some way when we lose a limb. Whether it is as significant as an entire arm or leg or just the smallest finger or toe, the appearance of a missing limb or amputation in a dream is reflecting some sort of invasion of your ability to navigate through life. Consider the use of the limb that is missing and you will have more information to interpret.

Anchor: An anchor connects to traversing water and in this way relates to some emotional experience you are having. It is designed to keep you steady and in once place in an atmosphere that is not naturally conducive to feeling grounded and stable. Therefore, in a dream an anchor represents this need or desire to stay put while some emotional process is underway. This image in a dream could be working to your benefit or your detriment, so you must determine whether the anchor is helping you stay focused on something that needs your attention or whether you are being held back and are unable to move forward because of a wound or a sense of grief.

Angel: Angels are major archetypal energies that were here before us. Over many thousands of years, humankind has formulated these huge energetic sensations into specific beings that appear in many religious and spiritual disciplines. These beings can appear in dreams and are evidence of a highly evolved moment in your spiritual development. Angels are also symbolic of divine intervention in process, where miraculous turns of events can occur through being guarded from a high level.

Animals: We think of animals as having intelligence that is basically instinctive. In this way, dreams that feature animals are helping us tap into our own instinctual nature. The first element of any interpretation of an animal that appears in your dream is to investigate the special trait that the particular animal represents. You will find many such interpretations within these pages, but a little research will yield great results if your dream animal is not listed. The animal's behaviors and habits will illustrate the instinct that is being highlighted. The second facet of your interpretation will come from what the animal is doing in your dream. The activity it is engaged in will correlate with some type of movement (or obstacle to movement) in your waking life. The dream may be asking you to stop trying to think your way through a situation and instead turn to your instinctive nature for an answer.

Ant: The ubiquitous ant is generally the smallest creature we think about on any regular basis. As such, ants represent our thoughts that are running their course at the very bottom of our consciousness. All animals in the dreamscape relate to instincts and thought patterns. The sheer number of ants in a colony and the supremacy of their organization connect them to anxiety and pervasive thoughts that crawl along the bottom of our consciousness and can irritate us and cause distress.

Anteater: The consciousness of the anteater is to consume and live off of very tiny pieces of sustenance. Ants relate to anxiety, and therefore the anteater is that which feeds off of pervasive anxious thoughts. A dream with an anteater is about perpetuating such states.

Apple: An apple has many possible symbolic meanings. Though not necessarily about money, an apple in a dream is a symbol of abundance and prosperity. There is a connection to health through the oft-used saying "An apple a day keeps the doctor away." The apple in your dream may also be associated with temptation from the mythology of the Garden of Eden and its use to tempt Adam and Eve. But remember, the apple is also connected to wisdom, as it is the fruit on the tree of life from the same mythology.

Arrow: As a symbol, an arrow has two meanings, one connected to aim and the other to how the arrow lands. You place an arrow where you desire with focus and intention, and in this way an arrow represents your ability to do so with a thought or an idea. On the connection side of the equation, an arrow relates to being penetrated by such an idea. If you are shooting the arrows, the dream is about your desire to focus an idea and have it land somewhere powerful. If you are struck by an arrow, the dream is about a sudden idea taking hold of you.

Art: A piece of art is an encapsulation of a previous experience that was creative and vibrant. Art might relate to memories of past expressiveness or passion. If the work of art is in progress, then some aspect of your creative expression is incomplete and wants your attention.

Art Gallery: A dream that takes place in an art gallery represents the place in your consciousness where you present your creative impulses to the world. Such a dream connects with the finished product as opposed to your creative process.

Artist: An artist in your dream represents an aspect of your own personality that is creative and expressive. What the artist is doing will relate to the ways in which your unconscious wants you to express yourself in your waking life. If the dream features behavior that is excessive or dangerous, you may be engaging in patterns in your waking life that are not serving you by being too impulsive. Consider the media that the artist works in as well. A sculptor is more grounded and earthy, whereas a painter is more connected to passion. A performance artist is more aligned with acting out behaviors.

Ashes: The presence of ashes implies that there has recently been a fire of some sort. Fire represents change and transformation on an intense level. Therefore, ashes in a dream may mean that some sort of great change has recently taken place. Often ashes are thought of as the grief associated with things that have changed against our desires, as in something being "reduced to ashes." Ashes are also the stuff out of which rises the Phoenix, so be aware that such a dream may portend the new beginnings that are just ahead after the termination of an old, outdated cycle, habit, or pattern.

Attic: The highest floor of any house corresponds to intellect and thoughts. Attics are often used for storage. In this way, they represent memories, information, and knowledge that accumulate over the course of our lives. The state of the attic in your dream will illuminate your current relationship with your thoughts and memories. Exploring any part of a house symbolizes an exploration of yourself. An attic indicates that your journey is taking you back to thoughts based on your past.

Aunt: All people in your dream represent aspects of yourself. An aunt connects to family history as it relates to the previous generation, and so she will have a loose connection to a life view generated by your parents. The fact that she is a sibling to one of your parents allows you to see the influence of the generational dynamic without the direct challenges of the child/parent relationship. An aunt of yours appearing in a dream is asking you to consider how some waking-life issue relates to family history and patterns. (See *Family*.)

Aura: An aura is the energy field that surrounds any living being and is the evidence of the higher self and the spiritual side of human nature. If you are seeing auras in your dream, you are connecting to this aspect of yourself and there may be an increase of your intuition occurring. If you perceive your own aura in a dream, this may be a moment in your life when the answers you seek ought to be of a spiritual nature. Since colors are an intrinsic part of how an aura is expressed, consider this as part of your interpretation. (See *Colors*.)

Automobile: *See Car.*

Baby: A baby is a new idea, relationship, event, direction, project, etc. The essential meaning of a baby as a symbol connects to the new life it represents. Babies grow up to become adult human beings, but in their infancy, they embody all the potential that has yet to be expressed. In this way, a baby in a dream is likely to be expressing some new chapter in your life that is just beginning and has yet to unfold into full manifestation. The age of the baby may give clues as to when the consciousness that it represents was born. A one-year-old baby may indicate a new shift in your life that began a year before you had the dream.

Backpack: Anything that allows you to pack certain items for transport is symbolic of having access to various tools for living. A backpack puts such helpful items easily at your disposal, with the implication of a journey on foot. Such a journey is symbolic of a trek into deeper places of your consciousness, and therefore the backpack is symbolic of the assistance you may need along the way.

Badger: The badger is a creature of the earth, so its power connects primarily to its ability to maneuver below the surface of consciousness. Badgers are tenacious burrowers, so part of their medicine is the ability to get to the bottom of things and keep going till a desired end is achieved. When a badger appears in a dream, it is time to get busy.

Bag: The interpretation of the image of a bag is directly connected to what is held by it. At the heart of it, a bag represents your ability to carry some object or objects with you. If you know what is inside the bag in your dream, use that to form your interpretation; in this case, the bag represents your access to the function of those objects and their potential use to you. If you do not know what is inside the bag, consider that any bag can hold the mysterious and perfect thing you may need at just the right moment. The structure of the bag may offer information about how strong your ability is to have resources nearby. A paper bag will not last as long as one made of leather. (See *Luggage*.)

Ball: The sphere is the purest shape that is easily understandable by the human mind. Anything round calls into consciousness this fundamental geometry that mirrors the globe of the Earth we call home and therefore symbolizes a sense of wholeness and integration. In the case of a ball, your dream may be connecting to a more playful part of your nature. A ball that implies a game ought to be played may be calling you to action, to participate more actively in the game of life. Balls can also relate to the testicles and symbolize masculine power and are more likely in a dream to be pointing to the masculine principle of doing things and taking action.

Ballerina: Dancing can be a metaphor for how we navigate life's complexities, and a ballerina is an example of supreme skill at this endeavor. The ballerina as a character aspect implies that a great deal of discipline has already been exerted, though the dream may be telling you to get hard at work at the skills needed to exhibit more grace in complicated scenarios in your current life experiences.

Banana: Any food is connected to self-care and nurturance, and a banana's nutritional value makes it almost a perfect food. Dreaming of eating a banana may point to a need or desire to increase your energy and strength. However, a banana has an additional meaning. The phallic shape of the banana brings an element of sexuality into the mix.

Bank: Thoughts around money, power, and financial security are coming up for you. A bank is a construct of modern society created around the concept of protecting the abundance of the average individual. When examined more closely under the scrutiny of symbolic meaning, a bank connects more to fears around money and the desire to hoard abundance to maintain a sense of security about future needs. You may be concerned with keeping your sense of prosperity safe and guarded.

Bar: You may be expressing a desire to escape your current stressful experiences if you have a dream that takes place in a bar. The primary focus of a bar is to consume alcohol, and thereby this symbol connects primarily to escapism. Because a bar is a public place and is rooted in the spirit of socializing, there is a second layer of meaning that connects with how we are interacting in our social environments in a spirited and uninhibited way. Your own personal relationship to bars and alcohol in your waking life will play a prominent role in how you would interpret a dream that took place in one.

Barefoot: You need to be more grounded in your life and experience a level of vulnerability around immediate choices in life. Feet connect to how grounded you feel. They can also indicate issues around how you are maneuvering through your current life choices. There is a direct connection between where you put your feet and where you go. If your feet are exposed to the elements, it leaves them vulnerable to injury, but can also help connect you more organically to the ground beneath your feet. This image also connotes feeling more down-to-earth and implies being laid-back and relaxed.

Barn: A barn is a building and in its essence is connected to some construct of your consciousness. Since a barn is found on a farm, there is an organic sensibility to its meaning. In waking life, a barn can have many functions, but it is generally used for the storage and housing of crops and livestock, both of which are deeply associated with sustenance, nurturance, and self-care. A barn in a dream is calling you to pay attention to grounded and down-to-earth matters, getting back to basics. The resources you need right now are natural and organic.

Bartender: As a person, a bartender is a character aspect of your own personality. As the keeper of the liquor, this is the part of you that has access to the desire to medicate against difficult feelings or stress. Your relationship to this person in your dream is asking you to examine your relationship to escapism.

Baseball: Life is a game, and a dream that features baseball is asking you to recognize this. Hitting a home run in baseball has entered the zeitgeist as a standard expression to represent a successful endeavor, such that baseball in a dream may connect to such a desired outcome in a future event in your waking life. There are a number of sexual connotations connected to baseball, including the phallic shape of the baseball bat. Also, getting around the bases has long been analogous to various elements of foreplay. "Playing the field" is a phrase connected to being sexually active with a variety of partners. Consider your dream's context in order to understand how to interpret a dream with baseball in it.

Basement: A dream about the basement is connecting you to deep secrets, hidden or unconscious thoughts. A house represents the self, and therefore the basement would be the *self below the self*. As such, any dream of a basement connects with unconscious material and anything that lurks below the surface of your psyche. Since many basements are dark and gloomy, they can have an aura of menace about them. This notion is exploited in the media—such as scary basements in films where no one escapes unharmed—making the symbolic meaning of this image connect to the shadow and those things we are afraid of in life.

Basket: A basket is a container, and the purpose it exhibits is the essence of the symbolic meaning. When you put things in a basket, you are more able to take them with you. In this way, a basket is a symbol of organization and efficacy around keeping with you what you desire. In a dream, a basket is asking you to consider how well you are able to contain all that you need. There is also an implication with this image that something will be or has been transported.

Bass: This musical instrument is responsible for keeping rhythm by expressing the lowest notes of the audible sound waves. Any musical instrument is ultimately a symbol related to the desire to be creative and expressive. However, the distinctions of the bass connect it to the grounded rhythms of life. When a bass is featured in your dream, you are being called to express yourself, but to honor the organic rhythm and not move too fast or too slow. Listen to your heart beat.

Bat: You are exploring the darker, more hidden side of your nature. The bat is capable of navigating through the night and without the benefit of sighted vision; as such, the bat represents your consciousness of what can be found when you trust the darker side of your nature. In dreams, the shadow (as represented by nighttime) is the most valuable area for truly understanding who you are, so the presence of a bat in your dreams indicates that this exploration is getting assistance from the unknown.

Bathing Suit: At the heart of it, the bathing suit is about modesty. The very act of swimming, immersing oneself in water for sheer pleasure, brings with it a likelihood of nakedness. Culturally, however, we are compelled to cover up. In this way, a bathing suit is a symbol of that modesty and the desire to keep a certain amount of protection. There is also an implication associated with this symbol of a connection to water that may not be present in the dream itself. If you are wearing a bathing suit, then you have in the past or may in the future connect yourself to water, the ultimate symbol of emotional expression.

Bathroom: A bathroom represents the consciousness of individuation and privacy. It is the room where we get to shut the door and be with ourselves in total intimacy. It is also a symbol of freeing ourselves of waste and toxins. Many dreams that feature a bathroom find us searching for one. Such a dream is about searching for the freedom to be our authentic self, often with the caveat of reaching that authenticity by releasing that which no longer serves us or is detrimental if we continue to hold on, such as resentment or other poisonous thoughts. A bathroom inside a home connects with personal issues, whereas one that is more public is revealing information about your outside interactions. A toilet is located in a bathroom. As such, it can relate to relieving yourself of the "shit" in your life that you no longer need.

Bathtub: The bathtub is used for relaxation as much as for cleansing the body. In this way, it can symbolically connect to either, depending on your personal associations with it. From a structural standpoint, because a bathtub contains a small amount of water, it is also an emotional symbol and should be considered from the perspective of containing small amounts of emotional expression that can either relax you or overwhelm you, depending on the dream context.

Battery: The primary purpose of a battery lies in its capacity to store energy for use at a later time and in a way that is portable. In this way, if a battery appears in a dream, it may connect to a need or desire to conserve your energy for use at a different time. A battery is also symbolic of the ability to bring energy to places that might otherwise be lacking it.

Battle: There is a distinction between war and battle. War implies an ongoing state of flux, whereas battle is the actual shift taking place in a small increment of upheaval and change as part of an ongoing period of transformation. If you dream of being in a battle, look to where in life your defenses might be running on high. Also consider where changes in boundaries are imminent, both in your outside world as well as within, as many battles are with yourself.

Beach: Land represents your conscious mind, and the ocean connects to your unconscious mind. Where these two forces meet is the ever-shifting shoreline. A dream that takes place on a beach indicates the meeting up of these two vastly different elements of the human experience. You can also think of the land as your rational, thinking mind and the ocean as the irrational, creative mind. The changing tides are your emotional moods and fluctuating cycles of expression, so a beach dream can connect to extremes of emotional change in your life. The sandy edges are the parts of your conscious awareness that are constantly changing shape as you learn more about who you are. The things that wash up on a beach are the repositories for that which was previously unknown to you but can appear suddenly from the depths of your hidden self. Anything that happens in a dream on a beach is to be considered even more significant because of the symbolic nature of the beach as the mysterious place where that which is conscious and that which is unconscious come together. Of course the beach is a primary destination for people to relax and let go of daily stressors. A dream that takes place at a beach may be connected to this desire.

Beams of Light: You are focusing your thoughts to create more penetrating energy in your life. Light is energy in motion. We generally think of it in terms of that which illuminates and makes things visible. However, light is actually a wave of energy, only a small fraction of which is visible to the human eye. In this way, the light we can see represents thoughts we are conscious of. Various forms of light can represent different levels and intensities of thought. A beam is a focus of light that has the ability to illuminate a particular area or object and is therefore symbolic of concentrated thought.

Bear: You need to be patient and conserve your strength for now; the time to act will come after a period of hibernation. Bear medicine is about the long stillness that is necessary in order for true strength to be wielded appropriately. When the time to act comes, the power of the bear in you will give you incredible resources. A dream with a bear in it is asking you to consider whether it is time for aggression or time to retreat and wait for the right season.

Beard: A beard is generally worn by older men and is a symbol of age and intelligence. In this way, a beard in a dream can be a symbolic expression of maturity and wisdom. A beard also blocks much of the face and in this way can connect to a desire to hide your true feelings.

Beast: The generic beast of the dream world is expressing the more animalistic aspect of the human condition. Since a specific Earth-dwelling animal will carry with it the meaning associated with its very nature, the beast as an archetype connects with the shadow side of this—the irrational, aggressive, and instinctive elements of who we are that we disown or prefer weren't so. Remember the fairy tale *Beauty and the Beast*, as these two opposing archetypes must be integrated in order to find balance and true happiness. It is very important to honor the beast within you in order to find your own true humanity.

Beast/Human: When the qualities of an animal are mixed with a human being, you are expressing the integration of primitive traits into your consciousness. Mythology is filled with creatures that combine physical attributes of various animals and the human body. These magical man-beasts appear in many cultural histories, and even the most bizarre dream-related combination may actually have a predecessor in the mythology of an ancient civilization. The interpretation of this symbol should start with the energy associated with the animal that appeared in the dream. Examining historical references that match your dream image can yield a treasure trove of information that your unconscious mind is attempting to convey to you.

Beaver: The beaver is industrious and skilled in a way that relates to working with earthly structures to create a watery home. This puts it in a symbolic relationship with the management of emotions. Many animals that relate to water also connect to our dream states, especially when a land animal interacts well with a watery environment. Thus, the beaver is present to bring you wisdom from the dream state. The beaver also assists us when we need to make sense of our emotional life and shift how we are feeling about some situation.

Bed: This object is the home of both sleep and intimacy. It is a powerful symbol of the sacred acts of rest and sexual expression. Many dreams take place in the bed in which you are sleeping. When that is the case, there is immediacy to the experience of interpretation; you are dreaming of your current state of consciousness and the actual idea of exploring that state in a significant way. The bed is a symbol of personal security since you are so vulnerable when sleeping, and in this way your own bed in a dream represents this safety. Conversely, a strange bed can be symbolic of a fundamental lack of safety. The state of a bed in a dream may be a comment on matters of security, sexuality, and restfulness in your waking life.

Bedroom: A home represents the consciousness of your sense of self and the bedroom relates to privacy and intimacy, as it's usually the most private room in one's home, where intimate acts occur. Because of its association with nakedness, sex, and the vulnerability that comes with being asleep, the bedroom represents the parts of ourselves that we are aware of but generally keep hidden and separate from our social and public life. On a primal level, the bedroom is the one room in a home where an individual's scent is most prevalent. We humans are the only animals that compulsively remove our own scent. This deepens the personal nature of this symbol.

Bee: One of the most communal of all animals, the bee is a master at communication and community organization. Through a complex societal structure, bees produce one of nature's most exquisite creations: honey. The medicine that bees offer as a totem connects to this precise, organized structure that they create combined with the effort they expend in creating something so profoundly sweet. When the bee appears in your dream, you are being asked to deepen your willingness to work in a structured manner in order to create enormous levels of abundance and prosperity.

Beehive: The bee is an animal that is associated with organization, communication, and the power to create great abundance and sweetness. Their home, or hive, is the central locus of this ability. The beehive in your dream is the home for your thoughts about the sweetness of life, but approaching it with too cavalier an attitude can have consequences.

Beer: Ultimately a symbol of escapism, beer can also be thought of as representing the desire to celebrate, kick back, and relax. Beer is the original fermented beverage and connects to processes that happen behind the scenes and slowly change and transform into something surprising and delightful. Good things take time, and this hidden meaning may be expressed in a dream about beer, especially if the dream includes the process of making this beverage.

Being Chased: Something in your life is creating a fear-based response to a threat. That threat may be real or imagined. When a person feels exposed at a very primal level, the built-in survival mechanism of the fight-or-flight response occurs. You may be running in terror without knowing that the secret enemy you are running from is yourself. If

you do not know your assailant, it may simply be you trying to catch up to you with something important that, if embraced, would allow you to feel more complete. If you know who is chasing you, the person may have more to offer you if you let him or her catch you. Even if being caught ends in being killed, that death could be a symbolic transformation of such significance as to be the very thing needed to bring your greatest heart's desires into reality. That is, of course, if you have the courage to stop running and turn around. Sometimes it is part of human nature to be afraid of success, and a dream of being chased is alerting you to stop running from your own magnificence.

Belly: Your instincts and emotions are being expressed by this dream. It is in our belly that we experience our feelings and our gut instincts about what is happening inside us and in our environment. When this is working well, the relationship you have with your belly is your great ally in navigating the world and knowing if you are safe in any given moment. When the belly is compromised, such as being layered in fat, it is your instincts that are being blocked. If you are sick in the belly, there are consequences for past inauthenticity or holding back anger, rage, or sadness.

Bellybutton: The bellybutton is proof of your humanity, the constant connection to multigenerational continuity. It is through the bellybutton that we are forever connected to our mothers and therefore back into time and to infinity. This is the part of the body that remains as proof that we once lived in a state of grace where every need was met at the instant of the thought of desire; the womb is the closest we will ever come to the Garden of Eden. Consider the context in which you are dreaming of this part of the body for a more detailed interpretation of your dream. Your own bellybutton relates to your own personal sense of connectedness and continuity. If the bellybutton in your dream is on another person, consider the character aspects of that individual as your focal point for the connectedness you are searching for.

Belt: A belt is designed to hold up the pair of pants that it is wound through. In this functional way, a belt is a symbol of support. However, belts can also be used to adorn and express, which adds a creative flair to the symbolic meaning they possess. If a belt is too tight, the constriction that results is also a symbol for limitation and feelings of restriction.

Bible: The Bible is a fundamental symbol of the word of the Divine made manifest here on Earth. Your relationship to this as a symbol must be rooted in your personal associations with it. This can be complicated, because for some the Bible is uplifting and powerful, while for others it is a powerful tool used to inflict hatred and separation. As a book, the Bible relates to thoughts that are made permanent and a part of the foundations of your beliefs. Add to this your personal associations and you may arrive at a satisfying interpretation.

Bicycle: Any mode of transportation is about how you are moving through your life. In the case of a bicycle, the speed is fairly close to being on foot, but certainly faster. There is an element of joy to a bicycle as well as the requirement of balance in order to get around effectively. Such a dream may be a throwback to a childhood sensibility unless you are an avid cyclist, in which case the dream may be about the desire to enjoy what that pastime brings you. A dream of a bicycle is about moving a little faster, but still in an organic way.

Bills: You are considering the cost of the freedoms that you enjoy. There is a price to pay for every choice we make, and bills connect to the sense of responsibility that comes with that freedom. If you are overwhelmed with your own finances in your waking life, you may dream about your bills as a result of that stress. If you are paying your bills, you are dreaming of taking responsibility for your choices. If you are avoiding paying your bills, your dream may be expressing your avoidance. If the bill you are shown in your dream does not belong to you, you may be feeling responsible for something that is not of your own making.

Birds: Birds are messengers, and a dream with birds in it may be trying to get you to recognize some information that is flying around in your consciousness, just waiting to be recognized. Birds also connect with a vantage point and the ability to see farther by virtue of their unobstructed view of things. They can also fly directly to a location without the impediments of obstacles on the ground. A dream with a bird or birds in it may be asking you what you would see if you could see farther than your limited viewpoint allows and where you would go if you weren't hindered by perceived obstacles in front of you. The type of bird will have additional meaning for you.

Birthday: This milestone marker is something everyone has each year, and it comes with a variety of strong feelings. Your personal associations with your own birthday must be considered in interpreting a dream that has a birthday in it, especially if it is your own. Such a dream may reflect feelings you have about aging. If the dream birthday celebration is for someone else in the dream, consider this to be an anniversary marker of an ongoing cycle as it relates to the quality of your personality assigned to the person whose birthday it is.

Black: The darker sides of life connect with the color black. Though it is thought of as the absence of color to some, in the world of physics, black is actually the presence of all colors in the object that embodies it. It is the color that absorbs the most light, retains heat, and is associated with death, as it is the opposite of life-affirming white. As the color of mourning, black clothing represents the social construct of receiving consolation in some cultures. When we are in mourning, we are surrounded by people who share in our sadness. In the same way that a black shirt will absorb all wavelengths of sunlight, a person in mourning wears black in order to absorb the light from those who surround him or her. In the world of fashion, black has a connotation of being trendy and sophisticated. Nighttime is when blackness reigns, bringing secrecy and the ability to hide into this color's symbolic meaning.

Blanket: A blanket protects against cold and offers comfort, and is most associated with bed and sleeping. As such, its primary symbolic meaning connects with being able to offer us these two fundamental qualities. A blanket that falls short of this by being too small or worn out reflects an inability to comfort yourself in times of stress.

Blind/Blindness: You may be unable or unwilling to see something clearly in your life. By dreaming of the inability to see, you may be expressing areas in your life that you may be blind to. We also use the term *vision* to express where we see our lives heading in terms of goals and desires. If you are experiencing a loss of vision in your dream, you may be expressing an unconscious fear of being unable to see what is coming next in your life. Consider that a person who is blind represents limited sight but also the increase of other senses, especially intuition. Being unable to see exactly how things are going to manifest is often the very ingredient necessary for them to do so. Blind faith is one of the most powerful energies there is. (See *Disability*.)

Blood: You may be connecting to a deeper sense of life force within you and an expression of passion for living. However, depending on how the blood is appearing in your dream, this could be a dream about the loss of such passion and energy. If your dream includes receiving or losing blood, this may reflect a message that you either are in need of more energy or are being depleted by some situation. A wound inflicted by another may reflect an external struggle, whereas a medical procedure connects more to an internal process necessary for healing.

Blue: Blue is the color of communication and connects to the body through the throat and the thyroid gland. There is a connection between our metabolic activity, which is regulated by the thyroid, and the effectiveness of our communication. Through our voice, we communicate with others, but it is through our energy levels that we commune with our immediate environments. Other communication concepts associated with this color are the blueprints that communicate the structure of something not yet created. The call of a hospital emergency is known as a "code blue." Before a brochure or magazine page is printed, the early version used to finalize the design and layout is known as the "blue line." When blood circulation diminishes due to a drop in body temperature, the lips will turn blue and communication will be hindered. These are but a few examples that may not relate to a specific image; however, when the color blue is prominent in your dream, incorporate issues of communication into your interpretation. (See *Colors*.)

Blue Jay: All birds are to be considered messengers from higher consciousness and other dimensions. The blue jay specifically is one of the more talkative birds, so its meaning connects with communication. Its blue color aligns it with the throat chakra, further emphasizing this communication sensibility to the medicine that it offers. When the blue jay visits you in dreams, it is time to take a powerful look at how you are communicating. (See *Birds*.)

Blueprint: A blueprint relates to the structure of something and the intention to bring an idea to fruition. What are you in the planning stages of in your life? A dream that features a set of blueprints may be illuminating issues around what you desire to create.

Board Game: You are looking to resolve conflict through structure and control. In a dream, a board game may be an analogy for the "game" in life it is designed to represent. Popular board games are created to convey certain themes of life experience through the process of playing them. If you are winning a board game in your dream, you may be expressing recent experiences of successful negotiation of life's complexities. If you are losing, the dream may be reflecting back to you where you are blocked or challenged.

Boat: You may be skimming the surface of deep emotional issues below the surface. Any vehicle in a dream refers us to our paths in life. A boat travels over water, the universal symbol for anything that deals with the emotions. The size and type of boat in your dream will illuminate your current ability to navigate emotional issues based on resources and levels of skill. The water itself connects with the nature of the emotional territory in which you currently find yourself. The destination of your trip will offer insight into what may be causing an upsurge of emotion and what you hope the outcome will be if you are successful in arriving at your intended destination.

Bobcat: All cats connect to the feminine principle in action. The larger the cat, the more powerful the medicine it has to offer. Bobcats are solitary in nature and are patient, stealthy hunters. When the bobcat appears in a dream, you are being asked to combine focused intention with great patience in order to get what you most desire.

Body Parts: The parts of the body all have meanings based on the basic functions of those parts. The feet represent feeling grounded, while the toes are about maintaining balance. The legs connect with freedom, choice, and movement. The knees are the symbolic home of humility, subservience, and/or surrender. They are also the place where you hold your fears. The hips are the center of the core and therefore represent the integration of systems and all the elements of your life that have to interact with one another in order to function. The ribs are about vulnerability and protecting yourself from emotional pain. The ability to withstand pressure and fulfill the needs of others is associated with the shoulders. The arms are the structures that allow you to take action and accomplish your goals and desires, while the hands give you the creative ability to do so. The individual fingers are how you relate to details and life's complexities. The spine is your moral center and where your values are located. The neck, though a part of the spine, has the distinction of providing you with discernment and choice. The skull is related to your beliefs, ideals, and opinions, and the bones that support your face connect with community and the desire to connect with others.

Bomb: When a bomb appears in a dream, things are changing drastically, very fast. A bomb creates an enormous amount of energy in an instant, and an explosion is a powerful symbol of great change. In this case, the changes that are taking place are likely to be creating a great deal of chaos and challenge. A bomb that hasn't exploded indicates changes that may or may not happen. The results of a bomb blast symbolize the havoc that is wreaked when enormous changes take place.

Bones: You are trying to connect with the underlying structure of things in your life and how you are being supported. The skeleton at the core of our bodies is the foundation on which the whole system is built. Since most of the human body is soft and moist, we rely on the solid, durable, calcium-based bone structure for what little solidity we feel. Nothing can be any stronger than the foundation that supports it. This foundational structure is normally invisible to us, so to be dreaming of bones is to be getting a glimpse of issues that are normally hidden but are now visible. Old bones might connect to issues in your past.

Book: The answers you seek are to be found in the intellect. Books relate to knowledge that has already been recorded, so this dream is not looking toward new information to be made known to you. Rather, the message of the dream is that the knowledge you seek is already within your awareness. The more books there are present in the dream, the more likely that this is a call to express your desire to learn and grow in ways of the mind.

Bottle: A bottle is about the ability to contain a small amount of something, usually liquid refreshment. If the symbolic meaning behind what's in the bottle is to nurture you or please your palate, then the meaning of the bottle is your ability to contain that desire in a portable way and enjoy it at your leisure. An empty bottle relates to something you had in the past being unavailable to you now. A bottle that is broken indicates an inability to contain something pleasurable. If you know what is in the bottle, add that for a great distinction of your interpretation.

Boulders/Rocks: You may be blocked in your life by things from your past. Rocks act as the primitive memory for our planet, and to dream of boulders and rock formations is to be connecting on some level to primal imagery rooted in the distant past. On a more mundane level, the past that is being represented by this image may be your own personal history. Rocks or boulders can represent obstacles or challenges if they obstruct your way or present you with some amount of danger. If this is the case, what may be blocking you in your waking life could be material that is deeply imbedded in your unconscious. Examine areas where you may be holding fast to old ideas that no longer serve you. Painful memories can often seem like insurmountable obstacles or enormous boulders that appear to be immovable.

Box: A box is about containing something or compartmentalizing elements of your life. When this image is featured in a dream, look to where in your life you may be keeping certain things separate and potentially hidden. This may be a benefit if chaos or challenges require you to maintain structure and organization in order to get through some significant shift. However, it can also reveal a deeper pattern indicating that things currently hidden may need to be revealed or elements of your life that you are keeping separate might be better if integrated.

Bracelet: Any adornment is ultimately about drawing attention to yourself. In the case of jewelry, the meaning is found by examining the part of the body that the item features. The hands are about creative expression, and the wrists add an element of flexibility in that arena. A bracelet in a dream is about highlighting a desire to be more creative and expressive.

Breaking Up: Something in your life is changing or may need to come to an end. This can be literal and connected to a phase of life or an actual relationship with another person. However, it can also be that you are ending a relationship with your own behavior. Perhaps you are "breaking up" with a habit or pattern that hasn't served you and it's time to move on.

Breasts: You need to find a deeper connection to the feminine resources inside of you and your ability to nurture. This can relate to self-care or to taking care of something in your outside world. Breasts are also a powerful erogenous zone and are therefore part of sexual expression and physical pleasure. Dreaming of breasts often connects to the level of self-care of the dreamer, whether the person is male or female. Even erotic dreams involving this symbol should be viewed through this concept. Breasts that are not real might indicate that the nurturing you are giving yourself as an adult is somehow false and not truly nutritious. Older or sagging breasts would indicate a resource that is no longer full. Breasts on a man could indicate a need to cultivate more sensitive and nurturing qualities.

Breathless (Out of Breath): You are having difficulty connecting with your life force. Underlying feelings of anxiety or panic may be inhibiting you from being fully functional. The breath of life is also the physical representation of our level of serenity. When breath is slow and nourishing, we are at ease. Any elevation of breath indicates that we are either in a state of fear, emotional reactivity, or intense physical activity. Being out of breath in a dream may indicate a heightened fear reaction.

Bridge: A bridge is essentially that which makes a connection between two separate entities. You are seeking to make connections within your own consciousness. A dream about a bridge indicates that some sort of transition is taking place or that you are in search of a solution to what feels like an insurmountable problem. Since a bridge takes you from one place to another, it also carries the meaning of a transition in life. Since many bridges are suspended over water, an emotional issue is often the underlying conflict being expressed by this symbol.

Briefcase: This is a symbol that represents having access to certain important elements of your life, usually associated with work and responsibility. If you have lost it in the dream, you may be feeling unable to meet your obligations or take care of business.

Broken Bones: You are dreaming of a loss to the foundational integrity of some aspect of your life. Bones as foundational elements indicate that the essence of the stressor that is being expressed has to do with how something is structured or being supported. If you dream of a bone being broken, it tells you that some area of your life is on shaky ground. The solidity or strength beneath that which is creative or expressive is what is compromised. If your dream included the injury itself, add the means by which your bones were broken to your interpretation, including if there was another person responsible. The more creative you are with your rumination of these symbolic meanings, the more successful your interpretation will be. (See *Bones, Body Parts*.)

Broom: One of the fundamental tools for keeping house, a broom relates to a need for cleaning up life's messes. There is a media-driven association with brooms and witches, so if the dream's context indicates this perspective, a broom might represent an ability to introduce magical thinking into a situation that needs attention.

Brother: See *Siblings*.

Brown: While most colors are found in the spectrum of natural light, the color brown is a mixture of many colors that results in something that is generally thought to be dull and lacking in vibrancy. This is the direction to go with your interpretation, especially if the object or environment that is brown is unnaturally colored in that way. However, also consider that brown is the color of earth, and so what you perceive in this color in your dream could indicate a need for a more grounded approach to some element of your waking life.

Buddha: See *Jesus, Buddha*.

Buffalo: One of the most sacred animals to most Native Americans, the buffalo connects to gratitude, abundance, prosperity, and provision. When the buffalo appears in your dreams, you are being called to recognize the amazing way in which your life rises up to meet every need you could possibly have. The spiritual principle of gratitude is connected to this majestic beast.

Bugs: See *Insects*.

Bull: Sometimes the greatest display of power is stillness, and the bull reminds of this. The bull is a mighty animal that spends most of its time not moving. The medicine involved here is to know your own strength and trust your ability to take powerful action when the timing is right. The bull is also connected to prosperity through several traditions, most notably Western astrology, where Taurus the Bull rules money and comfort.

Bus: You are undergoing a slow transition in your public or social life. As with any mode of transportation, a bus connects with one's path through life. When you ride a bus, you turn the reins of control over to another, take a seat, and go along for the ride. The type of bus offers shades of meaning. A school bus may indicate regression to an earlier mentality, whereas a public transit bus could point to a need to follow a course that requires being patient with the paths of others. A private bus, such as a tour bus, may indicate levels of abundance and the need to gather creative resources for future use. However, if the bus was used in place of a car, feelings of lack and limitation may be indicated.

Business Card: A business card is a form of identification and is therefore symbolic of the very thing of which it is symbolic in waking life: a person's business persona. It is a tool for connection and solicitation, and in a dream it is connected to the person to whom it belongs. If someone gives you a business card in the dream, consider the character aspect of that person and what he or she might have to offer you. The business card itself and the act of passing it along represents your ability to call on those character traits to assist you in some venture. If the business card in the dream belongs to you, this may connect to a desire to expand your reach in some arena of your life.

Butterfly: The medicine of the butterfly is resurrection and the capacity to undergo enormous change and transformation. The caterpillar relates to the binds and heaviness of a previous consciousness, whereas the butterfly embodies the freedom possible when we surrender to the unknown factors that precipitate change. When the butterfly appears in your dreams, you may be being asked to trust the changes that are happening, for freedom is just around the corner.

Cable Car: This image of urban travel may be all but extinct, but its iconic nature may cause it to be featured in the dream world. First, it should be considered as a symbol of the ability to navigate through more complex thought patterns, where the transportation element represents the navigation and the urban environment in which it is found represents the complexity of thought. Second, it should be considered through the lens of your personal associations with cable cars. There may be a harkening back to a slower pace of thought and openness to your process.

Cactus: The cactus is a succulent plant that manages to flourish in the desert environment seemingly devoid of water. Since water is the precious source of life, this hearty plant is a symbol of the ability to thrive despite challenging conditions. When a cactus appears in your dream, you are being shown your own capacity to find sustenance even when it appears to be absent.

Cage: A cage is designed to keep something captive while still allowing an illusion of open space. You may be feeling confined in some way in your life. Who or what was in the cage will feature largely in how you interpret a dream that has a cage in it. If it is you in the cage, then look to ways in which you have limited yourself.

Cake: You are finding reasons to celebrate and revel in the sweetness that life has to offer. We eat cake when we are recognizing important moments that are worthy of rejoicing in. A cake in a dream is offering such a moment to consider life's joy and bounty. (See *Food*.)

Calendar: Calendars mark time; they help us know where we've been and where we are going. In the abstract, they represent the concept of time itself. In a dream, a calendar is asking you to consider how time is a factor in your decision-making or how you are thinking about the life you are creating. The emotional sensation of the dream will help you decide how to interpret this symbol.

Calf: This young cow is an immature and undeveloped version of the nurturing and sustaining meaning associated with its adult parent. Add the element of innocence to your interpretation. (See *Cow*.)

Callus: A callus forms when a certain action is repeated over and over, hardening the skin with small amounts of scar tissue. This allows for these motions to continue without harm or damage. Calluses are evidence of hard work and accomplishment as well as the skill to create and build. In a dream, they are asking you to consider where you have been putting your effort and attention.

Camel: The camel is a desert animal and can survive for long periods of time without intake of water. Additionally, camels are hearty pack animals and have been helping nomadic peoples with their way of life for thousands of years. In this way, camels carry the medicine of strength and drive, helping to keep you focused on the goal at hand. When a camel visits you in your dream state, you are being given the gift of fortitude.

Camera: A camera allows you to record and document the important moments of your life. In this way, it is a symbol that relates to an extension of your memory. This is becoming more ubiquitous in modern culture with the advent of digital media, and the camera's reach is more and more about a constant collection of data and self-expression. A camera in your dream may relate to a desire to be public about your experience and to continually reflect about where you have been in your journey.

Camping: Camping is a back-to-nature activity that brings you closer to the earth. This image in a dream may relate to a need or desire to get back to the basics or fundamentals of living simply, without the complications that make life chaotic and stressful.

Can: A can contains something of value that you want to keep preserved for later use, usually food. The implication of this symbol is that something from the past has been stored and saved. This can be something of value, in which case it is a positive dream image. However, canned goods can spoil and become dangerous, in which case the can in your dreams could indicate it is time to let go of something from your past.

Candle: A candle is a symbol for the spark of life that we are all masters of. You ignite a candle to signify important moments and to represent your ability to create light where previously there was none. A dream with a candle in it may be indicating that such a creative moment is at hand. An unlit candle indicates the potential for light to come into some dark space. Lighting a candle in a dream may indicate a desire to celebrate life's milestones and key experiences. If the candles in your dream have particular colors associated with them, look to the symbolic meanings of those colors for deeper meaning.

Candy: You may desire more sweetness in your life. You may also be more focused on instant gratification. Candy is a food substance that delivers an enormous amount of sugar into the body, significantly altering its chemistry in rapid fashion. The brain responds almost immediately, and while there is an initial surge of energy, it is then followed by a rebound effect shortly thereafter. Much of the symbolic meaning of this symbol connects to this physical phenomenon, as there is an addictive quality to the experience of eating candy. Have a little and the body will want more. You may also be longing for some romance, as giving candy as a gift is often thought of as a romantic gesture. Also consider candy as a reward; are you seeking validation for a job well done?

Cap: You may want to keep some of your thoughts hidden. A hat covers the head, the symbolic representation of your thoughts. Wordplay using "cap" as synonymous for something that limits or contains means this particular type of head gear is likely pointing to a desire to limit or restrain your thoughts in some way. A cap may also point to a desire to connect to your sportier nature, as caps were originally designed for outdoor play, where blocking the sun was desirable. A cap in a dream might point to wishing to limit how much light you can see. (See *Hat*.)

Car: We move around in our lives through our cars, and your dream that involves a car is illuminating something about the journey of your life as it relates to how you are navigating your life, your choices, and your sense of creating your own destiny. If your car is crashed or broken, you may be feeling like the circumstances in your life have stopped you from moving forward, maybe very abruptly. To have lost your car is to be feeling confused about where to go next. The color of a car in a dream may offer some deeper meaning. A car moving too fast or too slow for your comfort level may be indicating a desire to have more control than you actually have.

Card: Sending a card to an individual is a way of honoring a particular expression and bringing that expression to a higher level. Usually associated with a specific message, the type of card should feature prominently in your interpretation. Consider the message; your dream is asking you to consider some idea as important enough to point it out in a ritualized fashion.

Carnival: A tightly knit community of fringe society, a carnival creates an atmosphere of fun and escapism for the person who attends one. In a dream, this image may relate to either the event itself or the people responsible for creating the event. If the sensation of the dream feels connected to being a guest at the carnival, then interpret this dream through the lens of play. If the dream is more a behind-the-scenes experience, then you may be connecting to your rebellious nature. (See *Circus*.)

Carpet: The floor in a dream always relates to how grounded you feel. It is the foundation upon which the consciousness of the room stands. The presence of a carpet relates to a desire for softness and comfort beneath your feet. The state, color, and texture of the carpet in your dream should inform how grounded you are feeling at this time.

Casket: The implication of a casket is that someone has died. Any death is symbolic of the rebirth that will follow. The casket itself represents the ability to contain the process of change and transformation that a death implies.

Cat: You are dreaming about unconditional love in the feminine principle. Cats of all types represent powerful feminine energy, which includes receptivity, creativity, sensuality, and stillness. They are hunters by nature, and their nocturnal behavior associates them with the feminine aspect of night. While their masculine counterpart, the dog, embodies a pack mentality, the cat is the symbol of self-reliance. First domesticated about three thousand years ago, cats were revered for their ability to control rodent populations that would have beleaguered the stores of grain that were so crucial to the emergence of civilization. Cats have long been associated with magic and witchcraft, with the classic black cat as the carrier of the most superstition.

Caterpillar: Before the transformation occurs that leads to the butterfly, there is the caterpillar. The caterpillar must do something tremendously courageous: it must willingly give up its own life. It has no idea of the miracle to come. When the caterpillar comes to your dream, you are being asked to consider total and utter surrender, to take a great leap of faith, trusting that miracles occur.

Celebrities: Celebrities are the gods and goddesses of modern life and represent archetypal human qualities with which we all identify. The essence of a particular celebrity's image can be distilled into a character aspect by the ways in which we perceive the person. Millions of people hold the same projected image of celebrities. The power of all that magnified perception endows them with superhuman status and removes any sense of the person underneath the persona. Celebrities show up in our dreams when the stakes are a little higher in terms of what we're dreaming about. By providing a more powerful image, the unconscious is telling you to pay more attention. Approach the interpretation the same way you would anyone in your dreams.

Cell Phone: You are dreaming of being connected to or disconnected from the people in your life. In this day and age, your cell phone represents the power and speed of thought. The instant you think of someone, you can connect to them. Whatever is happening with a cell phone in a dream relates to how strong that connectedness is at the time of your dream. Using your cell phone in a dream means you desire to feel instantly connected to others in your life. Static on a call is representative of anxiety or chaotic and disconnected ideas. A lost cell phone is to have misplaced your ability to express yourself and your thoughts with your extended community. (See *Phone*.)

Centaur: The centaur is known for having the head, torso, and arms of a man and the body of a horse. This combines the archetypal meaning of powerful, masculine energy with the intellect and reasoning capacity of a human being. A creature that attaches the legs of a goat to a male torso brings dark sexual energy together with the masculine principle and is often considered a guide for bringing you from one place to brand-new territory. Such an image in a dream is calling upon the aspirational influence to face some difficult circumstance in your life with greater skill and power.

Chair: The act of sitting implies a restfulness or the stillness between movements. Sitting in a chair relates to the choice to commit to what that chair's purpose has to offer. The chair in front of a desk implies a willingness to get to work; a dining room chair relates to taking in sustenance and nurturing; a comfortable armchair might indicate the desire to rest. The presence of a chair in a dream usually indicates that it is time to pause.

Chakras: In modern New Age thought, there is an understanding of energy as it relates to the body that connects to certain centers known as chakras. Each of these body vortexes can be understood symbolically based on the area of the body they relate to and the function of that area. There are seven of these energy centers that correlate with the physical body. The first energy center is the root chakra, located at the base of the spine. This connects to security, groundedness, and the sense that all your needs are met. The second chakra includes the sacrum and genitals and is where primal creativity is expressed. The third chakra is in the belly and is where instincts and gut feelings are located. The fourth chakra is the center of the entire structure and is the home of the heart. The fifth chakra is located at the throat and is where communication occurs. Intuition is located in an area at the forehead known as the third eye, which is the sixth chakra. The crown of the head is the home of the seventh chakra and is most connected to the higher self and spiritual awareness. If your dream features any imagery that highlights one of these areas on the physical body, you can draw your interpretation from the meaning associated with the chakra that is being highlighted. It is important to note that each of these chakras has a color that is associated with it. The order of the chakras corresponds to the order of the colors as they appear when white light is refracted into its separate vibrations. From one to seven, that order is red, orange, yellow, green, blue, indigo, and violet. For more distinctions in your interpretations, see each of these individual colors. (See *Colors*.)

Chased: See *Being Chased*.

Cheerleader: Cheerleaders inspire enthusiasm and confidence by expressing these traits in an organized way in a public forum. The cheerleaders in a dream are the parts of your consciousness that are appearing to motivate you to your highest level of performance in some task you are undertaking.

Cheetah: All cats relate to the power of the feminine principle. The larger the cat, the greater the power of this totem. The distinction of the cheetah is related to its speed; it is the fastest of all the large felines. When this animal appears in a dream, the medicine you are being acquainted with relates to rapid agility when facing transitions in your life.

Chicken: The chicken is the most consumed animal product in the Western world, making the symbolic meaning of the chicken directly connected to abundance, prosperity, and nurturance. The common phrase "like a chicken with its head cut off" brings the meaning of ignorance and stupidity into the symbolic mix. The chicken in your dream may be relating to one of these principles. There is some spiritual connection to the rooster through Chinese astrology. (See *Rooster*.)

Children: All people in your dreams are reflections of your personality. At the heart of this symbol, children represent innocence. However, the behavior and actions of the children may affect how you interpret their presence in your dream. Also consider the age of the child or children in the landscape of the dream. They may represent new ideas, patterns, and expressions of consciousness that emerged in your waking life at the time of their birth. For example, a seven-year-old child may connect to some element of your life that began seven years prior to having the dream. You can also look at the age of a child in a dream as relating to a pattern that emerged in your consciousness at that age. From this perspective, the seven-year-old dream child relates to something that happened to you when you were seven. If the children in your dream are your own, the dream is likely reflecting issues that are more literal and about your home life.

Choking: You are struggling to speak your mind and facing an overwhelming or dangerous block to effective communication. Any experience that connects with the neck and throat places us in the realm of communication. When someone is choking, their ability to speak is limited or even eliminated. Someone choking or being choked in a dream is dealing with communication issues that are intense enough to be, at least symbolically, a matter of life and death. Look to where issues of communication are connected to people, places, or things where the stakes feel very high. If you are choking someone else, consider that you may be trying to stifle a particular way of communicating in the world that may be out of control or not serving you in some way.

Church: You are dreaming of connecting to your spiritual nature in a more conventional way. Churches, temples, and mosques are the center of spiritual life for any community. Just like a house in a dream, any building can be interpreted as representing one's current sense of self. In this way, any place of worship ultimately points to your relationship with spirituality and religion. Because this element of life can be particularly controversial, it is very important that you make a clear distinction between the universal meaning of church as connecting to matters of spirituality and whatever personal feelings you harbor about organized religion.

Circus: You are dreaming of running away from your responsibilities in life. Any form of entertainment must be considered symbolically as connecting to escapism. With a circus, the additional texture of enormity must be added. This symbol contains a surreal element as well, as exemplified by the strangeness of clowns and the oddities of the sideshow. Additionally, the circus has a reputation of catering to those on the fringes of society, a closed community that is secularized from the rest of the world. The mythology that surrounds the circus is that it is a place where freaks, outsiders, and loners can find a home. In this way, the meaning of escapism also includes a fantasy element in which someone can literally escape the mundane world by running away with the circus. If you were an audience member in the dream, then escapism should be the main theme of your interpretation. If you were performing in a circus, you may be expressing some inner pull toward grandiose expressions of your sense of individuality and originality. If you were more connected to what was going on behind the scenes and the community of performers, look to where in your life you may be seeking agreement from like-minded people in a realm that is off the beaten path.

Climbing: You are looking to grow and expand in your life and are expending a great deal of effort to this end. A climb is the effort that must be expended to reach a particular goal. All goals require effort; many can involve struggle. As you identify what struggle in your life might be represented by the climb, the feelings and images in the dream can inform how you are approaching the current challenge in your life. A dramatic shift is akin to embarking on a journey of some kind, whether it is emotional, financial, spiritual, or

dealing with a health challenge. It may show up in a dream as a climb as your psyche tries to show you that you have the resources to make it to the top, despite the fear or intensity of the effort involved. By the same token, the dream may be telling you that you may be overemphasizing the struggles in your life and that you are applying more effort than is required. If this is the case, consider the lack of balance between effort and expectations you are currently experiencing. Your job is to define the journey and find the balance between intent and effort. This way, the ascent to your destination can be met with joy and enthusiasm.

Climbing Stairs: A staircase allows you to move from one place to a destination that is located above or below you. Stairs are symbolic of your ability to raise your consciousness to a higher plane or explore deeper territory beneath you. Any set of stairs or steps in a dream is an indication of examining a higher or lower level of your psyche, depending on which direction you are moving. If the stairs are in a home, it is your sense of self that is being examined. Social issues and how you operate in the world are connected to a stairway that is located in a building or public place. Moving upward could indicate an increase in awareness and a readiness to elevate your thought process. Moving downward might connect to reexamining your past or considering something more deeply.

Cloaked or Hidden Figure: This is a powerful archetypal character aspect and a messenger from the unconscious, often thought of as the archetype of death. This image has its essence in anonymity and may therefore never be clearly known to you. As a character aspect, it is a figure from your unconscious mind that has the capacity to visit you in the dream state and deliver a message. The context of the dream will tell you what the message is, or at least where to begin looking for it. However, if in your dream the figure closely resembles the commonly held visage of death—the cloaked figure without a visible face that roams the world snatching the living into the world of the hereafter—then you are definitely experiencing an archetypal dream.

Closet: You are attempting to hide something. This is a dream about having a hidden agenda or about some sort of avoidance. A closet is a place used for storage. The items found in a closet usually fall into one of three categories: frequently used items kept out of sight for the sake of organization, things stored for later use, and forgotten objects that we continue to hold on to even though they have lost their purpose. A dream that features a closet as a primary image or location may need to be considered through one of these themes. Many objects found in a dream closet connect to shame. The level of this will correspond to how hidden something is and/ or how much fear there is around it. Keep in mind, however, that a closet is also a storage space where we file away things we no longer need on a regular basis. There may be old thoughts, feelings, or ways of being that need to be recognized and discarded in order to make room for new growth that is on the horizon. The phrase "in the closet" has come to be linked almost exclusively to an individ-

ual who is hiding their homosexuality. However, in a dream, this can refer to any hidden side of the self. What you discover in a closet should be viewed through the focus of something you are hiding from or not wanting to face.

Clothes: Clothing is very connected to your own personal self-expression and to the principle of the persona. What we choose to wear has enormous implications for how we feel about ourselves and how we would like the world to perceive us. Symbolically, clothing represents creative personal expression. However, clothes can also represent the ways in which we cover up who we really are and alter what the world sees. Additionally, the clothing we wear at any given time can reveal things about our moods and emotional states that might otherwise go unnoticed. The quality and style of clothing in a dream will provide you with different shades of meaning for your interpretation. Old clothes might represent old ways of being that are being stirred up. New clothes could indicate a desire or need to match your inner growth and shifts with your outer presentation. A costume might illuminate roles you are playing in your life that are false, whereas your own clothes indicate that the issue at hand is with your present sense of self. Being inappropriately dressed represents your concern about fitting in with others. Wearing too many clothes can sometimes indicate a lack of comfort with your sexuality or body image. Having to deal with many layers of clothing denotes that there are obstacles between where you are and a deeper level of authentic expression. A desire to take clothes off may mean a need to break out of a stereotypical role you find yourself in, while adding more clothes could mean putting on a few more layers in order to protect yourself from perceived outside harm. No clothes usually reflects feeling very open and, therefore, vulnerable.

Clowns: Clowns are a complex symbol to interpret. They are expressions of playful energy, yet underneath there is a subversive and untrustworthy element to them, possessing an ironic ability to contain enormous contradictions. Clowns are playful and childlike, but also grotesque. There is a subversive quality to the concept of the clown: they are seemingly innocuous, but there is something possibly darker lurking just below the surface. Their expressions are permanently fixed and therefore not to be trusted. However, the entertainment they provide can be masterful and absolutely delightful when done right. A clown in a dream is an aspect of your personality, a thought or a pattern of thoughts. Such a dream may be asking you to explore more deeply to get to the authentic idea underneath the costume.

Coat: See *Jacket*.

Cobra: All snakes relate to change and transformation due to their ability to shed their skins. The cobra is a particularly venomous snake that is most remarkable for its ability to expand the hood that is just below its head. This neck-like placement connects it to the throat chakra, and when a cobra is present in a dream, issues of communication are being highlighted. (See *Snake*.)

Cockatoo: All birds relate to the messenger function and also represent our thought process and the movement of ideas. The cockatoo is less colorful than many of its brethren, so it relates to something more subdued, but still vibrant. The traits that are most directly associated with this type of bird are a very strong beak and a loud, shrill voice. This adds the texture of harsh and strong communication to the symbolic meaning if this bird should appear in your dream. (See *Birds*.)

Coffin: A symbol relating to death, a coffin in a dream indicates that some sort of a change is going on. A coffin is made to hold a person after death. As a dream symbol, it should be interpreted by examining the individual inside the coffin as a character aspect of the dreamer. This applies whether you know who is inside the coffin or not. Any death is symbolic of change. When examined as a character aspect, the death represents sacrificing a portion of the personality that is no longer a useful part of the whole. An effective shift requires clearing out old ways of being in order to make way for new, more evolved functioning. Death is always followed by rebirth, but when a coffin is present, it signifies being at the beginning of the transformation process.

Coin: Coins are a form of currency and so they relate to abundance, prosperity, and the power that comes with possessing the ability to trade for what you desire. A coin, however, has an added dimension as representative of finding luck and good fortune if you should happen to stumble upon one in your travels. The relationship between coins and wishes is evident in the gesture of throwing them into fountains. Coins are also potentially seen as sacred objects of a spiritual nature. (*See Money.*)

Colors: Dreaming in color is often viewed as a particular phenomenon that sets a dream apart from others you have. There is an implication here that if a memorable dream is thought of as being vibrantly filled with color, other dreams must be in black and white by comparison. However, all dreams are likely to be experienced with various intensities of color, and the memory of vibrant color is just one more way the unconscious is speaking to you. Light is experienced as white, but if it is refracted into separate wavelengths, the naked eye can perceive the seven distinct bands of color that make it up.

Computer: A computer represents highly sophisticated levels of mental organization, thought, and memory. A computer is a symbolic representation of the brain itself. There is an operating system that allows other software programs to run. This is like the network of nerve cells that make up the majority of brain tissue. There is also a hard drive, which stores everything that has ever been inputted into it. This is akin to the neural pathways created by the brain's recording of sensory data it receives in the form of memory and knowledge. There is RAM, or desktop memory, which is like your conscious mind. This includes your daily production of short-term memory that is processed each night when you dream. The process that occurs during REM sleep is much like backing up your computer files for protection on a daily basis. When a computer features promi-

nently in your dreams, you are considering how your mind is working. The state of affairs in your dream computer may very well be mirroring the state of affairs in your current thought patterns.

Cookies: You may be seeking reward and an extra dose of sweetness in your life. Cookies connect us symbolically to maternalistic nurturance, even if you didn't come from a home where Mom and cookies were synonymous. We think of these sweet treats as something we get to have after a job well done. This dream may mean that you are seeking such accolades. Cookies can also represent the insidious power of excess; have one and you're fine, but before you know it, having one can turn into having many. As with anything that is good in moderation, the dream world may be pointing out ways in which you are overdoing it.

Cougar: All cats relate to the power of the feminine principle. The larger the cat, the greater the power of this totem. The cougar is nocturnal and therefore relates more to shadow elements of things hidden and unknown. A stalk and ambush hunter, the cougar is associated with the ability to have your presence remain hidden, but take powerful action at the precise moment that action is necessary. A cougar can also be an older woman who is enjoying her sexual power with younger men, so this may be something to attribute to the appearance of a cougar in a dream.

Cow: The cow is rich with mythological symbolism in many cultures. However, at the heart of a modern interpretation, the power of the cow connects to basic sustenance and nurturance. Between the milk these animals provide as a food staple and the meat that is consumed by billions of people on the planet, the cow relates to having such basic needs met. Through the image of milk, the cow relates to fertility and the power of the feminine principle. In a dream, a cow is offering access to having basic needs met as part of its medicine.

Cowboy: You are dreaming about the part of yourself that is connected to hard work and an individualistic spirit of expansion and freedom. Cowboys represent the rugged individualism that is intrinsically bound up with the mythology of the American tradition of expansion and cultivation. The cowboy is often considered a lone figure, connecting with a sense of isolation and a dedicated work ethic. The media has turned the cowboy into an icon of enormous proportions. Cowboys represent the silent strength of the masculine principle at its absolute best. Any dream that features a cowboy is likely connecting to this spirit of independence. Are there new frontiers in your life that need exploring? Perhaps there is something to be done that must be done on your own. After all, the cowboy is ever riding off into the sunset, propelled by the belief that there is always something new just over the horizon.

Crab: The crab is a water creature and so relates to feelings, emotions, and the feminine principle. A crab's habitat is connected to the tides, which relates these creatures to the interaction of the conscious and unconscious minds as well as the cycles of the moon. Their medicine can be hard to connect to because of their pinchers, which keep them out

of our grasp. When the crab appears in your dream, powerful information is being offered from the depths of the unconscious, and that wisdom is best understood from a place of stillness and receptivity.

Criminal: Some part of your personality is expressing choices with a disregard for consequences. When a criminal appears in a dream, he or she should be considered as a character aspect of your sense of self. While criminal behavior is varied and can cover a wide array of activities, there is one common denominator for all crimes, whether mundane or heinous: there are consequences for breaking the law. From this perspective, any choice that ignores this societal agreement indicates a lack of regard for these consequences. Since crime is essentially antisocial in nature, the character aspect of a criminal in the world of dreams is shadow material. By examining the fundamental nature of the criminal in your dream, you will discover what part of your unconscious is being expressed. The severity of the act or intent reveals the extent of the darkness of your current emotional state.

Crocodile: See *Alligator*.

Cross: This symbol is most associated with Christianity, but in fact the circle divided into four equal parts is the most ubiquitous of all spiritual symbols found in almost every civilization back through time. The earth is a circle divided into a cross by virtue of the North and South Poles combined with the eastern and western horizons. This makes the cross a truly universal symbol. If you have a personal association with Christianity, then you must use this in your interpretation. If not, still consider this a primal symbol representing the spiritual energy of all beings on Earth. Its presence in a dream may indicate a stirring of a mystical nature.

Cross-Dressing: Clothes relate to our persona and the choices we make about how we want the world to see us. When gender lines are being crossed in a dream, the main theme of your interpretation will be the integration of either the masculine principle or the feminine principle, depending upon the direction of the switch. Taking on the garb of the opposite sex could mean a desire to incorporate more of those traits into the way people see you. A woman in drag could be expressing a desire to be seen as more aggressive or powerful. A man in drag might be considering what it would be like to be more receptive in the world and be perceived as more sensitive.

Crows: All birds are to be considered as messengers of some kind. There is probably no bird that exemplifies this more than the crow or raven. In Norse mythology, the two ravens Huginn and Muninn represent thought and memory; they fly around and report back to Odin every day and create our ability to name things and commit them to memory. They gather where humans do, and so they reflect our numbers directly in proportion to our population. In this way, crows and ravens bring us important messages when they appear in dreams. A group of crows in community is known as a murder, and this twist on words adds an element of shadow to their medicine.

Crying: You are feeling a heightened emotionalism in your life right now, powerful enough to bleed over into your dreams. Water represents emotion, and tears are the fluid expression of our deepest emotions as squeezed out by the body. If you are crying in a dream, then you are likely in some sort of mourning or expression of grief. If someone else is crying, then a character aspect that lives within you is involved in a powerful emotional process. If this is the case, then use the character who is crying to gain a deeper understanding of what part of your personality is undergoing a shift. Tears of sadness connect to loss. Tears of joy connect with gain and could indicate getting to the other side of a challenging transition. The more acutely you can feel the physicality of crying upon waking, the closer to consciousness the wound is. The level of disconsolation you feel may give you an idea of the intensity of the hurt you are cleansing. Remember that in your dreams, just as in life, crying is a healthy and powerful way of processing grief and facilitating transition and transformation.

Crystal: Crystals are mineral formations found buried in the earth. There are many different kinds of crystals, but all of them are thought to have certain vibrational qualities. To dream of any sort of crystal is to awaken your desire to embody your spiritual nature and your ability to connect to energy in an esoteric way. If a particular type of crystal appears in your dream, you may want to research the meaning associated with that crystal. (See *Stones, Boulders/Rocks*.)

Cup: The purpose of a cup is to contain something, usually a liquid. Therefore, the meaning associated with this symbol connects to your ability to contain something that you desire. Since a cup is most often associated with a beverage, the thing you may need to contain could connect to the principle of self-care. The state of a cup in a dream is a reflection of how well you are attending to this aspect of life. The sharing of a cup is a powerful symbol of connection and unity and may be reflected in a dream as well.

Cupcake: Any sweet food is most often associated with joyful moments in life. Cupcakes imply a celebratory moment that wants to be shared. Often associated with childhood, this mini-cake indicates that a joyful moment is at hand. (See *Cake*.)

Cut(s): A cut is evidence of wounding; protection that is instinctive. The skin is the largest organ of the human body, comprising three layers. Its primary function is to separate the outside and inside of the body, offering a mildly protective shell for the tissue beneath it. Cuts in the skin hinder the effectiveness of that protection, and the body quickly responds to any injury it may sustain. A cut leaves a mark that is the evidence of the wound. Whether the wound occurs in the dream or appears to have already happened in the past indicates where you are in the process of responding to some hurtful moment in life. (See *Wound(s)*.)

Cutting: The phenomenon of "cutting" is a ritualized addiction where a person deliberately cuts himself or herself as a stress-relief mechanism. People who cut will describe a satisfaction in having an interior experience of emotional pain expressed physically on the body. Being cut in a dream, whether self-inflicted or otherwise, is a similar action by the unconscious mind to express inner pain in an outward manner. (See *Wound(s)*.)

Dagger: Any weapon in a dream is a symbol of aggression and destructive impulses. A dagger is a small implement capable of making deep cuts. The dagger itself in a dream only implies that aggression may occur. The cut that a dagger may make could be symbolic of cutting remarks or the possibility of being stabbed in the back, both of which indicate betrayal of friendship or loyalty.

Dance: A dance is a gathering of people, and in the dream world those people should be considered as thoughts within your consciousness gathered around a common idea. The idea in this case is the expression of passion and sexuality through the symbolism of dancing. If there is a dance in your dreams, there is a compelling desire brewing in your consciousness to have more passion in your life.

Dance Class: You may want more passion and creative expression in your life and are willing to learn what you need to know more about in order to create some.

Dancing: You are searching for more grace and fluidity in the complicated relationships in your life. Dancing is also an elaborate mating ritual. It is a socially acceptable behavior that is designed to escalate toward intimacy and sex. Even dancing alone is a sensual experience that celebrates the ability to move in space. This results in a sensual experience of one's body, signaling a readiness for sexual expression. In group dancing, such as ballet or modern dance troupes, the symbolic conversation expands to the idea of poetry in motion.

Dandruff: Negative thoughts are creating mild but noticeable fallout. There may be some doubts about self-worth and attractiveness at the core of the issues at hand.

Darkness: The absence of light in any way brings a dream into the realm of the shadow. If your dream is more dark than light, add this element to your interpretation. It may be time for you to explore areas you have previously avoided and to be willing to look at things that usually remain hidden or fill you with fear.

Date: A date is an opportunity to possibly find romance and love. It involves taking a risk and the need to show up authentically. In a dream, it represents the willingness or the lack of willingness to take such a risk, show up fully, and possibly find a new level of self-expression, passion, and eventual integration.

Daycare: In daycare, an individual finds temporary freedom from one set of responsibilities in order to attend to another realm of responsibility. If a daycare environment features in your dream, you may be juggling obligations and need some relief or balance in the area of whatever you have a duty to accomplish.

Dead End: You have come to the end of one course of action; it is time to choose again.

Deaf: The ability to hear is part of our navigation system. The ears keep us balanced and upright and orient us to the space around us. To lose this sense interrupts your ability to receive guidance from your environment. If deafness is featured in your dream, you may want to consider how well you are listening to whatever direction you are getting in your life at this time. (See *Disability*.)

Death: This is the ultimate symbol of change at a transformational level. All change involves the cycle of something dying to be reborn again. This applies to all of life, from the changing of the seasons to the coming and going of relationships and the process of birth and death itself. Death in a dream signifies that an enormous shift is occurring in your life. If you know the person from life, decide what character aspect of yourself he or she is representing. How that person operates in life is what is changing within your own psyche. The change is so great that it is being expressed by the ultimate of changes—death. If the person is a stranger, then use whatever information you can remember about him or her from the dream to explore what elements of your personality are undergoing a transformation. The quality that is being shifted could be about behaviors, habits, or character traits. The more violent and sudden the death, the more combustive and intense the process you are going through is likely to be. A death that has already occurred could signal that you are in a later phase of change rather than at the beginning. If it is you who dies, the transformation may be so complete that it involves your entire life or lifestyle—e.g., moving, changing jobs, a breakup, a new relationship, ending destructive behaviors, etc.

Deer: Grace and beauty are the medicine of this timid animal. Also, the need to be on guard and self-protective is part of what is being called into consciousness when a deer appears in a dream. The deer knows its way through the woods and has the ability to guide us through unknown and hidden territory. If the deer has antlers, this increases its power to navigate through primal instincts.

Defecation: While the elimination of waste might be the first thought that comes to mind when thinking of feces, at the heart of it, bowel movements are our first connection to us as creative beings. Consider the power and intensity associated with potty training and all the effort that goes into guiding a child toward controlling this bodily function. This period in a child's life has a profound impact on how he or she operates in the world. Often the most effective method of this training involves helping a child make a creative connection to what comes out in the toilet. For the young mind, this is quite an impressive feat. From this perspective, defecation or feces in a dream are always going to connect *first* to personal creative power. Whatever that turns out to be, it is likely going to be about the state of your individual, creative affairs. Notice whether the experience in your dream is repulsive or not. Often in such a dream, there may not be an association to feces as dirty. If the experience is indeed repugnant, then you may be in some form of resistance to a deeper process that is going on that may require getting "down and dirty" with shadow material. Eating feces points to needing to integrate your own creativity into some aspect of your life. Playing with or handling feces (and how you felt about doing so) may indicate your level of comfort with a transition in your life that may be requir-ing you to go deeper into your "own shit" in order to find a new sense of self.

Defibrillator: When the electrical rhythm of the heart is in a chaotic overload, a defibrillator stops the heart with a jolt of electricity with the intention of supporting it to start up again on its own charge. In this way, this device essentially resurrects the life force of an individual suffering from a breakdown of this system. You may be feeling overwhelmed with so much stimulation that you are about to shut down, and this image in a dream indicates a desire to stop the current patterns and start again.

Delivery: A delivery indicates that something you have expressed a desire in receiving has finally arrived. In this way, a delivery in a dream is asking you to consider what you are expecting to come to you. The ultimate indication of convenience, having something delivered implies a level of abundance consciousness and your ability to feel deserving of having your wishes brought right to you.

Demon: The darker side of the spiritual realm, a demon is a being that feeds on fear and hatred. When a demon appears in a dream, you are being put on notice that your shadow side is out of control and things that are sparking fear are getting the better of you. A demon can also be an indication that you have been ignoring a destructive pattern for a very long time.

Demonic Possession: The idea of being possessed by something outside of your human self is connected to relinquishing responsibility for certain feelings that are deemed unacceptable. This is a fairly common dream image and represents a sudden outburst of any number of pent-up, dark emotions, such as guilt or rage. At the heart of this symbol, however, is the concept of not feeling responsible for the behavior in question or the intensity of the feelings being expressed. As the saying goes, "The devil made me do it." Such a dream is asking you to look at where you are either blaming someone else for your own overwhelming feelings or are unwilling to take responsibility for your own reactivity.

Desert: There may be an obvious lack of passion and life force in your life right now. In a desert, you have to look deeper for the signs of life that are actually there, so a dream that takes place in a desert may be calling you to do just that. Do not take the surface appearance of things at face value. Look below the surface and you will find that there is more going on than meets the eye. A dream desert is also inviting you to irrigate and fill your life with more emotion and passion.

Deserted Place: You are dreaming of unmet needs and the consequences of past choices that have not served you. Human beings are social animals. We have lived in community with one another since our arrival on the planet. To find yourself in a place that is deserted and devoid of the presence of other human beings would leave you helpless in many ways. The severity of this vulnerability would depend greatly on where you were, what resources you had access to, as well as your own fortitude and courage. Even in the best of circumstances, your very survival would be at risk; hence, the primary symbolic meaning of this symbol is connected

to risk and death. While loneliness might be thought of as the underlying emotional content of such an event, it is the absence of human resources that carries the interpretable weight of this symbol. Even if you found the absence of other people comforting, this meaning still applies. You may want to consider how relying on others for getting your needs met may be the root cause of the anxiety that sparked this dream.

Desk: When you are at a desk, it is a sure bet that you are doing work of some kind. In this way, a desk is a symbol of this consciousness. Work has different meaning for different people, so this symbol may be more or less literal for you if you are someone whose actual job involves sitting at a desk. A desk connects to left-brain sensibilities and a need for organization and structure in your life. What you were doing at the desk should be considered in your interpretation. If there was a person in the dream associated with the desk, add the meaning you assign to the individual as a character aspect of your personality connected to the need to get more organized and approach a problem from a more practical angle.

Dessert: You are looking to reward yourself or sweeten things up a bit. This is also a symbol that relates to overindulgence and attempts to control yourself. Dessert is often seen as something to be resisted, so your relationship to the dessert in your dream will offer you deeper shades of meaning.

Detective: As a person in your dream, a detective is a character aspect of your own personality. This is the part of you that is responsible for figuring things out as your life unfolds. If a detective appears in your dream, the implication is that whatever you are attempting to figure out still has mysteries associated with it that may yet be solved. Surrender to the process.

Detergent: An agent for cleaning, detergent in a dream implies a need to clean up a past mishap or hide the evidence of something that has already occurred that is causing you shame or discomfort.

Devil: Most people will fall into two categories regarding the Devil: the religious and the non-believers. There is a third category of people who don't necessarily believe in the Devil, but were raised in an environment that embedded certain beliefs that they may have consciously rejected but that still have great power in the unconscious mind. The first and foremost quality of the Devil is temptation. The ultimate motivation for the temptation is for ownership of a person's soul. In the world of psychology and dream work, the soul is akin to your spiritual nature and the totality of your experience as a human being. The presence of God and the Devil in our world offers each of us a choice: With whom will you align yourself and on what will you base your life choices? Your higher nature, through the choice of love, or your lower nature, through the choice of fear? The presence of the Devil in a dream indicates that a powerful degree of fear is being expressed. Bondage is another important element associated with the Devil. The contract he offers is permanent, with severe consequences. In symbolic terms, the Devil could illuminate areas in your life where you feel you have sold out. Look for situations in which you feel stuck for reasons of obligation, financial insecurity, or outmoded satisfaction. Often we make choices that initially provide us with something we desire, only to discover that we pay a price we hadn't counted on. Real soul-searching may be called for when the Devil appears in a dream. What thoughts or old ways of being must be cast aside for your greater good? From a lighter perspective, what devil-may-care attitude might be inviting you to discover that which your inner critic won't give you permission to explore? The phrase "the devil made me do it" can be either a misguided excuse for bad choices or a call toward letting go of judgment.

Dew: Dew is the result of water in the atmosphere that has yet to be evaporated away by the rising sun; it is considered beautiful and a touch magical. The water that makes up dew is symbolic of emotional content that appears when the cloak of night makes it safe to be more expressive. The fact that it will evaporate when the light of day shines upon it indicates a symbolic sense of temporariness and privacy. Dew is the secret expressions of subtle tenderness and nostalgia that come along with your daily life.

Diamond: The diamond is formed when carbon molecules are acted on by time and pressure to create the most precious form we know. Symbolically, the carbon molecules are the building blocks of all life's forms and therefore are related to everything there is. Time and pressure can be thought of as literal in this interpretation, for life is filled with both in great measure. Therefore, the diamond is the ultimate symbol of the gift and benefit that can be harvested from the challenges that life presents you with. As a precious gem, the diamond relates to that which we value above all other things because of the great challenge involved in its creation. (See *Stones*.)

Diaper: The purpose of the diaper ultimately points to the freedom it brings. By virtue of the diaper's presence, the wearer is able to be unconcerned with when and where the release of toxins and waste occurs. Since there is often shame connected with the acts of defecation and urination, the diaper can be thought of as a container for your shame. Are you holding on to things that make you feel bad about yourself?

Diarrhea: At the heart of the interpretation of this image in a dream is the lack of control that diarrhea represents. Feces have several meanings, one of which is powerfully creative, as they are something that you actually make with your body. However, feces also connect to the shame that is inherent in our fundamental humanity. When diarrhea is present in a dream, something is out of control.

Dice: The roll of the dice relates to blind luck and the impact of random chance as it relates to a desired outcome. We live in a world that is half divine plan unfolding and half random chaos. The dice relate to the latter half of this paradoxical equation. A dream that features dice as an image may be asking you to surrender to uncontrollable outcomes.

Diet: To diet is to limit the intake of food toward the end of maintaining some control over the shape of your body. This consciousness can run the gamut from healthy, balanced self-care to deeply destructive restriction combined with compulsivity. Your personal relationship to food must be factored into your interpretation of such a dream. Wherever you land, a diet is about restraint and control of something that is fundamentally about sustenance and nurturance. What are you denying yourself in order to get what you want? Is this a good idea? These are the questions to ask if dieting is featured in a dream.

Digging: You are expressing a need or desire to get to the bottom of something. Anything that is under the surface of the ground relates to hidden consciousness—available to be known, but not until some exploration is undertaken. Such an image in a dream may indicate that there is something to be gained from looking below the surface.

Dildo: The penis is a symbol of masculine power, and the dildo is a manufactured penis. It is a substitute for this masculine power and can represent a desire to stimulate this power within in the absence of projecting it onto an outside source. In a dream, the power being expressed, while inherently sensual in nature, may not necessarily be about the sex drive. Look to where in your life you have a desire or need to increase your sense of power.

Dining Room: Every room is an expression of the consciousness of that room's purpose. A dining room is a place where food is shared with others. There are two elements to this image that bear consideration. One is the act of taking in nurturance and sustenance; the other is the desire to share this act in community. Whatever is happening in the dining room of your dream is a reflection of these principles in your waking life.

Diploma: You receive a diploma at the end of a significant course of study. Therefore the symbolic meaning of the diploma itself is that the work and effort has happened in the past. The idea of being recognized for possessing a certain level of wisdom and knowledge is embodied by the presence of a diploma.

Disability: Anything that limits normal ranges of functionality, mental or physical, might fall under the broad category of disability. In a general way, the symbolic meaning of such a state relates to the limitations the disability creates. Since the capacity for excellence begins with perception, the interpretation of any disability begins with the notion that something is challenging because it appears to be so. If a particular disability in a dream is not one that is mirrored in waking life, then the dream is expressing a perceived diminishment of capacity and the call to overcome its sense of limitation. Use the specific disability for distinctions in your interpretation.

Dishes: These implements for eating meals bring a touch of civilization to the process of taking in sustenance. Food is symbolic of the different ways you nurture yourself, and dishes are ultimately containers of that nurturance. Look to the condition and usage of the dishes in your dream to reveal your current relationship to self-care.

Ditch: A ditch is a culvert in the earth that has been deliberately created by human intervention. With the ground being a symbol for consciousness, anything that is just below the surface of the ground is that which is just below the surface of our awareness. Most ditches are built to hide in or divert the movement of something. In this way, a ditch is the result of doing a little self-investigation in order to provide for something to be able to move without detection or other implemented strategy. What is just below the surface of your thinking in your life right now?

Diving: When a diver plummets into water, he or she intends to symbolically rush below the surface into both the world of emotions and the unconscious mind, as water represents both of these domains. The dive then becomes the ritualized expression of not only the intention to do so but also the skilled creative expression of the act itself. In this way, a dive is symbolic of the practiced and majestic way that someone has prepared to courageously explore the hidden depths of his or her own nature.

Divorce: A marriage is the symbolic integration of different character aspects. It can also symbolize the primary integration that is the purpose of all consciousness expansion. A divorce is the end of a level of evolution that is no longer viable. In order to grow, you must release elements of the past. A divorce in a dream is symbolic of the end of one phase of your development and the beginning of another.

Doctor: Every person in a dream is part of your psyche, and a doctor is an aspect of the self that can diagnose and heal. You may be looking for answers to some underlying problem or challenge, and the doctor in your dreams may help heal what ails you.

Dog: You are connecting to principles around unconditional love as expressed by the masculine principle. Dogs represent unbridled joy, constant affection, and enthusiastic loyalty. A dog in your dream connects to your own capacity to remain constant in love and affection. Remember to consider what the dog in your dream is doing and add that to this idea of unconditional love and you will understand what this dream means. The presence of a dog means a need to call this quality into your life, and this image being present in the dream indicates that the quality is readily available. Anything that inhibits this, such as a dog being injured, sick, lost, or challenged in any way, is pointing out your own inhibitions around being loving for love's sake. A dog in your dream connects to loyalty and love, which can indicate that issues of commitment and intimacy are being triggered by some event or circumstance. A positive dream experience could be pointing to places in your life that are sparking enthusiasm or requiring you to become more enthusiastic and joyful. Frightening images involving dogs may be inviting you to investigate unconscious fears around love and connection. A rabid dog represents inner fears of danger that may befall you if you get too close to an intimate situation. An actual dog bite represents the misuse of kindness or consideration. An obedient dog may point to a sense of control in areas of friendship and

trust. Different types of dogs can embody a variety of qualities, from the dog that rescues a person in danger to the harrowing attacker. Dogs range in shape, from something tiny enough to put in your pocket to large breeds that resemble small bears. The size and attributes of the dog in your dream will inform you of the scope of the unconscious notions being expressed.

Doll: A doll is a representation of a child for an actual child to have an experience of his or her own maternal instincts, and this might be expressed by a doll appearing in a dream. Conversely, a doll could indicate an infantilization of impulses that relate to maternal feelings.

Dollar: A dollar is the primary denomination of currency that we use in the United States. Any dream that involves money is connecting to the principles of abundance, power, and freedom. In a dream, money often represents your inner resources. Such a dream is asking you to consider your current relationship to these principles. (See *Money*.)

Dolphin: This is one of the most beloved of all animals and holds a very high place in many belief systems of the New Age. The dolphin's intelligence and beautiful song have been held in high esteem by so many cultures; there is hardly one that doesn't feature this beautiful animal in mythology of some sort. The primary qualities associated with this animal as a totem are grace, beauty, compassion, and playfulness. Dolphins live in pods and are known to exhibit highly complex social relationships, so they also connect to the care and uplifting of the community. There are two main themes to consider when a dolphin shows up in a dream. One is a reminder to be playful in all your dealings in life, as life is supposed to be filled with joy. The other is a reminder to always remember the breath, for as you choose to breathe, that is how you are choosing to live. The more dolphins there are in your dream, the more intense their message is for you. Dolphins are intelligent mammals, so they relate to the human experience in this way. They inhabit the vastness of the ocean, so they simultaneously connect to the collective unconscious. When a dolphin appears in a dream, you can consider yourself visited by a very powerful aspect of the collective conscious.

Donkey: The donkey is an indefatigable worker domesticated to be of selfless service to humans through its strength and fortitude. As such, its medicine as a totem animal connects to this dedication and determination to achieve any goal. When the donkey appears in your dreams, you are being connected to your willingness and discipline to face the hard work that your life demands.

Door: You may be facing an opportunity or choice to venture into the unknown. A door is the obstacle that separates a person from accessing whatever is in the room to which the door marks the entrance. It represents both opportunity and choice. What is on the other side connects with opportunity. The volition required to open it and cross the threshold connects with choice. Additionally, when one door closes, another one opens, suggesting a correlation with transitions in life. Even if you think you know what is on the other side, a closed door creates mystery and uncertainty and usually refers to something that is unknown. A door that is ajar or open is an invitation from the unconscious to check out what's beyond it. The more doors there are, the more complex the choice at hand may be. The size and weight of the door may indicate the importance of the issue being expressed. Shutting a door indicates the will to end something or the ability to set a boundary with certainty and clarity. A door being shut on the dreamer is an obstacle that is created by another person or a set of circumstances in the dreamer's waking life. The person creating the obstacle may in fact be yourself. If you are not in control of whether the door is open or closed, issues of forced choice or lack of choice could be indicated.

Doorbell: A door symbolizes a choice or a transition in life. In this way, a doorbell is connected to being alerted that something new is on its way into your experience.

Doormat: This is the symbolic preparation before something new is embarked upon. You stop for a moment and clean your shoes so that what is unwanted from your past will not be carried forward into your future. Also consider that a doormat is sometimes used as a term for a person who allows other people to wipe their feet on them figuratively, and this meaning may be reflected in a dream.

Dove: The dove is a symbol of peace and love, and if one appears in a dream, you are connecting to these principles through the symbolism of the dove itself as well as through the animal medicine that the dove brings.

Doves are also symbolically connected to romantic love.

Down: In this world that is divided into binary code, there are always two options in any polarity. The up-down continuum relates directly to the strongest force we deal with: gravity. When anything in a dream is moving in a downward direction, you are either exploring what is below the surface or being stopped in your forward movement by something that is forcing you down. Consider how this downward direction is being presented to you and then remember to explore what wisdom is available for you in the lower depths.

Down Syndrome: This genetic disorder is expressed as limited development both physical and mentally. Therefore, as a symbol in a dream, it may be pointing to some area of your life in which you are not expressing your full potential. Use the context of the dream to see what may need development. If there is someone in your life with Down syndrome, the dream may be interpreted more literally.

Drag Queen: The height of illusion, a drag queen presents an exaggerated presentation of feminine qualities. Often infused with exuberance and a sense of joy, this symbol means that things are not what they seem to be. The feminine side of nature is nurturing, creative, and patient. Perhaps these qualities need to be integrated in your life in a more authentic way.

Dragon: There are two very different dragons in the world of symbolism: the Eastern symbol of charisma and good luck and the Western symbol, which connects with greed, avarice, and overprotection. According to Western mythology, dragons are the guardians of treasure and virgins. These are things that are of no use to a dragon, a creature that does not need money to get what it wants and also cannot safely consummate a relationship with a woman. Despite this, a dragon will face all comers with a mighty ferocity, challenging the courage of the most able warriors. In this way, we can view a dragon as symbolically representing a fight for something that is of no use to you. The dragon in your dream may represent the battles you fight in life that you cannot win or that do not need to be fought at all. By the same token, you may have to fight an inner battle and face the part of you that is in the way of you getting what you want in life. Is it possible that your inner dragon may be keeping you from receiving the love you deserve and the abundance you desire? There is also an implied theme of confrontation in battle when a dragon appears in your dreams. What are the battles in your current life? Are you fighting for something that you do not need or cannot use?

Dragonfly: Change and transformation are part of this animal's totem power. The dragonfly spends an enormous amount of time in the larval stage, which represents the hibernation that must accompany great change. When the dragonfly emerges, it can fly with beautiful multicolored wings. The larva is aquatic, so the transformation that it connects to happens at the level of the unconscious mind. When the dragonfly's change is complete, the ability to fly and spread the translucent beauty of its wings represents messages of ascension that come directly from the depths of our soul. This is a powerful totem of change, transformation, and wisdom.

Drain: In the structure of plumbing, the drain is what takes away what is no longer wanted or needed. Often what is being drained would fall into the category of waste or things of an unsanitary nature. Therefore, as a symbol, the drain represents your ability to slough off the old and easily release the past. If the drain in your dream is functioning properly, all is well. If it is not, there may be some need to examine why you are unable to let things go.

Drapes: Windows offer a view from the outside world into the inner sanctums of a home. Drapes have the function of creating privacy as well as adorning this aspect of transparency in your consciousness. They can open and shut at will, adding the element of controlling who can see into that which you might want to keep secret. They also can be seen as your willingness to let light in or shut it out, with light being a representation of conscious awareness and life force. As a dream symbol, drapes relate to this choice, the free will to exercise it, and the state of affairs around doing so.

Drawbridge: A drawbridge functions in two ways and allows completely different modes of transportation to exist. In the world of symbols, the cars on land represent thoughts and consciousness and the boats on water connect to emotions and the unconscious. By being able to change shape, the drawbridge can distinguish between which is more im-

portant. In a dream, consider how the drawbridge is operating, for it will point to which mode has higher priority at the moment. If the drawbridge is not working properly, your own ability to distinguish between emotions and thoughts is being affected.

Drawing: The act of drawing is an effort to take something from inside of your consciousness and express it in the world of form. It is a creative act that results in something tangible. As a dream symbol, drawing relates to this impulse to allow yourself an outlet for creative expression and the patience to allow form to appear to you slowly.

Dream within a Dream: There are levels of consciousness that exist in the dream state that you can wake up to and still be asleep. This happens in waking life as well, but is less noticeable, like when you suddenly realize you were not paying attention to something that was happening and you snap into awareness. When this happens in a dream, it is an indication that you are waking up to higher levels of your own conscious awareness.

Dress: The dress is the staple article of clothing for women and as such is a symbol of feminine qualities such as creativity, receptivity, nurturance, and patience. If you are wearing a dress in your dream or there is a dress present, you may be considering what it would be like to try on these qualities. The design of the dress offers distinctions about how these principles are being worn by you in life.

Dressing Room: The dressing room is essentially about preparation for some heightened form of expression. Look to where in your life you are gearing up to be expressive in a particular way. Additionally, you may be hesitating to take risks around putting yourself out there by staying too long in the dressing room.

Drinks/Drinking: This symbol has a wide trajectory in the continuum of fun and relaxation on the one end and excessive escapism on the other. This activity in a dream may point to a need for more balance in your life by letting go or more balance in your life by reining in the ways in which you avoid responsibility. The dream context will help you with your interpretation, as will your waking-life relationship with alcohol.

Drive-In: All but extinct, the drive-in movie theater is an interesting mashup of the symbol of car and the symbol of movie. In a dream, a drive-in relates to the impulse to stop your movement through life and take some time to relax and escape. If the movie on the screen features prominently, there may be something to explore about thoughts that are in the shadow and usually hidden.

Drive-Through: Ultimately the drive-through structure connects to a desire to get what you want when you want it without interrupting the flow of your life. This can reflect a high level of positive focus or a sense of moving too fast and avoiding taking the time needed to more effectively meet your own needs. A drive-through in a dream is asking you to examine your priorities and need to control things.

Driving: Any driving dream connects to how you are moving through your life and the quality, sensations, and judgments you have

about how this is going at the time of a dream in which driving is a prominent image. If you are driving out of control in the dream, you must consider what area of your life might be beyond your ability to regulate. If you are in the back seat and need to gain control of the car, look for ways in which you haven't yet stepped up to the plate. You may not be able to do so yet because of circumstances beyond your control. If your car isn't responding to you, you may be feeling ineffectual about taking charge of some path you are traversing. Varying speeds might be reflecting movement in life that feels either too fast or too slow for your comfort. A vehicle other than a car might point to being in foreign territory. You may not be feeling confident in your ability to work with the circumstances you have been handed. Causing an accident could be inviting you to look at the consequences of your choices. Being a victim of an accident might encourage you to look at the ways in which you have abandoned your own direction because of another person or outside force beyond your control. Driving in the rain connects emotional issues to your current route. Icy conditions indicate that emotions are being frozen over, making your way treacherous. Driving down or up a hill would illustrate the sense of effort or ease involved in your life movement.

Drowning: You are feeling overwhelmed with deep feelings and need to surrender to your emotional issues and learn how to process them. Many people have free-floating anxiety associated with the idea of drowning. When this is the case, the universal meaning of peaceful surrender will often be overlooked when considering this as a dream image. No matter how deep your level of fear is around the frightening possibility of an actual drowning, the return to your watery roots and turning yourself over to the gentle embrace of the weightlessness of water implies a very serene experience from the symbolic perspective. Water, as a symbol, always connects to the world of emotions. To drown is to die. To die is to sacrifice part of the self in order to be reborn again. Therefore, to drown in a dream is a beautiful transformation that occurs by virtue of giving yourself over to inevitable emotional processes that lead you to a new way of being in the world. The presence of panic in a dream of drowning is a signal of resistance to the emotional change that is afoot. The more intense the panic, the greater the resistance you are expressing. Being able to breathe, or at least function normally, underwater is a common dream image. While this is not generally experienced by the dreamer as a drowning dream, the meaning connects to the same concept of grace and ease with emotional overwhelm.

Drugs: You may be looking for an instant but temporary shift of consciousness. All drugs dramatically alter the experience of the individual taking them. Hence, they represent a shift in consciousness that is controlled by the user and is instantaneous. Also inherent in considering this symbol is the matter of consequences. When many substances are abused, especially recreational drugs, there is a disregard for the potential harm they can cause and the often challenging afteref-

fects of their use. The desire for the high outweighs the difficulties that result from the overindulgence. When drugs appear in a dream, there may be a life situation where you are looking for a quick fix rather than the more difficult path of meeting things consciously.

Drugstore: The drugstore is a place where so many needs can get met, and it is in those needs that the meaning of such a location can be found. Pharmaceuticals may relate to a health issue or healing that needs to take place.

Drum: All musical instruments relate to passionate expression. The beating of a drum is most connected to the beating of the heart. If a drum features prominently in a dream, you are connecting to a fundamental and organic expression of the rhythm of life.

Drunk: If you are drunk in a dream, you are expressing a desire to avoid or escape some aspect of your life. If someone who appears in your dream is drunk, consider who the individual is through the perspective of being a character aspect of your own personality. Once you have determined what the person represents in you, consider that that area of your life is expressing avoidance or destructive tendencies. If there is an unidentified drunk in your dream, there is more investigating to do to understand where you are holding yourself back.

Dryer: A dryer removes the moisture from clothes that have already been cleaned. In this way, there is an element to this symbol that relates to the evaporation of previously powerful emotional experiences. Those experiences may in fact have made you feel dirty or unclean, so the symbol of the dryer has within it the implication that something has recently been cleaned or cleansed.

Duck: All birds are messengers of some sort. The duck is waterfowl and therefore connects to emotions. A duck's propensity for flying south during the winter connects it to the idea of moving toward warmth out of instinct. The medicine associated with the duck is this inner knowing of how to move in the direction of resources.

Dumpster: The dumpster is the intermediary between declaring something as no longer wanted or needed and the removal of the thing itself. Dumpsters are usually located toward the back of property, connecting them with elements of your consciousness that are somewhat hidden. They tend to smell bad, so they connect with old consciousness that has already been declared as no longer useful but that still requires some attention. What change or shift in your life is not quite complete?

Dungeon: You are tapping into unconscious negative beliefs. Dungeons are places of torture and imprisonment, and they correlate with deeply hidden and unconscious thoughts and fears. They were a place where people were kept locked up and tortured; therefore a dungeon is the part of the shadow where our most frightening ideas and thoughts create ongoing and unimaginable levels of suffering and pain. There is a sexual element to this image that connects to the fetishistic desire to dominate or be submissive in sexual role play. A dungeon in this case need not be a fear-inspiring dark and dreary place, but rather a private place possessing the appropriate equipment to facilitate the activities associated with such sex play.

Dust: Almost everything in our world that is organic in nature emits dust as a natural part of its aging or breakdown process. We consider that all things come to dust as part of decay. In our homes, most of the dust we experience actually comes from the human body. In this way, dust in a dream is the consciousness of things past, and if it is building up or obscuring your vision, there may be things in your past that still need to be cleaned up.

DVD: The DVD has entered our consciousness as our connection to an immediate source of entertainment and the escape that movies provide. As a symbol in a dream, DVDs relate to a desire to remove yourself from your day-to-day life and immerse yourself in a pleasant sense of escape and relaxation.

Dynamite: A blast of dynamite is a controlled explosion. Explosions relate to the sudden change they create. The destruction associated with dynamite is generally connected to the constructive elements they are involved in. The blast they create is usually designed to remove obstacles to growth and expansion. What old ideas, habits, or constructs in your consciousness need to be blasted away in order to build something new?

E-mail: E-mail is the communication venue of the new world order. We are simultaneously brought closer together and further isolated by this almost instantaneous way of connecting our thoughts to the minds of other people. The realm of the intellect is represented by this image. The newness of Internet technology imbues the symbolic meaning with a sense of uncharted territory in the world of thought and interpersonal expression. We live in a time where the technology has evolved faster than our ability to formulate a universal sense of etiquette and propriety. Its speed implies spontaneity. However, the ability to edit and alter our words prior to sending the finished product adds a dimension of control that should not be overlooked when arriving at an accurate interpretation. Words typically account for about 20 percent of any verbal interaction. Absent from the e-mail experience are the crucial elements of tone and body language. Despite this enormous limitation, most people approach e-mails as if they were clear and accurate when, in fact, they are subject to projection and presumption. In this way, an e-mail in a dream connects to communication that is assumed to be lucid but may not be received with the same intention with which it was sent.

Eagle: All birds are to be considered as messengers of some kind. The eagle, however, is perhaps the most majestic of these air creatures and their medicine is very powerful. It is one of the largest birds and its size and power have led many aboriginal cultures to consider it an earthly incarnation of a godlike presence. The eagle as a symbol embodies strength, courage, and the ability to soar above any difficulty. The vantage point of such heights is a part of what the eagle brings when it appears in a dream.

Earphones/iPods: Our ears are the sense organs over which we are able to exert the least amount of control. Sound enters the ears from all angles, even though they are constructed for directional optimization. The ears are open and vulnerable to all outside stimuli unless impacted by an external object. While people often use various items to minimize incoming sound, the purpose of the earphone is to replace the naturally occurring inflow of sound with something of the individual's choosing, usually music. This is where the element of escapism becomes an important consideration of the meaning attached to this symbol.

Earrings: To adorn the ears is to bring attention to them. Do you need to increase the quality of your listening and your ability to be compassionate and empathetic?

Ears: Hearing is ultimately about balance and orientation and so the ears are your conduit toward being in this state. Any interpretation of a dream that features the ears must be considered in these two ways: What is happening with the ears in the dream itself? Then filter that awareness through the question of how this is affecting your sense of balance or understanding of where you are in relation to the things around you. When you hear what others are expressing, you are able to tap into compassion and empathy, so the ears connect to these principles in action. Of course, a dream about ears is also about how well you are listening to what your life has to say to you.

Earth: We are extensions of the earth itself, and the presence of this as a dream image indicates some sort of archetypal connection to the concept of a collective consciousness where we are all united as one human organism. You may be dreaming about global issues and how they are affecting you on a personal level. This dream may be helping you see that you are not alone in your challenges, but are connected to a vast wholeness. The dream may indicate the earth as an object of comfort if the dream has pleasant imagery associated with it. An unpleasant or violent dream involving the earth could point to fears about the challenges and dangers of modern life.

Earthquake: There may be a lot of disruptive change of great magnitude in your life right now, perhaps under the surface of your current awareness. The shift of landscape that happens in an earthquake is the result of changes that originate in the subterranean world. This is representative of how unconscious thoughts and feelings can have an enormous impact when they suddenly become conscious. Earthquakes themselves are of relatively short duration, so the life event this image may be reflecting is likely something that occurred quickly or appeared suddenly. The symbolic meaning of an earthquake comprises three elements: First, a great change has already taken place. Second, the onset of the change originated in a deep and unconscious place. Third, things will never be the same.

Eight

Earwax: A buildup in the ears is a blockage to their effectiveness. What are you not willing to hear? Remember, too, that it is through the ears that we hear the cries of others. Ears that are blocked cannot connect to empathy and compassion.

Eating: The symbolism of eating primarily has to do with the taking in of sustenance and nurturance. This can relate to other things besides food, for such is the power of a symbol. If eating is featured in your dream, take a look at where in your life you are experiencing some issue around how well you are taking care of your own needs. The context of a dream that features this activity should offer many clues. The more excessive the eating, the more the dream may be pointing to issues of excess and gluttony. What you are eating should be considered for symbolic interpretation as well. Once you are clear about the meaning you ascribe to the food (or other substance) of your dream, recognize that the act of eating is expressing a desire to take that quality into your own body and integrate it as part of you.

Echo: An echo is created when sound waves bounce off of land masses and return in the form of a repeated frequency of the original sound. In this way, an echo is the symbolic ability to be aware of distant boundaries and limitations. In a very simple way, it is an indication of where the next mountain to climb is going to be. Additionally, the desire to be heard by another person in an experience of intimacy is also reflected by the concept of an echo. In both cases, the power of the echo is in the information it provides. An echo in

a dream is asking, "Do you feel heard and do you know where you are going?"

Eclipse: During an eclipse in the solar system, one body blocks the light coming from another body, most notably the moon blocking the light of the sun or the earth blocking the light of the moon. An eclipse is therefore the symbolic blocking of any light, where the light is a metaphor for consciousness, ideas, or life force. Eclipses were once thought to be omens of important things to come.

Egg: There are new beginnings afoot and your life is filled with possibility. An egg symbolizes the potential for life that lies within it. From this perspective, this symbol always connects to new possibilities and new life. The type of egg in your dream and what it might hatch should provide the foundation of your exploration.

Eggshells: The delicate casings that protect the insides of an egg are very easy to break, hence the term "walking on eggshells." If eggshells appear in a dream, this notion of care and delicacy is being expressed. If the eggshells are intact, there is a need to be most cautious. If the eggshells are already broken, there is an implication of a previous tactless maneuver that has left its mark.

Eight: After spiritual matters have been made manifest, great abundance is possible. Eight is the number of infinity and all that it implies. This includes wealth of every kind: love, money, bliss, joy, and every amazing experience life has to offer. The concept of infinity states that there is no limitation in the universe, that time and space continue forever and ever in a way that is beyond our ability to truly comprehend. When an understanding of infinity and abundance are combined, there is a realization that there is an endless supply of anything you could possibly desire, even those things that you perceive as limited and unavailable to you. Eight is the magic of seven in action. The shadow side of this is greed, hoarding, and withholding love.

Ejaculation: The sudden emergence of semen at the end of male orgasm is the key component of the sex act that relates directly to procreation. There is a tremendous buildup of energy that is released very suddenly, and this is at the heart of this experience as a symbol. Ejaculation implies that a great deal of tension needs to be released.

Electricity: Electricity is an invisible force that is present in our lives on a daily basis for most of us in the Western world. We generally take it for granted but trust it to be there when we flick a switch. In this regard, electricity symbolizes faith and the power to manifest our thoughts into reality. We don't necessarily know how it works, but we know that it does indeed work. We have become completely dependent upon it for our lives to function smoothly. In this way, it is like faith; it is most apparent when we lose it. When electricity is the theme in a dream, you are considering your relationship to the flow of creative energy that infuses life with possibility. Your emotional response to the dream can inform you of how much faith you have that something is possible even when there is no evidence of it in your current circumstances.

Elephant: The elephant's sheer size and strength are at the root of the symbolic meaning associated with it. The Hindu god Ganesh has an elephant head and is thought to bring luck by being the remover of obstacles. He will also bring an obstacle if that is in your highest interest. When the elephant appears in a dream, you are being given the medicine of patience, strength, and the capacity to move through anything. Also to be considered is the notion that elephants "never forget." Your dream of an elephant may be asking you to remember something about your authentic self.

Elevator: Elevators carry us from one floor to another at the push of a button. The different levels to which they transport us connect to various perspectives of our awareness. We choose our destination on an elevator, aligning this symbol with the choices we make about what areas of our consciousness we are willing to investigate. What happens in the elevator of our dream may reveal how well this process is going in our daily lives. The floors involved in a dream can hold significance. In a general way, moving upward connects with higher, more sophisticated levels of thinking, and moving downward indicates investigation of past issues and behavior patterns. Moving downward can also align with visiting hidden or shadow material. Most dreams about elevators are connected to this process not going well. To be going up when down is desired may indicate a pressing need to operate with greater insight than that with which you are currently engaged. Going down when up is anticipated may point to the need to uncover additional material hidden in the lower depths of your consciousness or your past. Being stuck on an elevator is to be midway through a process or shift. Your response to the lack of movement may reveal levels of impatience with your progress in some area of growth. An elevator out of control is similar to a falling dream, but the added components of transition and choice must be considered. While you may be falling, you have chosen to take the elevator in search of new information. Going sideways is to be confused about the direction in which a current transformational shift may be taking you. If the elevator is out of service, you may be stuck in some area of your life. Another possibility with a broken elevator is a need to stay where you are and not try to escape your current situation by rising above it or sinking to a lower level.

Elf: The elf comes to us originally through Norse mythology and was thought to possess magical powers. What survives today in modern media is still magical and also often mischievous. An elf in a dream is putting you in touch with the inner aspect of self that is impish and a bit of a trickster.

Elk: The elk is a member of the deer family, so any meaning associated with it will be based on a foundation involving grace, beauty, watchfulness, and the ability to navigate the symbolic forests of our unconscious. Being larger than a deer but less so than a moose, the elk carries a medium weight of power as an animal totem. If the elk in your dream has antlers, then the amount of his medicine is increased. Either way, when an elk appears in your dream, you are being guided through a journey into hidden territory.

Emerald: The emerald is a precious gemstone that is mostly dark green in color and symbolizes a great sense of comfort, luxury, and prosperity. The beautiful green shade of this gem connects it to the healing energy of the heart chakra. In the lore of crystals, the emerald is thought to be connected to luck and abundance. Additionally, the green color of this beautiful mineral relates to growth and the expansiveness of nature.

Engagement: The ritual of engagement is about intention rather than commitment. It is the declaration that a large undertaking is likely to occur in the future. As a symbol, this can be applied to any life experience that embodies a significant amount of dedication but is not yet requiring the action that the future will bring. Be on notice if an engagement is featured in a dream; you are preparing to take major action in the near future.

Engagement Ring: The engagement ring is a reminder of an intention that has been declared for future commitment. As a dream image, that future commitment can apply to any life experience and not just marriage. The power of the engagement ring is that it is visible to others as a symbol of this intention and has the energy of accountability associated with it. The great expense involved deepens this sense of accountability. What intentions are you considering in your life that are demanding a significant investment on your part?

Engine: At the very core of any combustion-oriented machine is its engine. In this way, an engine is symbolic of the heart of any matter. Since an engine represents the power that can be put behind a desire, the engine is the direct expression of the ability to meet the desire with the force and power it will require to manifest. The state of the engine in your dream relates to how much power you have access to in order to make things happen.

Envelope: The essence of the envelope as a symbol is privacy; it keeps what is inside hidden until it is ready to be opened by the rightful recipient. Also connected to this object is the concept of identity; an envelope usually bears the name of the desired recipient of the information contained inside of it. There is a mystery with an envelope and therefore some excitement about the information it contains, and this may be what is being presented to you in a dream that features one.

Eraser: When you no longer want something that you have previously created, you use an eraser to wipe the slate clean. An eraser provides the ability to eradicate mistakes and choices that no longer serve you.

Erection: The penis is the ultimate phallic symbol, an image that represents masculine power. An erection is the implication that that power is ready to be put to use. This is so no matter the gender of the dreamer. If you have the erection in your dream, you are ready to take action in some area of your life. If someone in your dream has an erection, then the aspect of your personality symbolized by that person is the one that currently needs to be called upon to provide the power you need.

Escalator: The primary meaning behind the escalator connects to its movement to upper or lower aspects of thought and consciousness. The direction in which you are moving will determine whether you are examining what is deeper and more hidden or are aspiring to higher levels of functioning. The slow, steady pace of an escalator symbolizes the gentleness and grace in the process of investigation that is going on. A broken escalator means that you will have to do more work to figure out what is currently challenging you.

Exams: Accountability and responsibility are the principles that lie behind the symbolic meaning of exams. When you were in school, the exam was a high-pressured demand to perform along these lines, and the exam is one of the most prolific dream environments to return to. In this way, taking an exam is a fairly ubiquitous anxiety dream and always relates to your experience of being held accountable for what you have recently learned. (See *Pop Quiz, Quiz, Taking a Test*.)

Executions: This dream indicates a need to sacrifice a way of being or thinking that no longer serves you. Such a sacrifice is a symbolic movement in the process of change and the evolution of your character. Something needs to die in order for something else to be reborn. In the case of an execution, the impulse to do this is coming out of some perceived wrong, shame, or defect of character. A particular way of being in the world as represented by the character being executed is no longer necessary. If it is you who is being executed, then it is your whole sense of identity that is being confronted with drastic change. If you are doing the executing, then your ego mind is getting ready for some dynamic housecleaning. If neither of these scenarios is the case, consider what you know about the person being executed. You will find what is currently up for transformation in the character aspect that the individual embodies.

Exes: This is one of the most commonly misunderstood images in the lexicon of dreaming. In archetypal psychology, we each have within us an image of the beloved. When we find someone on the outside who matches our image on the inside, we fall in love. When two people's versions of this align, it forms a relationship. When we dream of our past partners, we are dreaming about the part of ourselves that is prepared and aligned to relate with another person in an intimate connection, but from an earlier time in our emotional development. When such a dream comes along, the thing to do is to consider a few things and apply the one that fits the most. Ask yourself what you learned from that relationship and how would it be helpful in your current circumstances to tap into that knowledge. Additionally, you can consider the actual qualities of your ex and ask yourself how that person's specific attributes might be being called into activation in some area of your current life. The dream about the ex has nothing to do with the real-life ex.

Exit Sign: These ubiquitous objects are indications of how to shift your current environment. There is a sense of urgency connected with exit signs, as they are posted generally for the purpose of rapid evacuation. In a dream, they are the indication that your current level of risk is acceptable because you know where to move to reduce that risk when you feel the need. What situation in your life feels slightly uncomfortable such that you would prefer to know where the nearest exit is?

Expiration Date: The idea behind the expiration date is about safety; anything that falls before the posted date is safe to consume. If something feels risky to you, the presence of an expiration date is the confirmation you need to proceed. This can be applied to any aspect of risk in your current life. Also to be considered is the notion of time running out on something that needs your immediate attention.

Explosion: The essence of an explosion is combustion, and combustion means change and transformation. The distinction here is how fast change sometimes occurs, and in the case of an explosion, change is happening very rapidly. Remember that in a dream, an explosion is a positive thing and indicates that some transition in your life is happening abruptly and may be causing you fear. Change can be very frightening, and it is part of the human experience to fear change. The explosion in your dream may indicate that whatever is occurring is inevitable.

Eyes: The eyes are the windows of the soul, so the saying goes. They are also the dominant sense with which human beings navigate their existence. There are many things that can happen with the eyes in a dream, but whatever that is, consider that the interpretation should connect to how you are seeing things in your life at the time of the dream. Anything that involves your eyes should be considered as relating to you directly, but if the eyes belong to someone within the dream, look at the character aspects of that individual and consider what would occur if you saw things through that person's eyes. Eyes that are closed may point to not wanting to see something that needs your attention.

Face: You meet the world with your face, and everything that is occurring inside of your consciousness is either revealed or hidden there. When your face or the face of another is featured in your dream, consider any interpretation you make through the lens of how authentic you are being in your daily life. Whatever is occurring to a face in a dream will add layers of distinction to your interpretation. Marks, scars, pimples, or boils are all examples of ways in which the face inadvertently reveals things that are below the surface of a darker nature.

Facebook: The new world of social media offers an experience of instantaneous expression of elements of your daily life. Facebook is a community where you get to choose what you present to the world, so as a symbol it connects to this idea of controlling how others see you and how they may perceive your life. Facebook also represents a desire to feel connected to others without really experiencing the vulnerability of true intimacy.

Faceless: The face connects to the concept of the persona, the part of who we are that we readily show to the world. We hide our true self behind our face and choose what we want to present to others. This process can be oppressive, and a dream image of being faceless may indicate the consequences of either holding back too much authenticity or, conversely, exposing more than we are comfortable with. While your actions identify what you are committed to, it is through your face that you reveal your motivations. Without a face, the assimilation of an identity is impossible. An aspect of your personality that has no face may connect to a new way of being in the world. Lacking a face may indicate that this new way of being is not yet fully formed as an active part of your outward persona.

Facelift: Any alteration to the face is akin to exerting some measure of control over the mask we show to the world. When this alteration is reflected as surgical in nature, the resulting change is manipulated and inorganic. Plastic surgery is usually chosen in an effort to appear more attractive, desirable, or acceptable than one already feels. Ask yourself how authentic you are being in your interactions with others. This dream could point to something out of balance with how you feel and what you project.

Factory: A factory is ultimately a building in which something is built or made. The building itself then is a symbol of a clear foundational structure of thoughts, ideas, or a belief system that exists within your psyche. What is created in the factory provides an important distinction when considering such a dream. Whatever the factory makes offers the primary clue to your interpretation. Then recognize that whatever meaning you attribute to that, there is a great deal of permanence to that belief system or idea.

Fair: A fair is a public display of joy and frivolity that has its origins in agrarian society, where farmers showed off their accomplishments and a community joined together in celebration. In this way, there is a very grounded and earthy sensibility to the fair as a dream image. Dreaming of a fair or fairgrounds may be indicating that it is time to slow down and find joy in simple things.

Fairy: The tradition of fairies is quite ancient and ubiquitous in most mythologies in some form or another. Fairies have evolved and are fully present in modern media. They are very small magical beings who are thought of as harmless and even helpful in children's material of today. However, they originated as beings who were often tricksters and filled with malice and ill intent. If such a creature appears in a dream, be careful to see what its actual desires are. A fairy could represent a thought or idea that looks harmless but actually may mean you harm. Look to where in your life you may be falling victim to magical thinking.

Falcon: All birds connect to the essence of messengers, but the falcon has a very special medicine. Fierce and powerful, this bird has a rich history in a number of mythologies. Its vantage point is considered visionary, and when one appears in a dream, you are being guided from a very high place. You can be led to your life purpose through the vision of the falcon. These birds are also associated with hunting and warlike aggression, so not only are you being guided by the falcon, you are also being given the power to go after what you desire.

Falling: This is a dream about the loss of control. A fall is one of the most frequently occurring dream images, and all human beings have experienced this at one time or another. A fall can be very frightening; however, the real danger is not the fall itself, but the sudden stop that is likely to follow. Therefore, the real source of the fear associated with this symbol is what may occur, and the anxiety about not being able to directly impact the outcome of a situation. The deeper meaning of falling dreams is that the highest road to take in any difficult situation is to surrender yourself to the lack of control you are experiencing. In any situation where there is no control to be had, letting go is the only powerful choice to make. Most dreams of falling do not end in landing, further cementing the symbolic connection of this image with surrender. Where and how you land will be directly tied to the quality of your descent. The more graceful the fall, the more likely you will benefit from where you wind up. The context will offer you subtleties of meaning by examining the way you are falling in your dream. Falling backward indicates not being able to see the direction you are taking. Facing forward might enable you to see what you are facing, but your fall still indicates lack of control. Spiral twisting is an even stronger loss, as in spiraling out of control. The amount of fear felt in the dream is the barometer of how much unconscious fear is being suppressed. A fall that is easy and flows with a sense of surrender might be telling you that you are ready to let go of control in some situation. Falling in a dream could be compensating for some area in your life where you are reaching higher than is appropriate to your current circumstances or level of development.

Family: All the people in your dreams represent aspects of you, the dreamer. When they are known to you, the dream can also be reflecting your outside relationships in the waking world. However, the most value in interpreting such a dream still connects to how the people represent aspects of yourself. This is the most difficult to do when the people in your dreams are members of your family. You are who you are in life as a result of the role you played in the dynamics of your family. As you grow and mature through life, you will have a sense of your identity changing. However, if your family of origin creates the setting and characters of a dream, you can interpret such a dream as relating to your personality and identity as it relates to your first few decades of life.

Family Members: All people in a dream represent aspects of your own personality. This is also true of family members, although such dreams may also be reflecting your waking-life relationships as well. Your first relationships in life are with the individuals who make up your family of origin, and all the relationships you have for the rest of your life are reflections of these original dynamics. When interpreting a dream that involves a family member, consider the qualities of that person first and the relationship you have to the person second. Each person in your family lives inside you as an aspect of your personality based on these qualities. Parents relate more to a sense of personal authority. Siblings connect with different choices or behaviors in your waking life. When a family member appears in a dream, ask yourself what quality the person embodies that might be called for in some situation or circumstance in your waking life at the time of the dream.

Fan: The purpose of a fan is to cool the temperature around you by moving the surrounding air faster in order to create a breeze. In this way, a fan of any type has a primary symbolic meaning connected to the desire to reduce heat. That heat can be thought of as literal temperature or the heat of passion or anger. In a contradictory fashion, using a fan to move air can actually increase heat by speeding up the flow of oxygen toward a flame, as in "fanning the flames." A hand fan can also symbolize eroticism in this same way, symbolically heating and cooling ardor by using it to extend gestures as a language of seduction.

Fangs: The animal kingdom has many examples of fang-bearing creatures, and in almost all cases, the purpose of the fang is to hold on to prey. In snakes and spiders, there is the added distinction of injecting venom. The canine teeth of humans are not considered fangs, but in vampire mythology these teeth are elongated and are that creature's tool for extracting the blood he or she needs. If some animal, fictitious creature, or other human being is exposing fangs to you in a dream, you may be expressing fears of being dominated and consumed in some way. If you are the one who is sporting fangs, you may be expressing a voracious appetite that either needs to be expressed or is being expressed in the world. If the former idea resonates, look to where you can increase your passions. If it is the latter that feels true, you may be hurting others with your words or actions.

Farm: A farm represents the production of food to provide nurturance through abundance on a large scale. Evoking images of serenity and simplicity, farms harken back to a connection to the land that is all but forgotten in our current culture and history. Working on a farm points to a call to action to dig deeper and take responsibility for getting your needs met. Owning a farm connects to how responsible you are to your self-nurturing and perhaps to the dependence of others upon you for such needs. If you can eat only what you plant and tend, then farms connect to taking (or not taking) responsibility for your personal needs and how you get them addressed. A specific farm crop could add some texture to your meaning. A dairy farm might connect to emotional matters, maternal concerns, and thoughts around children. A farm that slaughters animals suggests more substantial issues around taking care of sustenance. Slaughter and sacrifice relate to having to let go of something in order to receive something else and thereby achieve balance. An organic farm points to radical measures urging you toward a healthier approach to meeting your needs.

Fart: This is an unintended slip expressing some small, hidden feeling of shame or embarrassment. If the release of gas is very large, you may be dreaming of finally letting go of something you have been holding on to that you have been afraid to express. If you are holding back from this in your dream, consider that there may be a need to release something that you would rather not be made public.

Fast Food: Any food connects to how you are nurturing and sustaining yourself and fulfilling your own needs. Fast food is nutritionally worthless, and a dream that features this as an image may be asking how well are you taking care of yourself.

Fat: We have very powerful associations with fat in our culture, but at the heart of this symbol, fat relates to increasing your level of protection and number of provisions for your needs to get met. At its most fundamental level, fat is the mammalian body's way of creating stores of energy to be tapped into during times of lack. For most people, being fat is associated with sloth, blame, and shame. The media virulently reinforces this perspective. Therefore, your personal relationship with regard to fat as a symbol must connect to your own experience of your body shape and size. Gaining weight in a dream could point out an unconscious need to protect yourself from emotional stress. It can also indicate a need to put a protective barrier between yourself and the outside world. Losing weight could represent either a shedding of old defenses or a depletion of resources. Look to areas in your life where you may be feeling a sense of lack or fears of future limitation.

Father: See *Parents*.

Faucet: A faucet is the access point to running water, a symbol of civilization, convenience, and abundant living. Water connects to the emotional elements of the human experience, and in this way a faucet represents what can be done when your emotional life is harnessed for good. In the Western world, we take this for granted, but as a symbol a faucet is expressing the rather amazing access you can have to the flow of your emotions and the ability to be productive with it. Some-

thing inhibiting a faucet in a dream is reflecting an imbalance in how you are sustaining yourself, keeping filled with life force, and possibly cleansing your emotional experience so that you can continually start fresh.

Feather: The feather is considered a sacred object by itself, and one of the reasons for that connects to what it originally is part of. Feathers are an integral element of a bird's wings and as such are a reminder of the power associated with flight. To find a feather in your dream is to remember your higher aspirations. If you have something created out of feathers, such as an outfit or object, then this aspirational consciousness is taking an even more significant form.

Feces: See *Defecation*.

Feet: The feet are the part of the body that make the most contact with the ground, and as such they are symbolic of how grounded you are. They also point to the direction in which you are walking through life. Dreams that relate to the feet are pointing out elements of your relationship to the earth and your sense of stability. The feet also connect to how well you are experiencing living in the present moment, for that is something that is experienced right where your feet are.

Fence: Fences mark the boundaries that we set in the world, and any dream that contains this symbol can reveal current issues as they relate to the boundaries in your life, both those that you set and those that are set for you by others. The size of the fence and the material of which it is made add texture to any interpretation of a fence in a dream. The more impenetrable the material is, the stronger the boundary is. Which side of a fence you are on in a dream will figure heavily in how you examine such a dream. A flimsy wooden fence could indicate that you are too exposed, while a high concrete wall may indicate shutting the world out for fear of being vulnerable. A break in a chainlink fence could indicate a weak spot in your ability to protect yourself in some area of your life. If the fence contains barbed wire or some other harmful material, this could represent the consequences of taking the risk to shift boundaries in some life situation.

Ferris Wheel: As a carnival ride, the ferris wheel relates to brief moments of escapism and a desire to change things up in your life. The specific nature of this particular ride is about rising to higher vantage points, but the repetitive nature suggests that it doesn't offer anything of true substance. If you get stuck in such a ride, you may be dreaming of a desire to see further without doing the real work to expand your consciousness. The ferris wheel is usually the most visible element of a fair that can be seen from a distance. In this way, it can be a symbol of joy and playfulness that is available for you to enjoy.

Ferry: Ferries have two distinctions that inform their symbolic meaning. First, they traverse water, which means they help us move through emotional territory. Second, they generally transport cars as well as their drivers. Since cars are the vehicles through which we traverse our lifelong journey along the path, the ferry is the emotional detour so that

we can get to territory we wish to explore next.

Festival: You may need to rally all your resources into some creative direction and have your efforts acknowledged at a public level. A festival is a large group of people all gathered for some specific focus. This has the implication that a great deal of your consciousness is focusing on one particular form of expression. In life, most festivals center on some sort of artistic or agrarian endeavor, implying that the more creative elements of your psyche are being stimulated. Consider what the theme of the festival is to get more clarity about what this dream means.

Fetus: A fetus is a developmental stage in the life of any animal whose young are gestated inside the mother's body. In this stage, all creatures resemble one another, so one of the significant distinctions about a fetus is that it contains a sense of infinite possibility in terms of what it is going to become. In this way, a fetus is an idea, a direction, a new path, or a concept that has yet to even be birthed. An aborted fetus is such an idea that is terminated before it can even reveal what it might have grown into. (See *Abortion*.)

Fight: A fight is a masculine-principle way of solving a problem by meeting it head-on with equal force. This approach may or may not be effective. Look to where in your life you may be fighting something that would be better surrendered to.

File Cabinet: There is a need to organize your thoughts and ideas. The state of the filing cabinet in your dream will reflect how pressing this need is. Other details of the dream will help you understand what areas of your life need attending to in a more detailed way.

Files: This symbol represents the coalescing of ideas or the various thoughts that are pertinent to one particular organized principle of different thoughts. A file in a dream indicates that previous efforts around a particular idea have been collected and are being stored for future use. The other elements of the dream will help you understand what area of your life is being focused on in this concentrated way.

Filling: If a filling makes itself known to you after it has been put in your mouth, there is likely something wrong with it. As such, most dreams about fillings have to do with the idea of one becoming loose or otherwise compromised. In this way, such a dream is about a long-ago problem coming back to challenge you once again, especially a problem around insecurity and having a strong and powerful voice.

Film: Almost obsolete, film is the substance upon which we imprint our creative expressions and the desire to capture a moment. Since film has essentially been replaced by digital media, the essence of film as a symbol embodies the idea that it must be processed first before you can see the image that is captured on it. In this way, any dream that features film in it may be asking you to be patient while you see what is developing.

Fingernails: Fingernails are often adorned to draw attention to them, but they can also be a place where anxiety is expressed in the bit-

ing of them. Either way, the creative expression associated with fingers as a symbol has the added distinction of adornment when fingernails are featured in a dream, even if that adornment is the evidence of a nail biter.

Fingerprints: Fingerprints are created when the unique pattern on the tips of your fingers mixes with oils that your skin excretes, leaving a mark that can be unequivocally tracked back to your presence. You may be leaving your mark where you do not wish to, or you may be unaware that your impact has been noted by others. Conversely, the presence of fingerprints in a dream may indicate that something you are investigating in your own consciousness is slowly being revealed.

Fingers: The hands are the most creative body part, and the fingers represent our ability to be finely tuned with details in terms of how we express our ability to direct that creativity into various forms. How effective you are feeling in the world may be expressed by a dream with fingers playing a prominent role. Consider that each finger has specific meanings: The thumb is connected to dexterity and the ability to get things done. The first finger is the pointer, which correlates to blame and making choices. The middle finger expresses disdain and anger. The fourth finger relates to commitment and collaboration. The last finger connects to expressiveness and gentility.

Finish Line: The mark at the end of the race, the finish line in a dream indicates that you are very close to completing some chapter, cycle, or process.

Fire: Things are changing in a dramatic way. The combustion of fire destroys everything in its path. However, remember that fire reduces what it burns to carbon, the building block of all life. So while the destruction of fire is absolute, like all change, it is making way for something else to be created. A small fire or spark may indicate that winds of change are approaching, whereas something raging out of control could be pointing to change and transformation that feels overwhelming and scary. Consider what is burning in the dream, and that will shed light on what a dream that features fire is reflecting. What is burning is likely the most important focus of your investigation. If it is something you are familiar with, it may indicate that a major transformation is occurring in your life in the arena represented by that thing. A house on fire connects to a transformation in your personal identity. A building that is more public relates more to your social identity. An object that you possess could be explored and the meaning you associate with it combined with the idea of radical change in that area. A fire in nature might point to a loss of resources, nurturing, or creativity. If someone dies in a fire, that person's character aspect will inform you of what part of yourself is being sacrificed in order for a new sense of self to emerge. The size of the fire and your emotional response to it will illuminate issues of overwhelm and loss of control. A large fire that is out of control could indicate broad-based changes that may be resulting in the total dissolution of the old landscape of your life. A contained fire could indicate that the change may be manageable and possibly even intentional. A campfire in the outdoors could represent your ability to create powerful change out of limited resources. A fireplace or wood-burning stove relates to harnessing change for your benefit or pleasure. While fire is dangerous and violent, it has the power to purify and create the possibility of renewal and new growth. When it appears in a dream, be aware that great change is afoot and that the future is likely to bring new life and new possibility. (See *Flame*.)

Fire Engine: Fire is a symbol of great change and transformation. The fire engine is the part of your consciousness that needs to be called upon when things are changing too fast for your own comfort and you wish to slow things down to a more manageable pace.

Fire Escape: Fire is a symbol of great change and transformation. Change is scary and we often avoid it. The fire escape is an image that implies knowing how to get out of a hot situation should it prove too dangerous or frightening. The challenge with this in a dream is to identify whether your fears are warranted or if you should turn around, go back, and face the changes that are inevitable.

Firefighter: The firefighter is an archetypal character that is called upon when there is great change occurring and that change is overwhelming or out of control. This is the part of your consciousness that can attempt to manage the level of chaos and the sense that things are out of control.

Firefly: This is a symbol for fleeting moments of inspiration. Something that flies through the air connects to the intellect, like thoughts. The sudden glow of a firefly's tail is evidence that it is there, flying around undetected, but suddenly makes itself known, just like an idea that briefly appears in your consciousness and just as quickly fades away. Your dream may be asking you to pay closer attention to the random thoughts of inspiration that pass through your consciousness lest they pass you by.

Fireplace: All symbols that relate to fire are about change and transformation. A fireplace is a humanmade construction designed to take the amazing power offered by a fire and contain it in such a way to provide any number of services. Fire represents change and transformation on an enormous scale. However, when it is enclosed in a safe and durable structure, that force of change becomes both highly effective and focusable. The usable power of fire lies in a very small window of the continuum on which it exists. Too little and it does little more than look pretty. Just a little too much and the danger is life-threatening and enormously destructive. A fireplace is the organizing principle around which great power can be harnessed to accomplish a very specific goal.

Fish: Fish are like ideas that are floating under the surface of your unconscious mind. Dreaming of fish means you are considering what is lurking just below your awareness, the thoughts and feelings that are close enough to be known to you but that you may have to make an effort to get to the heart of. If the fish are colorful and beautiful, they may be representing more creative aspects of

your potential expression. Fish in a tank may be the ideas from your unconscious of which you are actually becoming aware. Containing them in a tank may be considering taking action on them, but could also indicate being stuck in a cycle of limiting your creative expression. A live fish out of water reacts violently. In a dream, this could symbolize the awkwardness surrounding vulnerable expression. Eating fish is to experience satisfaction from the constructive use of your ideas and thoughts.

Fish Tank: Fish are symbolic of ideas that float around under the surface of the water of your emotions and your unconscious nature. A fish tank is a symbol that puts such ideas on display, like a reminder of the beautiful notions that are available to you if you look below the surface.

Fishing: If your dream involves the act of fishing, there is an entirely different interpretation to consider. The act of fishing is the search for an idea that matches a particular desire. The process requires the proper tools, an element of attraction (bait), and the most important ingredient—patience. (See *Fish*.)

Fist: This is a symbol for aggressive tendencies and the preparedness to fight. A fist implies an angry reaction to something and the readiness to take action or retaliation.

Five: What follows the foundational sense of four is the freedom of five. Once a structure has been established, there is now a sense of safety and security for exploration. The number five embodies this expressiveness. The human body expresses the number five as represented by the four limbs and the head. The ability for the body to move about through space is a vibrant and exhilarating experience. In this way, five symbolizes freedom, joy, and bliss. With this comes the shadow of freedom: indulgence. This expression of five can carry grave consequences, such as compulsion and addiction.

Flag: The flag is a symbol itself and always represents something such as a country, a state, or an organization. In a dream, the flag represents another thought or feeling, depending on the nature of the flag. Something that looks or feels governmental or political might connect to the structures of your life. A white flag suggests that you need to surrender something that is occurring for you. A red flag is a warning that is often unheeded.

Flame: The flame is the tip of the fire and could be thought of as the part of the fire that spreads from one thing to another. The flame of a candle or any fire may seem manageable at first, but it could easily lead to more combustion if left to its own devices. In this way, a flame is the potential for greater destruction if you are careless. (See *Fire*.)

Flamingo: The flamingo is a wading bird, so it is connected symbolically to the realm of emotions and things that are just under the surface of the unconscious. A flamingo's elegant visage and beautiful pink color give it the added dimension of signaling in a soft way something that may be brewing just under the surface. Flamingos stand in murky territory as if to say, "Something is lurking just under the surface here."

Flash Mob: A relatively new phenomenon, the flash mob is a moment of creative genius that arises out of chaos. It is a symbol of the ability of random thoughts to suddenly coalesce into a single magnificent idea, direction, or creative project. In life, such an event requires an enormous amount of preparation and teamwork to execute in a successful manner. Consider each person in the flash mob in your dream as an individual thought or idea that lives inside your own consciousness. When these random tangents of thought are brought together into alignment with an idea or project that you would like to manifest, amazing things can be accomplished through cooperation and organization.

Flashlight: Any light is symbolic of the desire to illuminate and see more clearly. A flashlight implies a sense of portability and the capacity to shed light on a situation at any time. A flashlight in a dream indicates that some sort of deeper investigation is at hand.

Flea Market: This gathering of people who are selling used items is symbolic of the notion that old ideas can be traded for currency or the idea of making room for something new by releasing that which no longer serves you.

Flies: Most insects are symbols of the underlying ideas and constructs that we generally consider repellent or undesirable. Flies in particular carry disease and are often associated with both fecal matter and decomposition. From this perspective, flies are associated with the possibility of such repulsive material being nearby. In this way, they connect to the shadow side of things we wish weren't close to us.

Flight Attendant: An airplane relates to sudden transitions in life, as you get on a plane in one place and get off it in completely different territory. The flight attendant is the person whose role is to make that trip more comfortable and safe. As a symbol, flight attendants are the parts of your consciousness that are designed to ease your way through difficult shifts.

Flood: Water in dreams relates to emotional issues and the unconscious mind. A flood is the destructive experience of being overwhelmed on an emotional level. This is a fairly common dream theme and will emerge when your life is offering you experiences that are stimulating deep responses on a feeling level.

Floors: A dream that involves anything to do with floors or flooring symbolizes considerations of feeling supported. The floor is the symbolic foundation of our identity. Buildings in dreams represent our different perceptions of consciousness. Houses, especially, connect to our sense of self. As such, the floor represents the foundation on which we stand as individuals. The quality and integrity of the floor in your dream informs how grounded you currently feel. A solid floor with structural integrity points to solidity of identity. Any type of damage or erosion indicates that there is change afoot.

Flowers: A flower is a symbol for expressions of love and beauty for its own sake. Flowers also represent fertility and the possibility of new growth in the future. There is a language to flowers that we have lost in modern society but that was once a vibrant way of communicating specific loving messages. For example,

a red rose signifies romantic love, whereas a yellow one indicates platonic love. No matter what distinctions you draw about the specific flower(s) that appear in your dream, consider that once flowers are picked, they begin the process of wilting and decay, representing the ephemeral nature of feelings of love and its expression.

Flying: You are ascending and rising above mundane life. You may also be avoiding something on the ground. This is one of the most common universal dream images. One of the most delightful aspects of dreaming, this cross-cultural symbol means that you are rising above everything that is on the ground. Since this can be a wonderful sensation, it is often associated with intense feelings of a positive nature. A flying dream could indicate strong feelings of freedom and bliss, which can represent moving toward a higher state of awareness or connection with spirit. It can also provide a broader perspective on your life by virtue of giving you a higher vantage point. However, it should not be overlooked that this very experience can be used as a defense by the unconscious. When this dream appears, it begs the following question: Is there anything that is being avoided or overlooked by rising above the conflict or simply not being grounded in reality?

Fog: You are having trouble seeing things clearly because of an illusory blend of thoughts and feelings. One of the interesting things about fog is that it mixes the symbolic meaning of two different elements: air and water. Fog occurs as a phenomenon in the air, yet it only exists when there is an abundance of moisture in the atmosphere, therefore connecting it to the emotions. By combining the two elemental aspects of air and water, fog is the symbolic phenomenon of what can happen when unconscious thoughts and hidden emotions combine. Fog can completely block your vision and impair your ability to navigate safely. Fog presents a potential danger to those who are traveling through it, whether over water or on land. It may be seen as the blindness that can result when your thoughts and feelings interact with each other in a confusing way. It also indicates a need to slow down and be more careful as you move about your environment. If fog is present in your dream, ask yourself if there is any area in your life that you may not be seeing accurately.

Food: Any dream with food involved is connecting to the principles of sustenance, self-care, and nurturance. If you exert rigid control over your eating in life, then you must consider food through the lens of control. If you abandon all discipline in the face of eating, you must consider food through the lens of indulgence. As this is a continuum, place yourself anywhere on the scale between these two extremes. If you are eating in the dream, combine the quality of that experience with your waking perspective. For control, eating might suggest that more nurturance is needed in some area of your life. If indulgent, you may be getting a warning of a need for discipline or a hidden impulse to stuff feelings that need expression. If you are having dream-hunger, then the control perspective could point to the impact that some

exertion of limitation or lack in your life is having. In what ways are you starving?

Football: Football is a game of strategy and brute force that mirrors the act of war, where each side is engaged in the struggle to take back certain amounts of territory from their enemy. As a symbol, this very popular game is a primal expression of the competitive nature of human beings that is also infused with a level of joy in expressing these urges. If football features in a dream, you may be looking for a healthy and socially acceptable way of expressing aggression and competition.

Fork: A utensil is a mechanism that assists in the process of taking in food. Eating is symbolic of self-care and nurturance. In this way, a fork is first and foremost a symbol related to meeting these needs. As a distinction, a fork relates to making specific choices and adding an element of efficacy around taking care of yourself.

Fountain: Your emotions are bubbling up in a controlled expression of joy and ebullience. Water in a dream is always connected to emotions, and a fountain carefully constructs the flow of water in a specific way and does so for the sake of beauty and pleasure. The larger the fountain, the more emotions are being dealt with. Something in public indicates the need or desire to control your emotional expression as you are out in the world. A small water fixture that you might find in a home has the same meaning, only on a smaller scale. One that is broken in some way indicates a need to give some attention to how well you are expressing your feelings in a way that can be easily received by others. Be willing to explore whether the control implied by a fountain is in your best interests or a way of avoiding the messiness of some emotional outbreaks.

Four: When you add a fourth point to a triangle, you end up with a square. Four is the number of structure. Once the creative impulse has been satisfied, it is time for solidification, which can be accomplished by the power of four. A wonderful weight-bearing shape, a square is what allows for building the foundation on which the creative energies of three can be supported. Four connects to the establishment of institutions, order, rules, and regulations. While a number of great strength, it can engender a sense of limitation and the concept of restraint.

Four-Leaf Clover: The four-leaf clover is the ultimate symbol of fortune. If you stumble upon it, you are guaranteed a measure of good luck. If you find one in the land of your dreams, you are expressing a desire to increase your sense of abundance and prosperity and unexpected income.

Fox: The fox is clever and a bit of a trickster. When the fox appears in a dream, you are being connected to the medicine of strategy and adaptability. What situation in your life right now is requiring a bit of cunning? The fox will help you with any endeavors that require a quick mind and a nimble response.

Frog: There is no escaping the fairy tale of the frog that might turn into a prince when kissed by a young maiden. The essence of this construct is potential. Potential can be a powerful force for change if it is embraced; however,

potential that is not met is of no value whatsoever. There are other meanings associated with frogs because of their amphibious nature. They represent parts of us that can survive both on land and in water. Unseen when under the surface of a pond, frogs can hop out at any moment, just as a strong emotional response can sometimes hop out of the unconscious without warning.

Fruit: The bounty of life on earth is expressed by all of the various edibles that Mother Nature has created for us. The sweetness of fruit connects to the sweetness of life. If you are dreaming of fruit of any kind, you are expressing a desire for life to feel abundant and prosperous. There is a cycle of ripeness associated with fruit that indicates a specific moment at which it is advantageous to benefit from a project, idea, or vision that may be at hand. If you wait too long to act, the fruits of your labor may be lost.

Funeral: You are processing a major change or transformation. While a funeral centers on someone who has died, the event is designed for the living. A powerful ritual, a funeral helps people process the death of someone close to them in a collective procedure that acknowledges the loss and marks the beginning of a new chapter in their lives without the deceased. In a dream in which you are at a funeral, the identity of the deceased will play an important role in your interpretation. By examining the person as a character aspect of yourself, you can consider what part of your psyche no longer serves you and has been sacrificed. In this case, only half the transformation is complete, because funerals mark a death and not the rebirth that inevitably follows. A common dream with this symbol involves the dreamer discovering that the funeral he or she is attending is his or her own. If this is the case, then the transformation that is taking place is more generalized and may connect to a developmental stage in life or a change of a large-enough magnitude as to imply a death of self. Another potential interpretation of this dream connects to feeling a lack of passion or life force in your current circumstances. (See *Death*.)

Furniture: A room has the consciousness that relates to the purpose of the space itself. The same can be said for furniture. The function of the object expresses the universal meanings associated with it. In a general sense, furniture is symbolic of your ability to express a particular desire, creative impulse, or structural function. Furniture in storage means that a change in how you are expressing yourself is at hand. Furniture that is old and battered may represent a need to update your ideas about how to express yourself. New furniture is symbolic of a new direction in some area of your waking life.

Gagging: You are stifling the impulse to rid or purge yourself of an idea, habit, or thought pattern. There may be a great deal of toxicity in your environment that you are not quite ready to deal with, and the gagging reflex is indicating that your level of tolerance is nearly at its apex. Vomiting is a symbol for the process of ridding yourself of something that does not serve you. Gagging is the simultaneous presence of this impulse along with the sense that it is not quite time. Gagging in a dream is a warning that something is about to be revealed and what that is may not be pleasant or healthy.

Galaxy: A galaxy is a bit like a unit of measurement that helps describe the known universe. It is easy for a modern human being to consider that our solar system is part of a larger complex known as a galaxy and that there are billions of these enormous systems that populate our universe. To be dreaming of a galaxy is to be contemplating life on this humongous scale. This could be a literal consideration of existential reality or a symbol for the bigger picture of your unfolding life.

Game Night: A social gathering to enjoy the spirit of competition in a fun atmosphere is at the heart of game night. As a symbol, it represents the need to express the fundamental drive to compete and win but to do so in a way that is harmless and playful. Game night in a dream may be pointing to a buildup of stressors and drives that need release in a constructive manner.

Game Show: A media-driven shared experience of skill and luck is what a game show is all about. A viewer lives vicariously through the experience of the player and his or her chance to win. If you are watching a game show in your dream, then the emphasis of your interpretation should be on the vicarious element of this symbol. If you are playing on a game show, you may be expressing a desire to take a chance for potential gain.

Gang: At the heart of it, a gang is an intimate social structure that provides its members with a sense of community and support. Because of the nefarious behavior often associated with a gang, this symbol is more reflective of the shadow and disowned qualities. The presence of a gang in a dream indicates a need for support around ideas that may feel scary to consider. Such a dream may show up when you are feeling cut off or disenfranchised.

Garage: This is a symbol for a temporary stopping point in your journey with the anticipation of movement in life. The primary purpose of a garage is to keep one's car safe and protected when not in use. The car is symbolic of how we maneuver through our lives. When a garage is prominent in a dream, some element of how you are moving forward (or not) is being expressed. The essence of a garage connects to being prepared to move out into the world. If the garage is a private one that is part of a home, then you must use the symbolic sensibility and apply it to your private life. A public garage indicates that the dream is reflecting issues that center around your social experience. Since there are many cars being stored in such a setting, it reflects a significant number of choices available to you. Being unable to locate your car in a garage is indicative of being temporarily stuck in some area of your life. Ask yourself where you would like to be heading and what you have to do to prepare yourself for the journey.

Garbage: Garbage is the waste product of our daily lives, that which we consider no longer of value. If we do not dispose of it in a timely manner, it builds up to a repulsive level and begins to decompose. Garbage then is a symbol of those things that no longer serve you and must be removed or recycled. A buildup of garbage in a dream may indicate a buildup of things in your life that must be discarded and released.

Garden: You are dreaming of abundance, prosperity, and your ability to create structure and the boundaries of self-care and nurturance. A garden is a planned, deliberate construct that creates growth in a confined area. Whether the growth is for beauty or consumption, it represents the feminine principles of creativity and nurturing. The structure and boundaries of the garden are the expression of the masculine principle in action. In this way, gardens are a microcosm of the act of creation itself. The act of gardening is often reported to produce significant levels of serenity, relaxation, and pleasure for the enthusiast. In a dream, a garden may represent a need or desire to produce an atmosphere of peace, abundance, or nurturance in your life. The type of garden, the state it is in, and what you are doing in relation to it reflect what area is being expressed and your current ability to be effective in it.

Gargoyle: A gargoyle is a representation of a demon or otherwise horrifying image that was placed on the edifices of buildings, pointed outward in an effort to ward off evil. Even though gargoyles have a horrific appearance, they are ultimately guardians of protection. Are you overprotecting yourself because of fear? What aren't you willing to face in your life right now?

Gas Chamber: An instrument of institutionalized murder, the gas chamber has both of these elements as part of its symbolic makeup. The murder portion suggests a need or desire to change some element of our consciousness, so much so as to need a death to represent the level of change that is being considered. The institutional nature of the gas chamber suggests that the impetus for this level of sacrifice or change may have more to do with what is good for the community than something personal. There may be some intense expression of guilt associated with this image showing up in a dream.

Gas Mask: The gas mask is an instrument of protection against airborne poisons. Anything that relates to air connects to the world of intellect and thinking. Poisonous gas is a symbol for thoughts, ideas, and consciousness that are floating around the atmosphere and can harm you. The gas mask is therefore a symbol for the protection needed to keep such ideas from harming you. Is the environment in which you find yourself in your life right now toxic?

Gas Station: The car is a symbol for how we move about on the path of our life, and a gas station is where we fuel up for the journey we are on. Whatever is happening in a gas station in your dream can be interpreted as reflecting how easily or how challenging it is for you to get to where you desire to go. You may need to recharge yourself before you can go any further in your life.

Gasoline: Gasoline is a highly flammable material that is cultivated primarily for fueling many of the vehicles we use to move about in life. The essence of its symbolic meaning connects to its combustibility and not necessarily its productive use. In an engine, gas is symbolic of the power that creates movement and power that can be harnessed. Outside of an engine, it represents the potential for such power that comes with dangerous consequences if it is not used with respect. Are you using your potential well, or are you in danger of experiencing an unexpected explosion by misusing your potential?

Gate: A gate is an opening in what is otherwise a boundaried enclosure. The symbolic meaning behind a fence or a wall is the separation that is constructed to keep different ideas or areas of consciousness apart. The gate, therefore, represents the choice to move into new territory. If a gate is locked and is blocking your way, you are at a crossroads. If you are on the inside of a gate, consider that choices you have made to be open may be leaving you feeling too exposed. A broken gate indicates the loss of the ability to protect yourself with appropriate boundaries.

Gay Sex: Any sexual act in a dream connects symbolically to the process of integration and the joining together of different aspects of the personality. In the case of gay sex, what is being highlighted is elements of the masculine principle such as taking action and aggression. It is not unusual for heterosexual men and women to have dreams about gay sex, and such dreams are not necessarily related to sexuality or the waking-life expression of it. However, if the dreamer identifies as a gay man, then such dreams should be explored more literally.

Gazelle: The gazelle is known for its swiftness and ability to burst into quick, graceful movement. Its medicine relates to this ability to take immediate and powerful action and yet remain in a state of grace. When the gazelle appears in your dream, you are being called to take swift action but remain in a state of peace.

Gemstone: See *Stones*.

Genie: The mythology of the genie states that if you grant it freedom, it will give you the fulfillment of wishes. There are always consequences to such easy solutions to life's difficulties. Additionally, most genie tales involve the genie itself as a character who brings chaos and destruction in the end. Dreaming of a genie may be expressing a desire to have a quick and instantaneous change in your circumstances without being willing to put in the effort to create something organically. Letting the genie out of the bottle may be asking for trouble.

Ghost: You are dreaming of the memory or imprint of a former idea, concept, or person. A ghost is defined as a remnant of a person's energy that remains connected to the physical world after he or she has died. Some metaphysicians theorize that a spirit can be stuck here due to unfinished business or an untimely death. There are scientists who explore the possibility of ghosts as bumps in the electromagnetic field of energy that can sometimes be perceived by people who are living. No matter what camp you fall into, a ghost is symbolic of something from your past that continues to have a presence in your consciousness long after the event or person that inspired it has passed. This can include memories, habitual patterns, and even obsessions. If the ghost is someone you know who is not actually dead, use the character aspect technique to discover what qualities are traits that you have let go of but that may still arise in your behavior or thought patterns from time to time. Someone who has actually passed away can be considered in the same fashion, but might represent the impact he or she had on you in life, whether positive or negative. This image in a dream could point to a need to face the ghosts of your past in the form of old choices and behaviors that still haunt you with regret.

Giant: A giant is a particularly large version of a human being. Such a creature symbolically represents an inflated or expanded version of any number of concepts. Consider what the giant or giants are doing in the dream to determine how to interpret the dream. If the dream is frightening, you may be experiencing more fear than a situation truly merits in your waking life. If the giant in your dream is more benevolent, you may be asking for a certain aspect of your personality to get bigger in order to face a particular situation.

Gifts: You are dreaming of unknown sources of joy. While gifts are often associated with events that merit them, the giving and receiving of a gift speaks more about the relationship between the two parties than the reason for the giving. If your dream includes another person involved in a gift exchange, examine that individual as a character aspect that is highly beneficial to you at this time. This is the case whether you are the giver or the receiver in your dream. Gift exchanges can be so charged with elation that many people are motivated to gift others in order to experience this elevated feeling. If the dream reflects this perspective, look for places in your life that might be in need of an injection of joy. If there was any mystery surrounding the gift in your dream, the unknown factor points to areas in your life that may be offering you gifts, the value of which is not yet known. Your unconscious mind will always know well in advance of your conscious mind when a seemingly challenging situation is really a gift. This symbol in a dream may be the first sign that something of value is on the horizon, even if it isn't yet apparent.

Giraffe: The neck of the giraffe is one of nature's quirkiest and most elegant expressions. By virtue of its height, the giraffe can graze where no other animal can. Herein lies its medicine: When the giraffe appears in a dream, you are being given access to higher places to find sustenance and nurturing. You are gaining a higher vantage point as well.

Girdle: A girdle is an undergarment designed to alter the silhouette of the body, creating a slimmer appearance through constriction. Girdles are uncomfortable to wear and represent valuing something superficial over something more authentic. Are you putting something out into the world that is not quite the truth? If so, the girdle in your dream may be pointing out the discomfort you are suffering in order to present the variation of truth you are perpetrating.

Glacier: A glacier is part of the landscape of the earth and thus connects with the conscious mind. Because it is made up primarily of water, there is an emotional sensibility connected with a glacier as a symbol. That water is frozen, which implies a lack of warmth and compassion. Glaciers actually move, but very slowly, and we use the expression "at a glacial pace" to connote this extreme sluggishness. In a dream, a glacier suggests that you may have turned off some of your emotional warmth and are slowing down all processes because of that. What is not moving forward in your life because you have turned a cold face toward it? Also remember that some changes in life happen very, very slowly.

Glass: See *Cup*.

Glasses: Glasses are a symbol for seeing the world in a different way, or improving the way you perceive some aspect of your life. If you have lost a pair of glasses, the dream indicates a need to find a better viewpoint. Broken glasses suggest that a way of seeing things that previously worked for you is no longer viable.

If you wear glasses in your waking life, then the dream may be about connecting to your personal way of viewing things. If you don't, the dream may be suggesting the need to correct your current viewpoint.

Gloves: Gloves both protect and hide your hands, so they connect with your talents, abilities, skills, and expressiveness. This can be deliberate or imposed, helpful or limiting. The type of gloves and how they appear in the dream will give you clues for an accurate interpretation. Because we gesture with our hands, a dream about gloves may connect to the part of communication that is beyond our words and part of our body language. Gloves represent the various masks we wear in our communication to present that which we want to while hiding our true skins underneath. Sexy, tight-fitting gloves connect to subtle elements of seduction. Work gloves might help you find areas in your life where you feel you have to work hard to conceal your true meaning. Lace gloves evoke delicate communication that is only thinly veiled or is hiding the authentic meaning. Boxing gloves point to a fight brewing from a challenge in your life. They might also be inhibiting your communication because of guardedness—hands inside of boxing gloves may be ready to fight, but they can't be very gentle or expressive. Mittens may connect to a need or desire to be more comfortable, but at the loss of the same expressiveness or effectiveness. Long gloves up the arms connect to the extensiveness of the hidden issues or the seduction at hand. Rubber gloves may be about projecting underlying messages of more serious vulnerability to communication that is toxic.

Glue: Glue is a sticky substance that is a tool for joining that which is either broken or desired to be permanently connected. In a dream, it indicates that something is broken and has split apart that you would like to mend. It can also represent the desire to bring two elements of your life together. Conversely, something may be stuck to you that you wish were not so permanent.

Gold: Gold is the most precious element on the planet. The theory goes that it arrived here from space in the early formation of the solar system. As a symbol, gold represents the highest and most precious thing to strive for, both as a material possession and in more amorphous constructs. In the myths of the alchemist, great effort was put toward taking baser metals and turning them into gold. This is symbolic itself of the notion that lower consciousness, such as fear, doubt, and lack, can be transmuted into the gold of consciousness: love. What are you valuing above all else in your life? Is your search for the gold in some situation bringing out the best in you or the worst? Let the context of your dream answer these deeper questions when gold shows up as a symbol.

Goldfish: Fish are symbols of ideas that float around just below the surface of our consciousness. In the case of a goldfish, this is the simplest form of an idea that is kept in full view. What interesting idea do you want to keep considering so much that you keep it nearby? Perhaps you are reminding yourself of the colorful notions that float around inside your imagination.

Golf: Golf is a game representing abundance of both money and time. Leisure, relaxation, and moving at a very slow pace are associated with this activity. In a dream, you are being called to slow down and enjoy life with a greater sense of leisure. If you play golf in your waking life, such a dream might be calling forth the feelings that playing golf provides for you.

Google: Google is symbolic of the ability to tap into knowledge and information instantly; the almost instantaneous connection between the desire to know something and the successful outcome of any search. This may be literal, as in connecting to the capacity to do this on the Internet, or it could be symbolically connected to the wish to search for anything longed for and have an instantaneous and successful outcome.

Gorilla: You may be engaged in a struggle for leadership or domination. Animals represent the instinctual part of our nature. Gorillas are pack animals that live in communities led by a dominant alpha male, which is usually the biggest and strongest of the clan. The media has perpetuated an image of the chest-beating ape that reinforces this collective view of masculine and aggressive behavior. Initially, any interpretation of a gorilla in a dream is likely to be viewed from this perspective, representing instincts of competition, aggression, and the need for domination. The fearsome outburst associated with an angry gorilla is, in reality, a posturing meant to establish leadership or a reaction to

being disturbed. Consider that an appearance of a gorilla in a dream may point to rage that is more a facade than genuine anger. This can reflect a moment when your reaction is greater than the situation merits. A gorilla in a cage might indicate feelings connected to feeling imprisoned, such as underlying aggression that is keeping you stuck in issues of anger management. A gorilla on the loose might point to the unsettling consequences of expressing previously locked-up emotions. Facing a gorilla in a dream might indicate some readiness to confront your aggressive impulses or receive the expressions of anger from someone in your life.

Graduation: A graduation ceremony is a symbol in and of itself; it indicates that some great accomplishment has been achieved and is ready to be celebrated. This symbol may come up in a dream when you have actually created something of significance. It can also emerge as the motivation to stay the course with some difficult project by reminding you of the sense of accomplishment to come.

Grain: Grain is a fundamental and basic food source and was, in fact, the substance that allowed civilization to flourish. As such, it has an archetypal connection to the sustenance of life, abundance, and prosperity.

Grandparents: Intergenerational family dynamics are being expressed by a dream that involves one or more of your grandparents. Consider them both as individual expressions of an aspect of your personality, and examine the family dynamic they may represent. (See *Family Members*.)

Grapes: Grapes are a great symbol of wealth and prosperity not only because they are a fruit that requires an enormous amount of cultivation to produce, but because from them is made wine, one of the oldest riches of Earth's bounty. Dreaming of grapes is connected to your feelings about abundance in your life at the time of the dream, so use the context of the dream to illuminate this. If you are growing grapes, you are connecting to the willingness to do what it takes to build prosperity. If you are eating grapes, you desire to enjoy the fruits of your labor.

Grass: Grass is something that those in the Western world, especially in the United States, grow in a controlled manner to represent a connection to the earth in the form of a yard. In this way, grass is a symbol of staying connected to nature. Grass in a dream can mean you are connecting to your ability to be grounded and safe no matter where you are. The phrase "the grass is always greener" is a powerful notion indicating that grass in a dream may be pointing to things you desire but do not have, or things that others possess that you covet.

Grave: This symbolizes a consideration of the past; a sense of identity that no longer serves you that has been put to rest. The presence of a grave implies that the death has already occurred. The person in the grave, if you know him or her, will give you clues to the consideration of what aspects of self are under consideration. Perhaps you are mourning something or someone from your past. A secondary symbolic meaning has evolved that has emerged through the media. A graveyard is also home to all of the dark elements associated with death: ghouls, goblins, vampires, and other creatures of the night. This setting in a dream may symbolize the fear of death and be an indication that you are in the realm of shadow material.

Gray: Gray is a color that is almost an absence of expressiveness. When gray is present in a dream, you are expressing a lack of passion and joy. Gray is also an indication of aging and an indication that some measure of joy is something of the past.

Green: Green means go. Green is the color of the heart center, which can be confusing due to the representation of the heart as red, made especially prominent in Western culture with Valentine's Day. However, green is the central color of the spectrum, and the heart is considered the center of both our physical and emotional bodies. This connects the color green to love, healing, and all matters of the heart. It may be easier to understand the meaning of this color if you consider the earth and Mother Nature's love affair with the color green. Keeping with traffic-signal analogies, if you go when the light is green, that is like following your heart's desire to move forward. When the heart is soured by hurt, green can turn into the menace of envy.

Groceries: Groceries are the specific items you bring into your home from the market. As a symbol, they represent the never-ending supply of abundance and prosperity that is the birthright of all human beings. Your relationship to the groceries that appear in your dream will inform you of your relationship to the principle that all needs get met. Are you living in lack or flow? If you are shopping in your dream, you are actively seeking to increase the amount of nurturance and sustenance your life has to offer. If you are bringing the groceries home, then you are even closer to receiving life's abundance. However, if there is something amiss about the groceries in your dream, consider that your dream is reflecting a distrust of your world to provide you with all that you need.

Gryphon: This legendary mythological creature has the head of an eagle on the body of a lion. The lion is the king of the beasts and the eagle is the king of the birds, so with this combination the gryphon rules over the entire animal kingdom. There is a ferocity combined with great dignity to this archetypal guardian of great treasure. This is a very powerful totem, and when it appears in your dream, you are communing with strength, leadership, and dominion.

Guard: The guard is an archetype whose job it is to protect. Guards can show up in a number of different settings, from the government to a prison, but their essence is the same. They keep danger and violence at bay. As a character aspect in a dream, any guard is the part of your own psyche that is there because of a sense of the danger that may befall you from the outside world. Conversely, a prison guard may indicate that there may be feelings of violence inside of you that must be contained.

Guitar: Any musical instrument connects to creativity and passion and the need to express both. Guitar players are elevated pretty highly in our culture, so the guitar enjoys more power as a symbol than most instruments. Its curvy shape is very evocative of the female form, so the playing of a guitar in a dream has strong sexual connotations.

Gum: Because gum is associated with the mouth, any dream that involves gum is going to connect to issues around effective communication. Gum is an obstacle to articulate and powerful speech, so gum in your dream may point to issues you are having about expressing yourself with strength. Having an endless amount of gum in your mouth is a fairly common recurring dream for some people and relates to being taken seriously and feeling the conviction of your words.

Gums: Gums are directly related to the teeth, and the health of the gums is a reflection of other things that may be going on in the body. Teeth relate symbolically to security, and in this way the gums connect to how well you are nurturing your ability to take care of yourself. Sore or bleeding gums in a dream put you on notice to increase your level of self-care. Issues of communication may be indicated as well.

Gun: This is symbolic of the desire to exert power over others. Whoever has the gun is in charge. Connected to the masculine principle, the gun represents male-oriented power in an extreme form. The masculine principle is related to action and the ability to make things happen. A gun of any type connects to this universal energy, but with an intensity that indicates a lack of balance or containment. While the presence of a gun may imply a sense of control in a chaotic situation, its deadly and unpredictable nature implies a breakdown of stability and the potential for lethal danger. The type of firearm is important to consider, as this indicates the amount of power being yielded. A handgun relates directly to personal power and should be interpreted as what is available to you as an individual. Something with more firepower, such as an automatic weapon, relates to the ability to express strength on a more social level. The proximity of the gun in a dream indicates where the power currently resides. Holding the gun puts the dreamer in a position of ownership, but the level of confidence (or lack thereof) should be noted. Having a gun aimed at you indicates that some character aspect of your personality is demanding to be heard and

dealt with. If this is the case, your interpretation needs to include working with whoever yielded the gun in your dream. Brandishing a weapon could indicate a need to be seen as powerful in some area of your life. A hidden or concealed gun indicates elusive power that is felt though not flaunted.

Gym: A gym is a location where the focus is on fitness, health, and the increasing of strength. As a symbol, it represents the part of your consciousness that is focused on getting stronger and more grounded in the masculine principle. The context of the dream may help you interpret what areas of your life you are attempting to work on and increase in strength.

Hair: In general terms, hair is a feminine symbol of beauty and attractiveness, but it also connects to strength and power as expressed by the Samson myth, where hair was the secret to great masculine power. Samson's strength was only accessible to him while his masculine body was integrated with the feminine principle as represented by his hair. Another phenomenon to be examined where hair is concerned relates to coveting: those with curly hair wish they had straight hair and those with straight hair wish for curls. Since modern chemistry allows for alteration with alarming precision, the color of hair in dreams can hold powerful symbolic significance. Consider changes in color as connecting with an unconscious desire for a shift in expression in your outward persona. The color that shows up has meaning as well. Blonde hair is most coveted but is also associated with a lack of intelligence. Intellect is the realm of the brunette. Red hair correlates with passion and magic. Given that hair is on the head, this symbol connects to thoughts, both conscious and unconscious. Dreaming of long hair can indicate thoughts based on a desire for beauty to be more fully expressed. Hair that is bound in some fashion might reflect unconscious feelings of constraint in the area of personal expression. Hair being cut, lost, or radically altered can point to the need for a shift in thoughts about attractiveness. A wig represents a desire to actively create a mode of expressiveness that is not organically your own.

Haircut: Hair is a symbol of attractiveness and strength, so a haircut is the act of attending to these notions and keeping them in the best possible state. If the haircut is extreme, you may be experiencing a drastic diminution of your sense of personal attractiveness and/or personal power.

Such an image could also be revealing a desire to shift how you are seen in the world in a dramatic way by no longer relying on ways of manipulation that don't feel authentic anymore.

Hallway: A hallway is a part of any indoor structure that leads to other more significant rooms. In the realm of consciousness, the hallway is a symbol of an inner transition or change. If your dream takes place in a hallway or features one strongly, then you are in some sort of process that has not yet led you to your final destination.

Hammer: A basic tool for building, the hammer forces one object to penetrate another. When this is the intended choice and all is working well, the hammer is a symbol of being more effective in joining things together in order to build something. However, a hammer can also be a symbol for attempting to force something that might actually require a bit of finesse. Let the context of the dream help you determine how to interpret this symbol.

Hammock: The hammock is a symbol of both relaxation and the notion of getting back to nature, since it is something that is generally connected to trees. As a symbol in a dream, it is calling you to let go of worldly cares and remember your natural connection to the earth and restfulness.

Handcuffs: Handcuffs are used to bind someone in order to restrict their movements, usually in the case of criminal activity. In this way, they connect symbolically to this sense of restriction and the inhibition of freedom, but also to the consequences of behaviors and choices you may have made that have resulted in such restriction. There is a secondary meaning to handcuffs as paraphernalia in sexual play where this type of binding is considered erotic. If the latter is the case, you may want to investigate whether sexual issues are inhibiting your freedom.

Hands: Hands have an enormous capacity for creativity and expression that are the exclusive territory of human beings. On a personal level, one's hands divulge an extraordinary amount of information. The condition and appearance of a person's hands directly reflect what the person does with them on a regular basis. Holding on to or hiding one's hands can be an indication of a need to exert a measure of control over personal expression. Overuse of the hands while talking could point to an excessive amount of embellishment in communication that may put a distance between you and others. A disembodied hand can represent actions without conscience. The act of making something with your hands could indicate a call do so more often in life. The notion of "getting your hands dirty" can apply to having a richer experience as a result of throwing yourself fully into something.

Hanging: A hanging has two symbolic connotations. The first is that it is a death and so it relates to the sacrifice that comes along with great change and transformation. The person dying by hanging represents a part of yourself that may be being released or let go of in order for something new to come along to replace it. Because hanging involves the neck, issues of communication and the voice may be part of the meaning of such a symbol. Consider again the person who is hanging in the dream. Once you understand the character aspect of what part of your personality the individual represents, you may consider whether that part of you is choking off your ability to have a more authentic voice in some aspect of your life.

Harbor: A harbor is a natural or humanmade piece of land that is connected to a larger waterway in such a way as to make the movement of ships easy and accessible. Land relates to the conscious mind, and the ocean represents the unconscious mind. In this way, a harbor is the symbol of your ability to receive that which comes to you through explorations of your emotional nature and unconscious mind. A harbor is a powerful symbol of abundance, as it is through the harbor that great wealth and natural resources from other lands are taken up. The state of the harbor in your dreams will give you a good idea of how well you are prepared to receive the richness that life has to offer you.

Hardware Store: Hardware is symbolic of all the structural and mechanical elements of life, and a store is your ready access to the things that can make your life run more efficiently. Also, since many of the tools and materials purchased at such a location relate to the act of building, a trip to the hardware store in a dream could point to the need to construct something new or reconstruct something that is no longer functioning effectively. What needs fixing?

Harp: All musical instruments relate to passionate expression, though the harp is very ethereal in nature. If a harp is featured in your dream, you may be expressing a need to be more aspirational and connect to higher callings. The harp is also connected to the notion of heaven, and there may be a connection to spiritual ascension reflected in a dream with a harp in it.

Harvest: The harvest is when all the benefits of any endeavor are reaped and enjoyed. This is symbolic of any effort to create something of value. If it is time to harvest something in your dream state, you are enjoying a period of great bounty and reaping the rewards of past efforts.

Hat: The head is the symbolic wellspring of our thoughts and ideas. Hats both adorn and protect the head. As such, a hat can represent specific ideas or thoughts themselves, but also the need or desire to contain them. In terms of adornment, a hat can be the outward expression of an inner idea. In the realm of protection, a hat can connect with keeping such ideas firmly in place. Wearing someone else's hat could be expressing the notion of trying on someone else's ideas. (See *Cap*.)

Haunted House: A house is always a symbol of the self. A haunted house then is a sense of self that is plagued by regrets of the past that continue to haunt you. What mistakes have you made that you cannot forgive yourself for?

Hawk: All birds are messengers of some sort, but the power of the hawk is its vantage point. Hawks have great intelligence and exceptional eyesight. Their majestic wingspan can take them to very high ground where they can see quite far. When the hawk visits you in the dream state, you are able to take advantage of this ability to see into the distance across both time and space. Hawks are bringers of messages and help point to new directions with confidence and clarity.

Head: The head is where the brain is and therefore is the symbolic home to thoughts and thinking. A dream that features a head may connect to the thoughts and ideas of the person whose head it is. A dream that features the head in a significant way could be pointing out that you are "too much in your head" and would benefit from giving a rest to overthinking things. The head also houses the face, which relates to your persona and how you present yourself to the world. Such a dream image may be expressing ideas about how you are being perceived. To "rip someone's head off" is an expression that relates to great anger, so a disembodied head in a dream may be the result of unexpressed rage.

Headlights: The headlights on a car or other vehicle illuminate the road so that travel can be accomplished at night. The ability to see in what is otherwise darkness is part of the symbol's meaning. Darkness connects with shadow and things disowned, rejected, or feared, and headlights allow you to move through your life despite such psychological obstacles. The headlights on a car resemble its eyes, and in this way they connect to the ability to "see" in the dark so that further movement on a particular journey can occur.

Headstone: See *Tombstone*.

Heart: The heart is the center of our being and is responsible for pumping life force through us every moment we are alive. It is a symbol of life, passion, and a kind of intelligence that moves slowly and powerfully in the direction of true happiness. Any dream that features the heart, either literally or symbolically through a shape or depiction of the heart, is expressing something about your current relationship with this intelligence and how it is operating in your experience. The shape of the heart has become a powerful symbol, especially through the celebration of Valentine's Day, where the sharing of such a shape is an expression of love and devotion to another person. If this is the heart in your dream, you may be feeling the impulse to make your feelings known. A broken heart indicates that some process is being undertaken in order to heal some past hurt. Pain, illness, or injury in the heart indicates that some very difficult change is occurring that may be causing a sense of grief and loss in your life. A heart transplant means that the change has been so great that you need to start over again in the arena of love.

Heart Attack: The sudden and destructive impact of a wounded heart is about abrupt changes and transformation around how you experience love. Results of a heart attack can range from innocuous discomfort to death. The heart is the symbolic center of love. When love is compromised for too long, the heart may rebel and attack. In this context, when we use the word love, we aren't necessarily referring to feelings of romantic attachment. Love is the primary principle on which life is based; anything that opposes love, such as anger, resentment, envy, or pride, is a quality that can have an impact on the heart. Often the causes of a heart attack go unnoticed for a long time before the actual event occurs. In this way, such a dream image may indicate that the underlying cause of your unconscious discontent may have been lingering below the surface for a long while before this time. If you are the one having a heart attack in your dream, then look to where in your life issues around love may be hurting you on a deep level. If someone else in your dream is the victim, then use that person as a character aspect of the part of your personality that is suffering due to a matter of love or the lack thereof.

Heights: You need to get a higher vantage point in order to achieve some objectivity in some area of your life. This higher perspective also offers you a higher level of consciousness. The higher your vantage point, the more expansive your view of your environment will be. This takes on the symbolic meaning of expanded consciousness. The higher your level of thought, the more enlightened you are considered to be. This is so because there is a correlation between expanded consciousness and making positive, life-affirming choices. In simpler terms, the more you see, the more you know. The more you know, the more informed you can be about your choices. This expansion, however, comes with a caveat. Choosing to live at higher levels of consciousness brings with it a great deal of responsibility. The higher you go, the farther you can fall should you lose your footing. The greatest issue here is whether your fear of falling from a great height is real or imagined. Even the most precarious precipice is safe as long as you practice stillness. However, stillness is perhaps the greatest challenge in the human experience. The key to understanding this symbol is relativity. The roof of a small building will afford you a view of everything that is near it. Conversely, being up in space can afford a view of the entire world. The greater the height, the higher the level of consciousness being expressed. Your emotional experience of that height in your dream must color the interpretation you assign it.

Helicopter: Like any vehicle or mode of transportation, a helicopter in a dream represents movement on your path in life. However, a helicopter is primarily connected to its ability to move up and down, hover, and move swiftly while staying close to the ground. Because of this, it is often used for observation or transportation across short distances in a very fast manner. In a dream, a helicopter represents these same concepts as they relate to consciousness: the ability to observe the lay of the land more effectively and to jump from one place to another with ease and speed.

Hell: When most people think of hell, they are relating to a Christian idea of an afterlife where people go when they do not subscribe to certain dogmas relating to behavior. The New Thought community thinks of hell as the experience of life on Earth when lived in the illusion of separation from the sense of Divine Source. No matter what your personal view of hell is, the principle that underlies it is separation and the pain that comes when you feel disconnected from love. This can manifest at any moment in life when you feel cut off from some source of warmth, affection, or even validation. At such moments, a dream of hell can be a powerful expression of this alienated state. Ask yourself where you feel separate from your ability to feel safe and loved.

Helmet: A helmet is something that provides protection. Since it connects with the head, the symbolic meaning relates primarily to thoughts and ideas. If the helmet in your dream is connected to a particular kind of activity, such as a sport, there may be a desire to have more joy in your life as long as risk can be averted. Your interpretation should include considering whether the presence of the helmet is necessary or is coming from fear and an unwillingness to be vulnerable in the expression of new ideas.

Heroin: The ultimate opiate, heroin creates an immediate and powerful euphoria that leads to tremendous withdrawal and often dire consequences. As a symbol, it relates to the lengths to which people will sometimes go in order to feel good in the moment despite the negative consequences of the choices that are made. Heroin also relates symbolically to the perpetual cycle of engaging in a certain form of escapism no matter what. Anything can be a setup for an addictive response. If this should appear in a dream, look to your life to what your current version of heroin might be.

Hidden Figure: The hidden figure in a dream always relates to a quality, character aspect, or skill set that has not yet revealed itself to you. Often a specter of fear, the hidden fig-

ure should be considered a positive element or a needed ingredient that you have yet to embrace.

Hidden Room: This is a universal dream about previously unknown or hidden resources. A house or home of any kind represents the dreamer's sense of self. If you discover a room that you didn't know was there, it is like finding a new aspect of yourself that was formerly unknown. This can be interpreted as something that is just becoming available to you, such as new thoughts, resources, or strengths that exist in you but were previously unavailable or untapped. What you find in a hidden room should figure prominently in your interpretation. Your association with anything you seek or discover should be considered as symbolic of a resource that you already possess but are just now able to utilize. Not all hidden room dreams are pleasant; some can be quite disturbing. If this is the case, remember that if you find something troubling within your psyche, accepting and incorporating such shadow elements is crucial to facilitating integration. If the room suddenly disappears, consider that the resource you counted on finding within yourself may not be as fully formed as you had thought. No matter what the sensibility of the discovery, this image is always an embodiment of the possibility that at any moment in life, more can be revealed.

Hieroglyphics: This symbolic written language is very different from any language in the modern era. As such, it represents the communication of thoughts and ideas that may be very difficult to make sense of. Hieroglyphics have a reverent aura about them, and if they appear in a dream, they could symbolize information of a spiritual nature that is still encoded in a sense of secretiveness. It is up to you to break the code and receive the higher wisdom.

High School: You are dreaming of being held accountable for your responsibilities; this is also the symbolic passage from adolescence to adulthood. The primary symbolic meaning for this image is deeply connected to your own personal experience of this period in your life. In a general sense, high school is where most of us learned life lessons of responsibility and sexual identity as well as where we built the foundation for the directions we took as grownups. However, the overall experience of this turbulent time varies from person to person and can range from fun and joyous to excruciatingly painful. When you dream of high school, your unconscious is expressing emotional issues that have their roots in this time in your history. This common dream symbol is often related to performance anxiety.

Hike: You need to explore the elements of your life that are off the beaten path and away from your normal routine. A hike takes us into settings that we normally would not traverse. In terms of consciousness, the natural landscapes you explore on a hike connect to your deeper, more natural human nature, free from the constraints of whatever in your life feels constricting. A hike in a dream may be expressing a desire to be free of obligations and responsibilities.

Hill: Life is feeling more effortful now. Land is consciousness, and if your journey takes you up a hill, you are feeling the challenges of things weighing you down or making your journey more arduous. The height of a hill will correlate with the amount of stress you are feeling. A hill in a dream may also represent the challenges you face that are exhilarating and will result in some sort of payoff, for as you reach the top of the hill, you will have the benefit of both the view and the trip down.

Hippo: The hippo is one of the largest mammals on Earth, and though it resembles the pig and the elephant, its closest living relative is the whale. Hippos are semi-aquatic, so their medicine is derived from this need to stay mostly submerged during daylight. The underwater posture connects them to the shadow realms of consciousness that are just below the surface and steeped in emotion. Despite their awkward shape and docile manner, hippos can be quite aggressive and can outrun a human. In this way, they connect to those strong feelings that are lurking just under the surface that can emerge at any moment and overtake you.

Hockey: All sporting events are symbolic of the way in which life itself is like a game. With hockey, the distinctions are its fast pace and the tendency toward violence. If hockey features in a dream, you may be giving yourself permission to be freer with your aggressive nature than you might normally be. Conversely, you may be noticing this tendency in others. The fact that hockey takes place on ice may indicate the agility needed to stay in the game in some chaotic and unpredictable experience that is currently unfolding for you. Ice is frozen water and water is a symbol of emotions. Hockey in a dream may reflect being graceful despite feelings that may have gone cold.

Hole: A hole implies that something is missing. Whether this is a literal hole in an object, a hole that has been dug in the ground, or the metaphorical hole that people describe having in their heart or gut, the basic symbolic meaning behind a hole is that a piece of something has been taken from where it belongs and there is an acute sense of something missing as a result. Allow the dream context to reveal the area of your life in which you are having this experience and the severity of the wound.

Hologram: Once a product of science fiction, the notion of a hologram has emerged as a possible explanation for the very structure of our universe. As such, in a dream, a hologram may be in the realm of what is known as sacred geometry and could be connecting you to higher wisdom in a spiritual experience. Allow the context of the dream to inform your interpretation. A hologram allows for something to be considered from all angles, so there is an element of objectivity present when it appears in a dream.

Holy Grail: The Holy Grail is a sacred object from the Christian tradition that is thought to have been the goblet used by Christ at the Last Supper. The metaphysical emphasis on this as a symbol connects to the feminine shape of any goblet as a container for the energy of the Divine. If this appears in your dream, you may be experiencing a connection to powerful spiritual impulses. If your personal religious affiliations are in this direction, such an image may have more meaning for you. At the heart of this symbol is the idea that a human being is a vessel for God's infinite love.

Homosexuality: At the heart of this aspect of the human condition from a symbolic perspective is the joining up of either the feminine principle or the masculine principle in greater force and emphasis. This is not sexual at all; the masculine principle is related to doing and the feminine principle is related to being. From an archetypal perspective, the individual who is homosexually oriented has the gift of being able to vibrate with both of these principles as a natural part of his or her energetic birthright, so a dream featuring some reference to homosexuality may be expressing this higher nature associated with such an orientation. Of course, sexuality is a complicated issue for many people, and a dream that expresses such themes may be operating on many levels. You will need to examine your own sexual mores and prejudices if you are not homosexual and such a dream should occur for you. If characters within your dream are known to be homosexual, you must interpret them as aspects of your own personality that are aligning you in either the direction of a need to be more or to do more, or to bridge the gap between the two with a higher level of intuitive grace. If you are made uncomfortable by the content of the dream, you may want to consider ways in which you are having anxiety about your own masculinity or femininity in a way that may or may not be sexual in nature.

Honeycomb: This complex feat of engineering is ultimately a storage unit. In this way, as a symbol a honeycomb relates to the capacity to keep on hand something that is valued or desired. Since what is generally kept in such a structure is honey, there is the added dimension of the thing that is desired being the sweet elements of life.

Hood: Since a hood is worn on the head, the first element of how to interpret it as a symbol connects to thoughts and mentality, either your own if you are wearing an outfit that includes a hood, or a part of you as represented by someone in your dream. A hood is ultimately about hiding something, so you might want to consider what thoughts or ideas you are trying to keep hidden or secret. There can be some menace associated with hoods, between historical references to hooded people engaging in secret acts of mystery or violence to the modern-day association of the hoodie and criminal behavior. What are you trying to hide?

Hoodie: The media has created a modern-day association between the hoodie and criminal behavior. If you see someone wearing a hoodie in your dream, you may want to consider the person as a character aspect of your own personality that you suspect is up to no good. If you are wearing a hoodie, the same may be true of you. This symbol, however, begs you to ask whether your suspicion is based on something authentic or on fear and prejudice. Check your motives closely in some area of your life.

Hooks: A hook is a tool used to keep something hanging in one place. As such, hooks represent anything inside your consciousness that an outside idea can be hung on. In order for you to accept something that someone else presents to you, it must first have a hook on which it can be hung. This is true whether that idea is positive or negative, helpful or destructive. Anything that is hung on a hook, or the presence of hooks in a dream, indicates a readiness for something to be hung there.

Horizon: The horizon is expansive and limitless as well as finite and constricted. It is the fixed point that is not fixed at all but ever changing, even as it seems to remain the same. The horizon is a symbol of the experience of nature as infinite and limited at the same time, which is why in life it inspires such awe and wonder. As a symbol in a dream, it reminds you of this part of your existential nature. A dream that features the horizon is asking you to consider the higher elements of your nature.

Horse: The horse is the ultimate symbol of power. We even use the horse as a measurement of an engine with the term "horsepower." When harnessed, this mighty beast can take you to extremes of speed and strength. As a totem animal, the horse will visit in a dream when you need to be in touch with this visceral energy to move.

Horseshoe: St. Dunstan is said to have put a shoe on the hoof of the devil, and in this way the horseshoe as a talisman with the power to keep the devil away was created. A more modern consideration of the power of the horseshoe relates to grounding and harnessing the power of the horse through the symbol of the shoe that protects the horse's ability to move. No matter how you relate to this symbol, if it appears in a dream, you are connecting with the idea of good fortune and the providence of luck.

Hose: A hose directs water in a specific direction for various constructive purposes. Water is always a symbol of emotions and feelings, and in this case, the hose represents your ability to take whatever is going on with you in this way and utilize it to your best advantage.

Hospital: You are dreaming of the need for healing and a restoration of health, whether that health is literal or symbolic. Hospitals tend to evoke powerful reactions. The discomfort that colors most people's associations tends to overshadow the benevolence connected to them as places of healing. A common reaction around hospitals is to fear them, adding a touch of irony to our relationship with the healing process. Healing is transformation, and the first step to any major change is the breakdown that precedes the breakthrough. Since the breakdown is the scary part, we avoid it, just as some people avoid hospitals in waking life. It is easy to forget that in order for surgeons to heal a patient, they must first cut the person's body open, creating a wound. And since not everyone who checks into a hospital is fortunate enough to check out, these places are indelibly connected to the fear of death and dying. However, remember that death is always followed by rebirth. In this way, being in or near a hospital in a dream is always going to indicate that some healing is either underway or necessary. If you are the patient, then consider that your sense of self

is undergoing a significant shift. If you are a visitor, then the healing transformation is connected to a character aspect or particular way of being as embodied by the person you are going to see. If you are playing the part of healer, the dream may be helping you step into that role in some area of life that is undergoing a transformation. The fear or repulsion that is present in the dream will give you an idea of how much resistance you may be unconsciously engaged in. If you are experiencing a health issue in life, the image of a hospital may be literal, in which case your dream relationship to the hospital will inform you of any underlying resistance to surrendering to your body and its functioning (or the lack thereof).

Hot Spring: A natural hot spring is an opening in the earth that connects to an aquifer below that is being heated by the geothermal system that exists below the surface. In this way, a hot spring first and foremost relates symbolically to emotional expressions that are of a more passionate nature and that bubble up from below the surface of consciousness. For the most part, since a hot spring is associated with relaxation and health, this is a very positive symbol relating to the benefits that can be gained when you allow feelings from below the surface of your consciousness to slowly and methodically surface and be expressed.

Hot Tub: All water in dreams connects to your emotional experience. A hot tub is warm and relaxing and as a symbol connects to the powerful and beneficial experience of allowing yourself the luxury of leaning into feelings of passion and intensity.

Hotel: Any home-like dwelling in a dream is representative of the self. A space of transitional living such as a hotel or motel room connects to the self in a temporary state of being. This symbol usually appears when there is change afoot, indicating that the sense of self is in transition and not yet fully "home." Given this transitory nature, such a dream may indicate the need for a temporary respite in order to consider being more authentic with regard to your identity. If the dwelling is dilapidated, as in an inexpensive motel, then you may be experiencing downward movement in the area of abundance. If the hotel is grand and lavish, you may be preparing yourself for an increase in abundance. Hotel rooms can also be connected to both sexuality and mortality, as they are often used in life for sexual encounters and suicides. Hotel-room sex could indicate a self-investigation that involves looking at an area of your sexual expression. If the latter image is present, ask yourself what part of you may need to commit suicide (be sacrificed) so that the rest of you can move forward with your life.

House: Anything that is a home in a dream connects to your sense of self. A house is a clear reflection of identity at the time of the dream. The sense of identity that the dream is trying to express relates directly to the qualities of the house as it appears in the dream. A house from your past and/or childhood relates to your identity as it was generated at the time you lived there. A house from your imagination also relates to your sense of self, and you must use the context of the dream to inform you of the meaning to associate with it. A mansion is an expanded sense of self, while something small or more rundown is asking you to look at issues of self-worth. A house under construction is the self being built up, whereas one that is being destroyed takes on the view of deconstruction or reinvention. The same ideas should be applied to any living space, from an apartment to a hotel room, a great big house or a hovel.

Humming: The act of singing represents the expression of passion and excitement. Humming is the less intense version of this that is often done in the background, just below the level of conscious awareness or when the desire to express is present but slightly inhibited. Humming often indicates that joy is present.

Hummingbird: All birds are messengers of some sort, but the hummingbird's primary medicine is related to your ability to connect with joy. The hummingbird can easily maneuver into any sort of space in order to obtain the nectar of a flower, a symbol of the sweetest that life has to offer. When the hummingbird appears in a dream, joy is available to you with grace and ease.

Hurricane: A hurricane is a wild and potentially terrifying combination of wind and rain. Wind symbolically relates to thoughts and ideas that are being whipped up to proportions of frenzy. The presence of rain indicates that such an experience is also emotional in nature. If there is a hurricane in your dream, look to where in your life some person or circumstance is causing you an enormous amount of pain, sadness, and rage. Such a dream may be a response to significant and stressful changes in your life.

Ice: Water represents emotions, and ice is frozen water. Symbolically, ice represents emotional content that has been dramatically altered. The resulting substance is cold and hard—adjectives that do not conjure pleasant sensations when applied to one's emotional nature. From the world of physics, we know that ice is not created by adding cold, but rather by the loss of heat. This tells us that when ice is present, warmth has been lost or given away. Ice can also be dangerous, especially when one must maneuver over it. An icy road has the symbolic connotation that a lack of emotional fluidity can be treacherous on your path through life.

Ice Cream: The ultimate in comfort food, ice cream is a superb treat and functions symbolically as the rewards that life has to offer and a desire for sweetness at this time. Conversely, ice cream can be a symbol for indulgence if your own relationship to food and weight loss is such that ice cream is a guilty pleasure.

Ice Skates: Ice represents emotions that are running so cold as to freeze over. Therefore, ice skates or skating on ice is symbolic of your ability to navigate well when there is an absence of warmth or passion. Ice is very slippery and hard, so ice skates may be a symbol of your ability to move gracefully in circumstances that are delicate, hence the phrase "skating on thin ice."

Iceberg: An obstruction that sticks up from below the surface of the ocean, an iceberg is a symbol of stuck emotions or patterns that pose a danger to you navigating the surface of your unconscious mind. There is the phrase "the tip of the iceberg," which suggests that you must look deeper to find the true source of a problem or challenge.

Icing: The sweet surface of a cake or other treat is symbolic of the added benefits of any situation, hence the phrase "the icing on the cake." When icing features strongly in a dream, you are looking for the gift that a situation has to offer.

Identification: In modern civilization, the carrying of some form of identification is a part of everyday life. Your sense of identity is what is being expressed by a dream that features this as an image. To lose your ID in a dream is symbolic of feeling disconnected from your ability to manage your day-to-day affairs.

In-Laws: Many dreams of in-laws will connect to waking-life issues sparked by the relationship you have with them. However, you can go to a deeper interpretation by considering them as character aspects of your own personality. In-laws are similar to parents in a dream, but are more connected to who you chose as a spouse and the challenges of marriage. (See *Family Members*.)

Incest: This is a complex issue in waking life, and there is a very big difference between the symbolic meaning behind incest as a universal concept and what a dream of incest indicates if you are someone who is an incest survivor. If this is the case, then dreams of incest may be an important part of healing and processing a very difficult experience. However, if this is not the case, then the appearance of this discomforting behavior in a dream needs to be understood from a symbolic perspec-

tive and absolutely not in a literal fashion. Any sexual experience is a symbol of integration and the joining together of different elements of consciousness. In this way, it is a powerful and positive symbol even when the people participating are unlikely partners. In the case of incest, the people involved are family members. In this way, the character aspects that are being integrated have to do with family traits, values, and the actual characteristics of the people who appeared in the dream.

Incubus: The incubus is a mythological creature that is itself a feature of dreams. The incubus is the male version of this type of creature, and it is thought to be a phantom that removes life force from its victim and is often a feature of night terrors. If you are visited by an incubus in your dream, look to where in your life some man or other experience is draining you of passion and power. (See *Succubus*.)

Infidelity: This symbolizes a circuitous route to meeting needs and an avoidance of crucial matters. There is no intimacy need that cannot be met in a primary relationship. Going outside of a marriage or partnership for sex or affection is a way of meeting a primal need in a roundabout way. Simultaneously, there is an avoidance of some underlying problem. Therefore, this image represents both a circuitous route to connection and an avoidance of confrontation. If you discover an infidelity in a dream, you may want to consider areas in your life where you are avoiding taking care of yourself. If you are engaged in an affair, you might need to examine your life circumstances for signs of being manipulative or indirect in getting your needs met. As getting caught is always reflective of an unconscious desire to effect a change, being discovered as being unfaithful could indicate a desire to shift some area of your life. Always be willing to look at issues of responsibility when this dream image appears. Where in your life are you not allowing yourself to be accountable for your actions? If the dream involves details of constructing an affair, you may want to examine how genuine you are being in terms of expressing and manifesting your desires in life, both relationally and otherwise. Where in your life are you not being authentic? How might you be betraying your own needs? It is safe to assume that this image in a dream indicates a theme of intimacy issues in waking life, no matter what the marital state of the dreamer. This may have literal implications if you are actually involved in an affair or believe your partner to be.

Infinity: The principle of infinity is something that is a feature of a particular sort of dream that can take many different forms. In a general sense, a dream of infinity features a landscape that feels extremely large and infinitesimally small at the same time. Such a dream is a spiritual calling that is asking you to wake up to the mystical nature of life.

Injection: An injection puts a substance into your body in order to alter the chemistry of your system. One element of the symbolic meaning of an injection is that it takes a very small amount of something and creates a fairly big change. The phrase "to inject something into" often refers to the act of increas-

ing an idea's power by adding some measure of passion or purpose.

Insects: Your dream is reflecting disturbing thoughts and hidden fears. Insects and bugs are generally found to be repulsive by most people. For some, they can evoke great fears that are often wildly irrational. As any animal is symbolic of some element of thought, any dream insect represents some small but frightening unconscious thought. To arrive at an accurate interpretation, you may need to do a little research about the insect in question. Once you know a bit about it, you can come to an interpretation of what it might represent. As an example, bees exhibit sophisticated forms of communication and a communal production of honey that represents enormous industriousness and the power of collective thoughts gathered for a common purpose. Cockroaches are famous for being hearty enough to survive a nuclear blast. They can therefore be said to represent the staying power of the creepy thoughts that live in the shadow. Certain beetles manufacture a substance similar to paper or cardboard, embodying the powerful transformation that is available by attending to small details. The silk made by any number of different insects connects to the amazing power of creativity and strength that actually has its origin in the shadow. Flying insects connect to the great mobility of our darker thoughts. Slimy ground dwellers point to the ever-present underbelly of our psyche. If you have an insect show up in a dream, take a moment to look up some details about it. What you discover may trigger an important message that your unconscious is trying to give you.

Instrument: Any instrument connects to music, and music is a symbol of passionate expression and heightened creativity. Musical instruments are the tools of such passion. If they appear in a dream, they are calling you to step up your creative exploits and increase your level of passion.

Intercourse: You are dreaming of the joining together of personality character aspects, of integration. The essence of sexual intercourse is the joining of two individuals in a process that allows them to be as close to each other as the human body will allow. This translates into the concept of integration as the symbolic meaning of sex. Additionally, the potential for this act to result in the creation of a third entity reinforces this definition. If you remove all sense of eroticism, embarrassment, shame, or titillation, the purity of this symbol is profound. Any characters that appear in a dream engaged in sexual intercourse are expressing an unconscious desire to merge the character aspects of personality of the individuals involved. If you are participating in sex in a dream, the focus of your investigation will be on your dream partner. The character aspects that person represents are the qualities that your unconscious is expressing a need to integrate into your present level of functioning. These qualities will be easier to identify when you know the person from your waking life; however, this can also be the very element that makes examining such a dream uncomfortable. It is common to dream of having sex with people with whom you would never

ordinarily do so or even think of doing so, such as co-workers, family members, or acquaintances. When using the character-aspect technique in relation to sex dreams, you must add to your interpretation an element of transformation of the qualities that you identify. The process is not literal or concrete.

Internet: The emergence of the Internet has radically changed the way we interact with the world in which we live. Through it, people can interact with others of like mind and connect with information and ideas that are shared by multitudes. In this way, the Internet is an exact symbolic representation of the collective consciousness of human beings today. The speed with which it has evolved is alarming, and it has created a global culture faster than our ability to comprehend the rules that govern it. A dream that features the Internet as a prominent image is inviting you to investigate your personal relationship with the overwhelming changes that have taken place in our world over the past two decades. If you are Internet-savvy in life and are logged on in your dream, you may not find this a particularly powerful image; therefore, consider this symbol as representing expanded and accelerated thinking. However, if you are someone who harbors resistance to the Internet, its appearance in a dream is inviting you to look into areas of your life that are overwhelming or moving too fast for your comfort. In this way, the Internet would be a symbolic depiction of anxiety or chaotic thoughts. If the dream has you utilizing the Internet as a tool, you may want to look at areas in your life that are requiring a higher level of functioning or thought processes.

Iron: An iron removes wrinkles from articles of clothing. As a symbol, a wrinkle represents something that is out of alignment. As such, the iron then is the symbolic ability to smooth things over and create more uniformity in your life.

Island: Land represents the conscious mind, and the ocean is the unconscious. An island is an isolated idea or construct in your consciousness that is separated from the rest of your awareness by issues that are of an emotional nature. An island in a dream can represent the sense of isolation that occurs when you are going through a difficult period.

Itch: Something just below the surface of your consciousness is troubling you and asking you to notice it. The challenge with interpreting a dream with an itch in it is that the itch itself will not tell you whether it is a good idea to scratch it or not. An itch can be the persistent underlying thoughts that, if you dive more deeply into them, will result in pain and suffering, like addictive tendencies or other persistent anxieties. At the same time, an itch could be asking you to go a little bit deeper in your consideration to see why something may be bothering you, the solution to which may be just under the surface. The source or cause of the itch is important to consider. An itch emanating from a wound is usually in a healing process. This might mean that resentments or unspoken thoughts about a recent emotional battle have left potential scars. An itch that spreads a toxin, such as poison ivy, would represent the addictive quality of what happens when you open the door to harmless satisfaction only to find the challenging compulsion to repeat harmful behavior. An itch in a socially sensitive area, such as the genitals, connects to thoughts and desires that are private, secret, and sexual in nature.

Jack-in-the-Box: This symbol in a dream indicates that there has been an ongoing buildup of pressure that will ultimately result in a surprising or jarring occurrence. The real tension indicated with a jack-in-the-box is not if, but when. As you wind the spring, you absolutely know that a sudden burst of energy will result. It is in not knowing when it will hit that anticipation builds. The state of this toy in your dream will offer more information. If it is unwound, there may be a desire to have more stimulation in your life in order to feel more excitement. If it is damaged, your capacity to delay gratification or take later action may be broken.

Jackass: See *Donkey*.

Jacket: This piece of outerwear is designed to protect from the cold. Any article of clothing relates to a mode of personal self-expression. The type of jacket in the dream also has shades of meaning. A dress blazer relates to prosperity and responsibility, whereas a parka connects to protection against life's harsher elements. Once you figure out the meaning associated with the type of jacket in the dream, you must add the context of the dream itself to your meaning. A jacket that is ripped or in disrepair indicates feeling vulnerable and unprotected. One that doesn't fit means you aren't quite aligned with your intentions. A lost jacket is to be temporarily removed from the needs the jacket represents.

Jackhammer: This incredibly noisy tool of destruction is capable of busting through very strong material in order to build something new. In this way, it symbolizes the ability to break open structures of the past that seem permanent but with great effort can be released in order to create a new set of habits, ideas, or consciousness about your life. The presence of a jackhammer or the evidence that one is being used in a dream signals that great change is taking place and that change is an eradication of things from the past that used to seem permanent.

Jaguar: All cats relate to the power of the feminine principle. The larger the cat, the greater the power of this totem. The jaguar is the third-largest feline, after the lion and tiger, so it has a certain gravitas in the symbolic world. The jaguar is more of a climber than a runner, so its totem power is connected to stealth and the ability to maneuver through difficult terrain, where that terrain is synonymous with life challenges.

Jail: Jail is the place where criminals go when they are awaiting trial and before the major incarceration of prison. You can be quite innocent of a crime and still be in jail. In this way, jail is symbolic of any powerful sense of restraint and limitation that keeps you from enjoying a sense of freedom. If your dream takes place in jail, examine your life for a situation or limiting belief that is holding you back.

Janitor: The janitor is a low-level employee whose responsibility it is to keep a space clean. All of these factors must be considered when interpreting a dream. As a character, a janitor will represent an aspect of your own personality, one that is operating on a simplistic and basic level and whose responsibility it is to clean up after higher levels of thought,

ideas, or choices that you have made. How much cleaning up is there to do after you have taken certain actions?

Jar: A jar's purpose is to contain something, generally for the sake of preserving it as long as possible. In this way, a jar symbolizes the ability to capture the essence of something and keep it accessible for later use. Anything that holds something is a symbol for the feminine principle of containment.

Jaw: The jaw is very involved in preparing food for digestion, and in this way it ultimately connects to the principle of self-care and nurturance. However, a tight jaw strongly relates to unexpressed anger and tension. If your jaw or the jaw of a person in your dream is featured, there may be issues of anger in such a dream. Consider whose jaw is prominent. If it is a character in the dream, then that person may represent a part of your personality that is causing you to either hold back anger or otherwise reflect issues of unexpressed rage.

Jeans: Now a fundamental part of the American uniform, jeans originally were worn for doing vigorous labor. Today, they are the ultimate in casual wear, so as a symbol, they may reflect a need to take yourself less seriously or dress down some situation that the dream is reflecting. If someone in your dream is wearing jeans as a noticeable image, the part of you that the person represents may offer you a way to incorporate more relaxation into your psyche.

Jeep: Any vehicle is a symbol for how you are moving through your life. A Jeep indicates a moment when what is needed is a more rugged and no-nonsense approach to your choices.

Jester: An archetype of playfulness and trickster energy, the jester is present when you need to be distracted from serious matters.

Jesus, Buddha: You are dreaming of one of the ultimate archetypal character aspects that connects to the highest consciousness available to a human being. In this symbol resides the ability to manifest thought into reality. Jesus and Buddha were remarkable teachers who were able to live the principles of pure love and manifestation in a fashion that can only be described as divine in nature. To limit this term to just these two is in no way meant to dismiss the many other prophets and teachers who have embodied this spirit. While both of them once lived as men, they should be treated as archetypes. Dreaming of one of them indicates that you are experiencing a high level of self-discovery and integration. Jesus and Buddha exemplify the masculine principle at its highest level of evolution. The masculine principle connects to the power of thought. Through very different teachings, both of these mystics taught the concept that what you think and believe becomes your reality. They exemplify that it is possible, through love, to experience states of bliss in this often challenging life. The appearance of one of these great teachers in a dream is to put you on notice that you are in a moment of elevating consciousness and self-integration. It is not uncommon for an archetypal figure to be silent in a dream, as it is the figure's mere presence that can be significant. If words and messages are present in the dream, take them to heart and do so literally. However, if this is not the case, your best use of such a dream is silent gratitude for the gift of a rare and powerful experience of elevated consciousness.

Jet: A jet is the fastest mode of transportation that is currently part of the day-to-day human experience. An airplane represents a significant change or transformation based on the fact that you get onto a plane in one location and wind up somewhere very far away in a very short amount of time. A jet is the fastest of these vehicles and in this way indicates that very rapid change is at hand.

Jewelry: Any adornment relates symbolically to self-expression. Jewelry has the added connection to abundance and prosperity and the desire to show the world your ability to attract wealth. People often place great value on their jewelry, so it becomes a symbol of anything that is considered valuable. Look at the context of a dream in which jewelry is featured, as your dream may be letting you know what you value.

Jewels: Jewels are precious objects made from the rarest things on Earth, and as such, they are great symbols of wealth, prosperity, abundance, and that which we treasure. A jewel can also be considered a sacred object, and to see one in a dream may indicate spiritual aspirations.

Jigsaw Puzzle: The essence of a jigsaw puzzle lies in the way minute pieces of something are considered piece by piece and put together to create a slowly emerging image of the whole. This is symbolic of mental considerations where an idea is examined bit by bit until eventually clarity emerges. This symbol may appear in a dream when you are engaged in such a process.

Joint: Smoking pot is a symbol for the desire to escape from your day-to-day stressors and especially from overthinking and mental overwhelm. A joint in a dream represents the ability to generate this form of escapism whenever it is desired.

Journal: A journal is a symbol for inner thoughts and private ruminations. Since many people who are interested in interpreting dreams keep their dreams recorded in a journal, there may be a literal connection between a journal in a dream and the actual process of gaining inner wisdom through considering the dream itself. Whatever is happening to a journal in a dream is a direct reflection of your relationship to these inner, private expressions.

Judge: The judge as an archetype relates to the warrior energy that divides everything into two camps: either right or wrong. The distinction with a judge is the notion of guilt and innocence and how this connects to the consequences of choices you may have made in the past. When a judge is present in a dream, you may feel that life itself is like a trial at this time and you may receive harsh punishment or a reprieve.

Juice: The juice of anything is the liquid essence of the thing itself. In the case of a fruit or vegetable, this is a literal liquefaction of the food and contains all of its nutrition. In this way, juice is symbolic of the benefit that exists in any substance or construct. Since juice is something that is easily digested, the presence of juice in a dream indicates a desire to easily assimilate something of value.

Jungle: This is a symbol for exotic, foreign territory, off the beaten path. By definition, a jungle is any land that is densely vegetative and essentially impenetrable by standard means. Only found in tropical climates, these vast, moisture-laden habitats are isolated, mysterious, and, for most Westerners, completely foreign to our civilized mentality. This can make for a romantic view of such a setting in a dream. If the jungle atmosphere in your dream evoked a sense of wonder and enchantment, you may be tapping into some new and interesting territory in some area of your life. The flip side of this coin would be this image expressing a desire for experiences that are new and different. Your dream could be a request for life to bring you a taste of the exotic. Jungle terrain can be quite inhospitable; with everything from deadly animals to insects carrying disease, your life could be in peril in such a place. If this is the case, you will want to find an association with your waking life where a sense of isolation or foreign sensibility may be causing you fear or stress. The rainforests are the lungs of Mother Earth and are responsible for much of the oxygen that is released into our atmosphere. As we continue to decimate these precious resources, we put our very existence in jeopardy. Whether you consider yourself an advocate for saving the rainforests or not, you are connected to every inch of our planet through the collective unconscious. Your dream may be representing the callous destruction of resources, both globally and in your personal life. Consider both when forming your interpretation.

Jury: A jury is supposed to be made up of your peers, so this group of people in a dream connects to your social identity. Because a jury is the ultimate decider of right and wrong, such an image in a dream may be an indication that you are feeling judged in some area of your waking life.

Kangaroo: One of the most well-known aspects associated with the kangaroo is that as a marsupial, the female carries her young in her pouch for a long time after birth. In this way, the totem for the kangaroo is first and foremost aligned with this maternal instinct. The kangaroo's ability to jump and kick adds the distinction of sudden shifts and changes that can propel you into new directions, especially in the realm of self-care. When the kangaroo appears in a dream, you are receiving the medicine of powerful and aggressive instincts around taking care of yourself.

Karaoke: At the heart of karaoke is singing, and in this way, as a symbol it connects with passion, creativity, and the impulse to be expressive. However, this public display of such activity carries with it the connotations of drunkenness and the unnecessary presence of talent to merit such activity. If you are singing karaoke in your dream, you may be expressing a desire to be free from the constraints of self-doubt and inhibition.

Kayak: A kayak is a vehicle that allows you to navigate water in a very masterful way, even when the water is moving very rapidly. All water in dreams is about your emotional state, and a kayak indicates a moment when you are able to ride just about any level of fast-moving feelings and emotional situations with skill and acumen.

Key: A key opens a lock. In the world of symbolism, a lock can represent any number of problems, challenges, obstacles, or desires yet to be attained. Therefore, the key is the representation of that which you need to have in order to begin facing whatever needs to be addressed to solve the problem you face. Most dreams about keys relate to the need to find a lost key or to the possession of a key without knowing what lock it belongs to. Life is an ongoing process and is filled with many opportunities to fit the right key into the right lock, but that is only the beginning of the next process. The key is perhaps the ultimate symbol of working effectively with the mystery of life.

Keyboard: A keyboard turns your fingers into a masterful communication tool. Fingers relate to dexterity and creativity. Words are everything in the realm of communication. A keyboard is your access to everything that occurs in the vast landscape of the Internet. Therefore, anything that is focused on a keyboard in a dream relates to your access to this enormous world that exists at your fingertips. A broken or otherwise compromised keyboard means that you are feeling ineffective in connecting to your world.

Kidnap: A kidnapper takes a child and holds him or her for ransom. In this way, the child becomes the symbol of something treasured and valuable, such as innocence or possibility. The ransom suggests that this quality is being forced as a sacrifice for something of more material value. Such a dream may arise when you are feeling like you must compromise your values in such a way to accomplish a goal. If you are a parent, such a dream could also be a reflection of parental anxiety.

Killer Whale: There is a shadowy and inflated connection to the depths of awareness that the whale brings. If the dream presents you with the distinction of a killer whale, you are examining fears that live deep below the sur-

face, but are still available to be visited and explored. (See *Whale*.)

King: An archetypal figure, the king in your dreams represents the ultimate sense of authority. This is the part of your higher nature that governs the choices you make in your waking life. Consider the sensation around this character in the dream itself. Are you governing your life as a benevolent ruler or a cruel despot?

Kiss: A kiss in a dream is always going to be connected to some form of communication, either desired, needed, or underway. A kiss is stimulating, so a dream kiss may be pointing toward some need to stimulate a new or needed way of incorporating a certain quality into your communication style. Consider who is kissing in the dream. If it is you, the person you are kissing may indicate a part of your personality needing to be evoked. If this person is an object of your affection from your waking life, it may indicate a desire to speak of your feelings. If two people are kissing in your dream and you are witnessing this, consider the traits of both people and ask yourself what the resulting communication would be if the qualities of those two people were to merge.

Kitchen: As the nurturing center of a house, the kitchen represents the heart and hearth of the self. It is where the family is fed and comes together in community. It is the room where people tend to congregate during parties. It is the symbolic realm of mother and the feminine principle as it is expressed by the family structure. Food is stored and prepared in the kitchen, so the symbolic food for your soul is located in the kitchen of your dreams. Consider how your dream may be informing you of how you are responding to your own spiritual cooking. If your life experience of family, mother, and kitchen was different from the ideal in your dream, your personal focus must include your individual paradigm. For example, much of a family's abusive interactions can occur in the kitchen, so such associations should be considered when interpreting a kitchen dream. The activity in the dream will outline your current internal view around issues of nurturing, self-care, and healing. Any people who appear are key components in the process of exploration. If they are known to you, use the character-aspect technique to integrate their qualities into your interpretation. If there were people in the dream not known to you, consider whatever you can remember about them from the dream. Any dream that takes place primarily in a kitchen has the capacity to offer you an overview of the status of your heart center. Use it to examine whether you are experiencing healthy levels of self-nurturance or are in need of adjustments in this area.

Kite: A kite flies effectively only when the person flying it is well grounded. This symbol of soaring to new heights while remaining on the ground represents the value of extending your reach downward as well as upward. Anything that relates to the sky connects to higher realms of thought, to the intellect and/or spiritual aspirations. The kite itself is the part of consciousness that can soar upward as long as it is firmly connected to the ground.

Kitten: A cat represents the feminine principle of unconditional love. A kitten is this energy in its absolute most innocent expression. It is not uncommon for people to have kittens as a recurring dream image, and this is an expression of a connection to love and comfort for that individual. Conversely, a kitten can also represent a less mature approach to love and intimacy, where independence is an expression of fear and resistance.

Knife: This implement offers a sharp edge as an extension of the hand in order to cut at will. It is a powerful masculine symbol of aggression and protection. When it is used wisely, it extends the skills represented by the hand's ability to create. The presence of a knife in a dream can be menacing and frightening and may indicate a need to cut something out of your life that no longer serves you.

Knight: A knight relates to the warrior archetype. The warrior divides the world into two camps: right and wrong. He is the defender of the innocent and can be called upon to right any wrong.

Knot: Anything tied into a knot is reflecting disparate elements that are bound together. Sometimes this is a positive construction, but it can also relate to the resulting chaos and confusion. The presence of a knot in a dream may indicate that a complicated element of your life needs to be unwound.

Koala Bear: The koala is an extremely slow and docile creature, so its symbolic meaning is connected with this sedate energy. When the koala appears in a dream, you are being offered a dose of calm serenity and the power to slow things down.

Komodo Dragon: Survival instincts are the domain of this somewhat rare creature. Any reptile in a dream is connected to your deeply primitive responses to life and the basic functions such as breathing and body regulation. When a Komodo dragon appears in a dream, you are reminded that your instincts are to be trusted.

Koran: The sacred text of Islam, the Koran is the word of God for many people. Its poetry is a beautiful expression of a life lived through spiritual principles. If your waking-life religious beliefs involve this holy book, then the dream is to be taken more literally. If this is not the case, you may be dreaming of the fundamental spiritual principles that underlie all perspectives.

Label: A label offers insight and structure to whatever it is identifying. As such, we rely on it to understand what something is. A label in a dream represents your relationship with this level of comprehension—the need for it or the impact of not having it. If a label is featured in your dream, you may be seeking to have a greater understanding of something in your life. A label that cannot be read for some reason indicates that you must operate in the unknown.

Laboratory: The laboratory is a setting of the advancement of knowledge or the clear identification of something of great importance that is initially hidden. Often connected to health and illness, the lab as a setting for a dream indicates a desire to get more information about something in your life. You are approaching things from a scientific and methodical view in order to get to the bottom of something.

Labyrinth: In its essence, a labyrinth is a confusing and mazelike structure found in the underbelly of a building. As a symbol, it represents a journey to the very center of something in which the journeyer can get quite lost and turned around. A labyrinth can be found as a symbol in many spiritual and religious settings as a pattern imbedded into a floor where an individual goes on a symbolic hero's journey. In a dream, the interpretation is the same, whether it is a freeform hidden and shadowed labyrinth or a beautiful symbol of such an inward journey. You are engaged in a deep exploration of the inner self where confusion can occur and changes of direction are imminent.

Lace: Delicate intricacy is what is being expressed with this symbol. Lace is a beautiful combination of the masculine principle of engineering and the feminine principle of patience and creativity. As a symbol in a dream, it is suggesting that the part of your nature that is being expressed can tap into both of these sides of your nature and come up with something truly beautiful.

Ladder: You are dreaming of risky transitions and the desire to get to a higher vantage point that may feel unsupported. A ladder is an effective but unstable method of getting to a higher vantage point. Anything that helps a person move from one level to another is symbolically connected to transitioning from one realm of operating to another. However, a ladder is a tool used in the construction or fixing of things, so in this way, the symbolic meaning connects to the ability to achieve some sort of goal. The presence of a ladder in a dream suggests that there is a transition afoot that may also connect to achieving some goal or fixing some area of your life that requires attention. If the dream merits the use of a ladder, but the ladder is either ignored or inaccessible in some way, you may be missing the very thing needed for success with some goal in life. A broken ladder may be a warning that you are not following the necessary step-by-step process to achieve your goals. The instability of a ladder requires a slow and centered approach to your climb, signaling a need to take each step in your life with care, grace, and ease.

Ladybug: A symbol of good fortune, the ladybug is connected to renewal and regeneration. When a ladybug appears in a dream, you are being graced with good luck.

Lake: All water in dreams relates to your emotional life. A lake has a measure of depth and plenty that is hidden from the initial view, but is not so deep that it cannot be explored. As a mostly placid body of water, it represents your feelings and the possibility of drawing sustenance and comfort from connecting to that part of your nature. Anything that happens in and around a lake in your dreams is revealing elements of your emotions and emotional issues at the time of such a dream. Consider the size of the lake and the movement or lack thereof of the water within it for clues as to what sort of consciousness is being expressed.

Lamb: As a baby sheep, the lamb adds the quality of innocence to the symbolic meaning. (See *Sheep*.)

Lamp: Any light is a symbol of ideas and the ability to see things more clearly. A lamp is a small amount of this light designed to illuminate a small area in order to focus on something specific. Since it is portable, it represents your ability to focus the light of consciousness on various areas that need to be explored or highlighted. The state of a lamp in your dreams is revealing your current ability to see clearly in some area of your life.

Land: We are divided into the two realms of the conscious mind and the unconscious mind. The earth is equally bisected into land and ocean, with the land connecting to the conscious mind. Everything we can see and are easily aware of is like the land of our minds.

In this way, any land formation in a dreamscape is asking you to consider some area of your self-concept that is part of your conscious domain or that you have the natural human capacity to be aware of. Land represents parts of yourself that are not hidden, but are exposed and available for exploration. Use the terrain of the land in your dream to understand more deeply what the dream is asking you to look at. High terrain and mountains are the areas of consciousness that can only be explored by looking upward, into higher ground of thought and consideration. A deep jungle is still consciousness, but more of your hidden nature. Chasms or land masses separated by water indicate that there are thought processes or patterns that are separate, distinct, or in need of integration.

Languages: This is a symbol of unconscious messages that are not yet decipherable or understood. This interpretation applies only to a language that you do not know or that was created out of the dream world. If you know more than one language, then dreaming in different languages is a reflection of where you are in your life and what the language in question means for you from your past. Words are the basis of all thought and all reality. When words that you do not understand show up in a dream, the unconscious is deliberately masking some information by changing the rules. Use the context of the dream to assess the height of the stakes. This would apply both to the information that is being expressed by the unconscious and to the emotional meaning attached to your reaction to being unable to decipher any literal meaning. If you recognize the language being spoken by virtue of sounds and cadences, then apply whatever associations you have with that culture to the dream interpretation. If the language is made-up and you can remember any specific words, sounds, or phrases, use them in your process to see if you can draw any parallels with words you know. There may be a rhythmic or phonic connection to the nonsense words of your dream. Do not be afraid of being overly literal. If someone else is speaking to you in the dream, then the message is coming from the deep unconscious. If you are speaking the foreign tongue yourself, it may indicate that the new information is already integrated as part of you. More investigation will likely need to be done before you will be able to understand and utilize the information being presented.

Lap: Your lap is both about the body and about a particular posture of making space on which to hold something or someone. It is a sign of intimacy and connection to sit on someone's lap or allow someone to sit on your lap. In this way, anything that involves a lap in your dreams is asking you to consider your relationship to intimacy and affection. Holding someone or something in your lap indicates your perception of that individual or thing as dear to you. You sitting in someone's lap expresses a desire to be comforted in some way. Consider the meaning of the other people involved as aspects of your own personality that either are in need of nurturing and care or that can offer those things to you.

Laptop: A laptop offers the power of a computer as a completely self-contained and portable commodity. A computer represents highly sophisticated levels of mental organization, thought, and memory. A computer is a symbolic representation of the brain itself. (See *Computer*.)

Laryngitis: The voice is central to all expression and communication for human beings. Laryngitis is the losing of one's voice and is a symbol for the limitations connected to not having the ability to express yourself with power and certainty. A dream that involves laryngitis is exploring the consequences of not being able to find your own voice. If a person in your dream has laryngitis, consider the character aspect that the individual represents; it is that quality that is unable to speak through you. Laryngitis is a temporary condition, so the limitation that such a dream is expressing should be considered to be something that will eventually pass.

Laughter: Joy is one of the most fundamental principles of life at its highest expression. Laughter is the expression of joy itself, so it is the principle of joy in action. A dream that features laughter is expressing a desire for more joy. If someone is laughing in your dream, interpret that character aspect of self as a quality that is needed to connect more deeply to joy. The shadow side of this symbol is the embarrassment that can be associated with feeling that others are laughing at you. If you are suffering from feelings of shame in any area of your life, such a dream may be helping you process this.

Laundry: Laundry is about cleaning and cleansing. Most laundry is made up of clothing, and this relates to protection and self-expression and the periodic need to clean off old energy and things that have happened in the recent past.

Lava: Lava is molten rock that emerges from below the surface of the earth's crust. As such, it is a symbol of the pure potential associated with land that is completely new. Land represents the conscious mind, and in a way, lava is a sort of pre-consciousness that is beginning to make itself known, but in such a raw form, it is still dangerous to experience. A dream about lava is connecting you to this primal process of reinvention that is sometimes a part of the evolution of a human life.

Lawn: A house is a symbol of the self, and the lawn is the land around a house, representing the public persona and an individual's relationship to health, growth, abundance, and prosperity. The state that a lawn is in is a reflection of these concepts at the time of the dream. (See *Grass*.)

Lawyer: A lawyer deals in details, structure, and left-brained organization. As a character aspect, any lawyer in a dream is the part of your personality that can be called forth when there is a need to identify specific distinctions around some issue in your life that might be initially confusing.

Leak: A leak is a breakdown in the structural integrity of something such that its ability to contain a liquid or gas is compromised. As such, there is a barely noticeable diminution of the contained substance. The source of a leak can be difficult to find, and unless it is repaired, the leak will continue to do more and more damage. As a symbol, a leak can relate to anything that is slowly robbing you of passion, life force, energy, substance, or some other valuable essence. Look to your life where some persistently challenging person or circumstance is eroding your sense of power little by little.

Leash: A leash is about connectivity and control. Whoever holds the leash is in charge. If you are holding a leash in a dream, then you are exploring issues of control. Consider to what or whom the leash is attached and add that distinction to your dream. A dog on a leash might be about attempts to control love and loyalty. Another person on a leash is a symbol of attempting to rein in the qualities represented by the character aspects of that person. If you are on a leash, there may be a need to submit or surrender control to another person, institution, or circumstance in your life.

Leaves: Leaves are a plant's respiratory system and the structure through which they turn sunlight into energy. As such, they are a symbol for the power and abundance associated with the earth's never-ending supply of life itself. Consider the state and structure of the leaves in your dream. On a plant or a tree, leaves are a symbol of the ability of life to sustain itself and how that lives in you. If the leaves are in the process of falling, turning colors, or decay, they are more connected to the way in which life unfolds as a series of cycles. Leaves that are compromised in some way are reflecting some breakdown in your

ability to take energy in and convert it to proper and productive use for personal gain.

Ledge: A narrow shelf-like structure found high above the ground on buildings and in nature, a ledge has the almost contradictory nature of being traversable, but not without some danger of falling. It is this precariousness that holds its symbolic meaning. To be "on the ledge" is synonymous with being highly stressed and in danger of becoming more so. A ledge in your dreams is pointing to this state in some arena of your life. Where are you at the very edge of your ability to hold things together?

Leeches: Leeches are from the family of worms whose primary association is their capacity to feed off the blood of mammals. Even the term "leech" refers to the slow siphoning off of something, and in this way the leech itself is a symbol of a slow, methodical loss of passion, energy, or life force. Since leeches are mostly aquatic, there is an emotional quality to the meaning of them as a symbol.

Legs: The legs primarily function for standing and walking. In this way, they are symbolically linked to all the ways in which you must stand up for yourself, take a stand on something, or stand up for the rights of others. In terms of the mobility function, legs are linked to how you are moving about in your life, your power and efficacy in how you are walking your talk. Consider what is happening with your legs or the legs of a person within your dream and apply the qualities being exhibited to these principal ideas. A broken leg is an indication of something that is inhibiting your powerful movement through life that will eventually heal. Legs that are too weak to support you indicate a moment when you are unable to give yourself the foundation you need.

Leopard: All cats relate to the power of the feminine principle. The larger the cat, the greater the power of this totem. As with the jaguar and the cougar, the spots of the leopard are connected to the beauty and sensuality that this animal totem represents. The leopard is very adept at climbing trees, which extends its symbolic reach into the upper realms of consciousness. When such a cat appears in your dreams, you are being called to your predatory nature.

Lesbian Sex: This is symbolic of the integration of character aspects of the feminine principle. Any sexual act in a dream connects symbolically to the process of integration and the joining together of different aspects of the personality. In the case of lesbian sex, elements of the feminine principle such as nurturing, caretaking, and creativity are being highlighted. This symbol is included as a separate term, as it is not uncommon for heterosexual women to have dreams of lesbian sex when life events focus on this energy. Dreaming of sex with another woman is often reported by women during pregnancy. If the dreamer identifies as a lesbian, then such dreams should be explored through the concepts outlined in the terms *Sex* and *Intercourse*. Watching lesbian sex is a waking-life fantasy for many heterosexual men. However, this image has more to do with integration of inner aspects of the feminine principle for a man when such a dream appears.

It is a natural process of evolution for every man as he matures through life to become more in touch with his feminine nature. A truly integrated man has access to his own creativity, receptivity, nurturing qualities, and sensitivity.

Letter: This almost obsolete form of communication is a symbolic expression of ideas being transported from one area of your consciousness to another. Such a dream may be asking you to consider slower, more restrained ways of expressing yourself.

Levitation: The floating of a body has to do primarily with the break from gravity that it represents. Gravity is symbolic of shame, depression, and any quality that weighs you down and keeps you unable to move freely through life. Levitation has a spiritual connotation that takes the freedom from gravity and adds an element of mysticism to the experience. Such a dream may indicate a moment of heightened spiritual exploration or awareness.

Library: The world of knowledge is calling to you. You have within you the capacity to connect to all the wisdom in the world if you choose to cultivate a relationship with that part of your nature. A dream that takes place in a library is expressing that part of your own consciousness where information is held in high regard. Such a dream may be asking you to seek out more information and do some research to find the answers you are seeking.

Life Jacket: A life jacket keeps you afloat in water in order to save your life. Water is a symbol of emotions, and needing a life jacket in a body of water implies that an overwhelming amount of feelings is causing you great fear and/or discomfort. The life jacket is therefore a symbol of your ability to surrender and not allow the overwhelm you are experiencing to do any damage. If you dream of a life jacket, you are connecting to whatever will keep you safe while you ride out some difficult emotional experience. If someone in your dream is wearing a life jacket, consider what that person represents as a character aspect of yourself, as that may be the quality that is needed right now to keep yourself afloat.

Light: Light in general is a symbol for life itself, for the creative force that some people refer to as God or the Divine. Judeo-Christian doctrine tells us that the very first thing that came about in the creation myth was light. Many dreams will express an aspirational spiritual sensibility through the presence of light as a symbol for your connection to this part of the human experience. If there is a sensation of light in your dream, you may be expressing your own spiritual nature. Light also connects to your ability to see and become consciously aware of things about yourself and in your life. In this way, light may be a symbol of your expanding awareness of things that used to be in the dark and are now coming to light.

Light Bulb: This image is immediately recognized as a symbol for a new, bright idea. It has permeated modern media as such. Therefore, a light bulb in your dreams is a representation of your capacity to be inspired by new

thoughts. If the bulb is functioning well and is lit up, you are expressing this efficacy in your thinking. If the bulb is broken, burned out, or otherwise compromised, you are experiencing a moment of being cut off from inspiration and wisdom.

Light Switch: You are dreaming of your access to creative power and the ability to connect to that power at will with the assumption of success. Turning a switch reflects the need to make a change in some situation. Since most switches have only two positions, the desired effect is likely connected to causing something to start or stop. We go through life with an expectation that our light switches are always going to work, barring any unforeseen circumstances. This implies a level of trust and faith in our ability to bring about the desired effect when this symbol appears in a dream. Light connects to the power to create. Being able to access this energy and turn it on and off is the essence of this symbol. Turning a switch on may point to a need to begin unleashing the creative force within you. Turning one off could mean a need to stop and take a break from some ongoing process. Be equally willing to consider that turning off a light can indicate an unwillingness to look at something as it really is. A working switch means your sense of control is intact, whereas one that is ineffectual means some area of your life is no longer responding to your demands. The safety of the switch is also important. Exposed wiring could mean that danger or uncertainty is present when tapping into your creativity.

Lighthouse: You are finally being guided through confusing territory, and while you may not quite know where you are going, you are at least experiencing some emotional safety. A lighthouse is located on a shoreline and provides perspective in an otherwise concealed landscape. During a fog, the lighthouse emits both a visual and an audio clue to allow travelers to navigate through what would otherwise be dangerous territory. To get to the core of this symbol, we begin with where a lighthouse is located. The ocean represents the deep emotional unconscious parts of the human psyche. Land is what is conscious and within our awareness. The shoreline is where these two vastly different landscapes meet. Because they are so very different in nature, the boundary that exists between land and sea can be a strange and sometimes treacherous place. This is true of the shoreline, where the land meets the sea in the real world. In the world of symbolic meaning, these two dichotomous elements of the human condition interact with each other in a dramatic and sometimes violent way. The lighthouse keeps you safe in this dangerous territory.

Lightning: You are being inspired by sudden awareness or enlightenment born of divergent, confronting ideas. Consider how lightning is formed. Thick clouds contain both positive and negative charges. The positive charges gather on the top of the clouds and the negative charges drop to the bottom. When they are thrust together by the right weather conditions, the reaction of opposites explodes in an electrical charge of great violence. Therefore, lightning represents the flashes of brilliant awareness that come when polar-opposite views come crashing together. These contradictory views should actually cancel each other out. However, what actually happens is that they reveal a brand-new viewpoint that would otherwise have not been knowable. How you experience the lightning in your dream is key to your interpretation. If it is harmful or feels dangerous, then your dream is reflecting shadow material. This could be anything that might inspire the kind of fear that comes from gaining knowledge or information; as the saying goes, ignorance is bliss. Look to where you are being guided to choose a path that you are resisting even though you may know it is your highest choice. If you are delighted by the beauty of the lightning, then your unconscious may be expressing gratitude for the sudden new awareness that is present or right over the horizon.

Lingerie: Lingerie as an article of clothing falls into the category of self-expression. Since all articles of this nature are undergarments, there is an implication of a hidden agenda associated with them. The last layer of interpretation connects with the erotic nature of lingerie. Wearing lingerie in your dream may be helping you cultivate more intimacy and sensuality in your life. This may be the case for either a man or a woman, but for a man wearing lingerie there may be more fetishistic elements being expressed as well as the possible need to move toward a softer, more feminine approach to sexual expression.

Lion: The king of the jungle is a cat and thus resonates as an embodiment of the feminine principle. Courage, decisiveness, leadership, and strength are all parts of this majestic animal totem. When the lion appears in a dream, you are being blessed with some of the most ferocious power available in the world of animal totems.

Lips: You are dreaming of communication and intimacy and your ability to control these elements of life. The lips are the sensuous guardians of the center of communication and intimate exchange. They are the first mechanism of control over what comes into the body with regard to nurturance, and they are the last mechanism of control over what goes out from us in terms of communication. The color of lips can range from blue to red, with the former associated with a lack of warmth and the latter seen as filled with life-giving blood and therefore passion. When someone's lips turn blue, he or she is literally freezing to death, making this a potentially high-stakes image. These details should be considered if the color of lips was prominent in the dream imagery. How much control are you exerting over your communication and your willingness to be intimate with others? The color of your dream lips may reveal this. The essence of this symbol is intimate connection, whether that is to the world through words or to another person through a kiss. Just as when lips meet in life, there is a mingling of fluids and all that implies. Lips meeting in a dream can indicate a need or desire to mingle with and absorb another mode of communication. Lips that are too loose can allow communication to flow indiscriminately, whereas those that are pursed too tightly can indicate holding back. It is your job to decide whether this restraint is necessary or is a function of fear and/or resistance.

Lipstick: Anything that is associated with the mouth is going to connect to aspects of communication. Lipstick highlights the mouth in an overt way that also has some sexual overtones. For a woman, lipstick may be indicating a need to pay more attention to the strength and command of your voice. For a man, it may be calling for a need to soften and adopt a more feminine approach to what you feel you need to say. If someone is wearing lipstick in your dream in a way that seems important, that character aspect may have something to communicate to you.

Living Room: A home is a symbol of the self. Each room in a home has a different specific meaning. The living room is the consciousness of shared experiences. It relates to the parts of yourself that are less private and are accessible to the people you connect to in the world.

Lizard: The lizard connects you to the most basic of primitive instincts. The reptilian brain is the part of the human brain that controls our fundamental impulses. The medicine associated with the lizard in the dream world is adaptability and survival.

Lobby: The lobby of any structure is the antechamber that precedes your entrance into the main room of that building. In this way, it has some symbolic meaning that indicates a need to prepare for what is about to come.

Consider the type of lobby to round out your interpretation, as a theater lobby is not the same as one connected to an office building. No matter what associations you make with the building, any dream that takes place in a lobby indicates that there is another step to potentially take before you can benefit from the consciousness that the building has to offer.

Lobster: A creature of water, the lobster relates to the depths of the unconscious mind. Lobsters continually grow throughout their lifespan and can regenerate a lost limb. In this way, the power of the lobster as a totem connects to spiritual regeneration and the ability to continue growing in wisdom as a result of continual self-exploration. When the lobster appears in a dream, you are being asked to look at things on a very deep level; be willing to explore that which is hovering just below the surface of your unconscious.

Lock: A lock is a mechanism that keeps something impenetrable. Inherent in this as a symbol is the notion that there is someone who has the key. If you come across a lock in your dream, there is something that is being kept from you or is not yet available for you to access. For a well-rounded interpretation, consider what type of lock it is and what it is keeping you from opening. A lock in a dream could indicate a thwarted desire to get something you want. A lock that is broken may leave you feeling unsafe if you are on the other side of what the lock is supposed to be protecting.

Locker Room: The essence of the meaning of a locker room is the event that is being pre-pared for or returned from, usually a sporting event or some other physical fitness experience. There is nakedness, and therefore vulnerability is associated with this imagery. Consider whether or not your dream suggests that the locker room as a setting is connected to the before or the after of the implied event. If before, then you are preparing for some sort of challenge ahead. If after, then you are coming down off of some measure of exertion or effort. Your own school-age associations with locker rooms should be taken into consideration with your interpretation.

Lollipop: You are searching for more sweetness in your life, perhaps a return to a more innocent sensibility. Since the mouth can be connected to self-expression, your wish may relate to a style of communication that is softer or gentler than what you are currently utilizing.

Lost Objects: Your dream suggests a preoccupation with lack and limitation, for we are usually looking for something that we already have. The feeling of searching for something important and being unable to find it is challenging enough when it happens in life. In the language of symbols, it also taps into a deep fear shared by all people: the elusive search for meaning that all of us have to face from time to time in our lives. On the face of it, a dream of searching for a lost object has a primary purpose of helping us relieve stress so we can wake up the next day and face our day-to-day lives with greater psychic balance. This is the purpose of all recurring dreams of this nature. If you have this dream on a regular basis, it may simply be a convenient way for your unconscious to process the pressures of everyday living. What it is that you are searching for should be your first consideration. Your personal associations with this object will reveal what you sense is currently elusive. When in doubt, ask yourself, "What does this thing do, or what is it for?" Keys represent your access to the various compartments of your life. Your wallet connects you to abundance and the ability to meet your needs in the world. A more personal or specific item should be viewed through whatever meaning you assign to it. If there is no specific thing that you are searching for or you do not know what it is that you have lost, the dream may be pointing to a free-floating sense of being inadequately prepared for some situation in your life. Where you are looking offers the next shade of meaning. Your own home connects to your personal sense of self. Any other environment should be used to guide you; where you feel that something has been lost may be telling you that a certain area of your life has left you feeling incomplete.

Luggage: Luggage is a container used to transport certain desired objects so that you can function in any location. As a symbol, any piece of luggage represents your ability to have access to various tools for living that you may need in any given situation. There is a strong cultural association with the "baggage" that you are carrying in your life as representing unhealed wounds from the past and the difficulties that you unconsciously bring to all of your current relationships. Use the sensations of the dream itself to determine whether your dream is relating to luggage as a tool for effective living or connecting to the work you may still need to do in the realm of intimacy. (See *Bag.*)

Lynx: All cats relate to the power of the feminine principle. The larger the cat, the greater the power of this totem. This medium-sized cat is actually named for the brightness of its eyes, so the medicine that it carries connects with sight and vision. When the lynx appears in a dream, you are being gifted with the ability to see clearly and navigate stealthily as a result of such vision.

Machete: A machete is a very large knife-like implement designed for cutting through thick brush and undergrowth. The overgrowth of plant life that a machete is used on is a symbol of tangled thoughts and ideas that are impeding your easy progression through life. The machete then is a symbol for your ability to cut through old habitual thought patterns that block your way. This image often appears in a dream where the character aspect wielding it is a dangerous or scary individual. Remember that all dreams are for your benefit, and such a scary figure with this tool is really capable of helping you face those fears and clear a new path.

Machine Gun: A machine gun's power rests in its ability to repeat its intention over and over again in rapid succession. The image of a bullet landing on its target is about violent penetration, driving some point home aggressively, or being attacked by the ideas, thoughts, and expressions of someone else. The machine gun takes this entire sensibility to another level through automated repetition. Any association that you make with shooting a gun, such as anger or retribution, could be escalating if a machine gun is featured in your dream.

Magazine: Magazines connect to the pop culture of the day. They reflect the sensibilities of the area of life that their content expresses. Your waking-life relationship to magazines should be considered in any interpretation of a dream that features one. In a general way, a magazine is a symbol of benign escapism.

Maggots: Maggots are flies in the larval stage that feed on decomposing flesh and therefore have a connection to disgust and decay. This is a classic example of a symbol that has a disgusting image but a numinous meaning. There are some implications to the presence of maggots, and the first is that something has recently died. Death is a symbol for transformation and change, so maggots imply that a change has recently taken place. Maggots are instrumental in the process of turning flesh into the nutrients to support future life. If you dream of maggots, you are in the process of coming out of a change that has taken place in the past.

Magic: You are relying on distraction and manipulation to get your needs met. This may or may not be a positive use of your energy; only you can decide that. At the heart of magic tricks is the power to distract and hide the true intentions of the person performing the magic trick or illusion. This has the benefit of getting a need met, but by means that are ultimately inauthentic. The person performing a magic trick in your dream will yield some important distinctions for your interpretation. If it is you, there may be a need to hide your true motivations. If it is someone else, you may be being deceived by a particular choice you are making in your life.

Magic Carpet: A staple of the genie, the magic carpet is about the power of magic, of course, but consider that anything that flies through the air is also working in the realm of the intellect and the mind. Magical thinking can be an uplifting boon or a defense against life's more practical and difficult circumstances. Consider that a magic carpet in a dream could be an invitation either to put a little uplifting spiritual faith into your thinking, or to look to where you may be avoiding something that is on the ground that needs your attention.

Magician: You are connecting to your own power to manifest the unexplained or unexpected. The magician is one of the primary archetypes that make up the human condition. Magicians represent the part of us that can use magic, divine power, and the forces of will to create anything we desire. However, there is a large distinction between this as an archetypal figure and the popularized image of a stage magician engaged in the act of entertainment. The modern-day entertainer in the world of magic is an illusionist who presents us with the impossible. We know that there is a trick to what he or she is doing, yet we find ourselves awestruck nonetheless. This type of magician relates to the concept of manipulation.

Magnet: At the heart of a magnet's symbolism is the power of attraction that it possesses. As such, if one appears in your dream, you are exploring the concept of drawing something to you that you desire. Sometimes a magnet may bring something that is unwanted through this power to pull things in. Let the context of the dream indicate whether the magnet in your dream is acting in your highest good or not.

Magnifying Glass: A magnifying glass makes something small appear larger so that it can be examined more closely. It is symbolic of the desire to investigate something at a deeper level.

Maid: A maid is a person who is responsible for cleaning and house chores. As a character aspect of your own personality, the maid is the part of you that is there to keep things clean and straightened up in the world of your thoughts and feelings that sometimes feel as if they are in disarray or need cleansing.

Mail: Your dream includes some sort of communication, perhaps something you anticipate hearing about. Our relationship to postal mail has changed greatly since the advent of e-mail. It is now considered so slow that it is routinely referred to as "snail mail." While our current perceptions of mail have changed, the essence of this symbol connects to the origins of mail and its impact on the world. Communication between two parties is symbolic of intellect and the inner process of deduction and decision-making. The slow speed and back-and-forth nature of mail add the texture of anticipation. Putting a thought in writing connects to the permanence of a thought expressed. Mail in a dream could connect to communication that is slower than desired. Junk mail is akin to anxiety and the background chatter in the mind, where information like an important letter can get lost in a pile of unwanted catalogs. A dream could connect to the need to ferret through the unimportant to find clarity. Since the majority of mail comprises bills to be paid, this might symbolize being put on notice for the price you will have to pay for some choice in life.

Mail Carrier: You are dreaming about your connection to important communication. This symbol may soon be going out of the collective consciousness. As computers and modern technology become the norm, the delivery of mail to our homes is becoming a less primary way of staying connected to the outside world. While this may be true, we still live in a time where on an almost daily basis there is a human being that comes to our residence and delivers items of interest and importance to one degree or another. As a character aspect in a dream, a mail carrier is the part of your own personality that remains connected to the larger circles of your life but is detached from your core personality. The term "going postal" has become synonymous with violent outbursts connected with overwhelming stress. If the dream has any dark or shadowy elements to it, you may want to explore the mail carrier as a character aspect of an undercurrent of violent feelings that are just waiting for an inciting incident to allow them to explode. What a mail carrier is delivering in a dream offers an important second layer of meaning. What new information is your unconscious trying to send you?

Makeup: Makeup is associated with the public persona and creating the illusion of more beauty than you actually possess. There is an element of inauthenticity being expressed through this as a dream image and a desire to present a face to the world that may conceal the truth beneath the surface. What is happening with the makeup within the context of the dream should enhance your interpretation. Putting on makeup is to cover up something true with a false presentation.

Taking makeup off is to desire a more authentic way of being seen in the world.

Mall: This is actually a fairly ubiquitous setting for many dreams. A mall is a location that offers a variety of retail establishments, so on one hand it represents your access to a certain form of abundance, prosperity, and freedom. On the other hand, it has a connotation of a lack of sophistication that must be taken into consideration when interpreting a dream that takes place there. There are many choices at a mall, and this is a strong element of the symbolic meaning associated with such a location. If your dream takes place at a mall, you are exploring your consciousness of choices that you have about abundance and prosperity in your life, but the ideas being expressed may be more connected to the social pressures to experience wealth in a very particular way that is not necessarily aligned with abundance as a spiritual principle.

Mammogram: The breasts connect to the feminine principle of nurturing and the maternal instincts. They are also connected to sexuality and eroticism for many. A mammogram is a symbol of breast health and making sure that all is well in this area, like getting an inside view of how you are aligned with these principles in your life. (See *Breasts*.)

Manatee: The manatee is a mammal and thus relates to us more directly as beings of consciousness. Manatees are, however, fully aquatic animals and as such connect to the unconscious as represented by the ocean that they call home. Therefore, first and foremost they are a totem that allows for conscious exploration of realms that are ultimately unconscious in nature. Though they are large in size, manatees have a gentle nature and graceful movements. In this way, they vibrate with the principles of peace and surrender. When a manatee visits your dreams, you are experiencing the medicine of serenity.

Mandala: A mandala is one of the oldest symbols in the world, having been discovered by anthropologists in just about every ancient culture on the earth. It is a circle divided into four equal parts, which relates to the sphere of the earth divided into the four hemispheres. A mandala is perhaps the ultimate symbol of unity and totality, and if one appears in your dream, you are having an aspirational experience of a spiritual nature. Such a dream indicates an important moment in your spiritual development when a new level of integration and wholeness is at hand.

Manicure: A manicure highlights the fingertips. The fingers connect to creativity and the things you can do with your gifts and talents. To dream of a manicure is to seek a certain amount of recognition for these abilities and to be recognized as someone who can be productive. There is also an association with a manicure to prosperity and the relief of stress, so a dream that features one could be indicating a need to relax in this way.

Map: A map is a detailed description of an area so that navigation of that area is possible. As a symbol, a map represents the guidance you need to go where you desire. Since most maps deal with land, the focus here is on traversing areas of your conscious mind. There is an implication, however, that you may be going to places as yet unexplored. The map shows up in your dreams when you are about to go on a trek of self-investigation and is an indication that you are being guided by forces beyond your comprehension to help you do so.

Marching: Marching is about keeping time and aggregating what might otherwise be separate entities and coming together in unison. If you think of the people marching in your dreams as thoughts and ideas, the image of marching is a symbol of agreement and aligning what might otherwise be chaotic and random thoughts into one focused idea. Think about who is marching and the setting in which this is occurring for details to round out your interpretation.

Market: The market is a place where you can obtain many things you need and desire with an emphasis on daily living wares and especially food items. In this way, it is a symbol of the sustenance and self-care associated with feeding yourself and the principle of abundance as it relates to the bounty of the earth. In a dream, the market is the place in your own consciousness that represents what is available and what you are ready to receive in this arena. Such a dream will have this concept as an overall theme, and you must use the things that occur and the characters that appear in this setting to gauge your current relationship to these principles.

Marriage: You need to integrate some aspects of your character. Marriage is a joining of two energies into a third entity of cooperation and harmony. Symbolically, it relates to habits, patterns, thought processes, or belief systems that at one time were experienced as separate but now are either integrating or need to. If you are one of the marriage partners, consider the spouse in the dream as representing the quality of personality that is being called forth at this time.

Mask: A mask covers the true face and presents a particular version of one's persona to the world. This is a symbol for the way in which human beings never quite reveal all of who they are, but there are masks that are presented to the world. This occurs in degrees of authenticity, and a mask in a dream indicates a stronger separation between what is being presented and the true identity that is hidden below. Consider the mask itself from the dream; if you know what it looks like, you will have a better idea of what you are trying to portray at the time of the dream. If the mask is being removed, you are stepping into a more genuine version of your self-expression.

Massacre(s): You are dreaming of an enormous transformation in personal ideology. A massacre is an event of great magnitude by virtue of the number of deaths caused by a single force. Any death is a powerful symbol of transformation and change, as it always portends a rebirth of some kind. A mass death can be interpreted as any death would be—change so great that it can only be understood as the passing of something old to make way for the rebirth of something new. Look to your life for evidence of some change or shift that feels inordinately large in scale and you will probably find the stimulus for this dream. Since people in your dreams represent parts of your personality, the loss of large numbers could indicate that many old thoughts or patterns are being left behind.

Massage: A massage can be a relief from stress as well as a tool for healing certain muscular injuries. At the heart of this image is the connection to the essence of relaxing and in a dream may point to a need to dig deep in order to let go of stress. There is a sensual element to having a person touching your naked body, and this may factor in the interpretation as a need to stimulate your own sensual nature.

Mastectomy: The breasts connect to the feminine principle of nurturing and the maternal instincts. They are also connected to sexuality and eroticism for many. A mastectomy is a radical response to the presence of cancer in the form of complete surgical removal of one or both breasts. As a symbol, such an act is reflecting a deep loss of connection to these powerful feminine forces. There may be a literal connotation to the dream if you or someone you know is going through a waking-life experience of facing breast cancer. (See *Breasts*.)

Masturbation: You are looking to stimulate some sort of self-expression, from power to creativity or even sexuality. Any image that involves sexuality is going to be complex and is best interpreted by starting with the symbolic meaning first, by breaking down the image into its basic parts. Masturbation has a specific purpose, which is to induce orgasm. There are two functions that might be assigned to orgasm. One is the pleasurable relief from stress that it provides and the other

serves to remind the person of his or her sexuality. Also of importance is the current state of your sex life and your relationship to your sexuality in general. If there is another person involved, consider that individual as a character aspect of your own personality. If you are watching someone masturbate (or you are masturbating someone), then the qualities you assign to this individual may be the part of you that has access to elements of your sexuality at the time of this dream. The same is true if the person is masturbating you; however, this distinction connects more to an aspect of your personality that may be trying to stimulate a sexual response in you. The gender of this other person should be considered as well, no matter what your sexual preference. A man connects to the masculine principle of taking action, whereas a woman embodies the feminine principle of being receptive. The human sex drive contains the same power as the creative instinct. Masturbation in a dream may not necessarily be expressing the need to be sexual as much as the need to be creatively expressive. Look to where your life might be calling you to wake up your sense of passion.

Matches: Matches hold the potential for fire and therein lies the symbolic meaning. The presence of matches represents the desire and possibly also the intention to light a fire. Fire is a symbol of change and transformation. When matches appear in a dream, you are considering making a change in the near future.

Math: Math is the language of the entire universe. Every single element of what we know life to be can be expressed by mathematical equations. Math is very analytical and left-brained and thus represents this aspect of thinking. In a dream, the interpretation of math can be as mundane as expressing a need to call upon your logical mind to help you through a life circumstance. It can be as profound as a dream of sacred geometry, where you are considering existence itself. The context of the dream will illuminate which way to go with your interpretation.

Measurements: Taking measurements is usually about planning to do something with exactness and precision. There are times when being well prepared is very important, and the presence of this activity in a dream is an indication that this is the case. "Measure twice, cut once" is the saying.

Meat: Meat is a staple of most protein-based diets. Its symbolic meaning connects to sustenance at a fundamental level. If you have a dream that features meat in it, there is something that needs to be fed in order to be strengthened; this could be an idea, a project, or a new direction in your life. The state of the meat in your dream has significance. Raw meat indicates that there is still some work to be done in order to strengthen your objectives. Meat that is rotten means an opportunity may have passed you by. If you have a waking-life relationship with meat that generates strong feelings against the eating of it, this personal association must be considered as an interpretation.

Mechanic: Any person in a dream is a character aspect of your own personality. A mechanic is responsible for keeping your car maintained and running properly. A car is a symbol for how you move effectively through your life's journey. Therefore, the mechanic in your dream is the part of yourself that can be relied upon to handle the breakdowns and challenges that happen along the way.

Medicine Man/Woman: The medicine man or woman is an archetypal character aspect; they are part of your personality, but at a much higher, aspirational level. The medicine man or woman has two functions. The primary one is that they are the keepers of wisdom and healing power. You turn toward this archetype when you need to face great change or heal something at a profound level. They are also the part of you that perceives change before it happens, as these shamanic figures possess a heightened level of intuition and energetic sensitivity. If such a figure appears in a dream, you are having an aspirational experience at a very high spiritual level. In the case of a male figure, you are connecting to the masculine principle of taking action. In the case of a female figure, you are connecting to the feminine principle of stillness and receptivity.

Meeting: A meeting is a staple of the world of business. It is a symbolic gathering of consciousness or different ideas in order to create some sort of unified direction. All of the people who attend a meeting in your dream are to be understood as aspects of yourself whose qualities are needed collectively in order to accomplish some current goal or objective in your life. This is more of a rational mind symbol and calls into being the part of your nature that can plan, schedule, organize, and carry out movement.

Menstruation: The power of the feminine principle is represented by menstrual blood, as the force for the creation of life is at the heart of the feminine side of human nature. In this way, menstrual blood is a symbol of the power to create at the most fundamental level. However, there is grief present with menstruation, as the periodic bleeding that all young women experience is evidence of fertility that is not going to materialize. As such, you may be dreaming about regrets around accomplishments not realized and creativity that has not been expressed.

Mermaid: The mermaid is a mythological creature with the torso of a woman and the lower half of a fish. In this way, she is an archetypal figure that embodies the feminine principle coupled with the capacity to connect to the unconscious mind and the emotional realms. In modern media, the mermaid has been transformed into something lovely and beguiling; however, her origins are dark and are associated with peril, death, and seduction. A dream that features a mermaid should be considered aspirational, and you must keep in mind all of her qualities, light and dark, when formulating an interpretation. In any case, such a dream is connecting you to the spiritual side of your nature.

Microphone: The primary use of a microphone is to amplify the voice. The voice is the center of your power as an expressive human being. A microphone in a dream connects to a need or desire to increase the power of your convictions, your ability to declare what it is that you desire, and the authority you wield in your life through knowing how to command your words. If the microphone in your dream is not working properly, you need to make some adjustments in order to get your voice heard.

Microwave: The principle behind a microwave is its ability to speed up molecules such that heat is created. Heat is symbolic of energetic increase, passion, change, and power. A microwave in a dream relates to a desire to make things happen at a much faster pace than is natural. This may or may not be beneficial, and you must take into consideration the potential consequences for overriding the natural flow of things if a microwave is featured in a dream.

Military: Anything associated with the military falls under the auspices of the warrior archetype. The warrior's job is to divide the world into right and wrong, black or white. He then defends this distinction with his life. This is a powerful aspect of human consciousness, and anything that relates to the military that appears in a dream is connected to this profound power. There are more pedestrian elements to this symbol that include regimentation, rigidity, and inflexibility.

Milk: This mammal-made drink is considered a fundamental food source, especially for infants and children. As a symbol, it is the ultimate source of nutrition and care from the feminine principle. There is a harkening to the maternal instincts with milk; hence the term "mother's milk" to connote the very essence of that which will comfort and sustain us.

Mine: A mine is essentially a tunnel dug very deep underground for the purpose of cultivating some raw material. Since land is associated with consciousness, a mine represents what is possible to gain when digging beneath the surface. If you know what the product of the mine is, you can add that distinction to your interpretation. There is a great deal of danger associated with mining, and a mine is a place where tragedy can occur in an instant. The same could be said of the fear that is sometimes associated with self-investigation.

Mine Shaft: A mine is a place beneath the surface of the earth where raw materials are found and cultivated. The shaft is the portal through which you get to the place below. From the surface, it is the evidence that an excavation has already taken place and that access to what is available has already been established. This is a fairly common dream image and indicates that there may be a need to revisit the dark and scary places below the surface of your consciousness in order to reap the benefit that is hidden in those realms. If the mine shaft seems abandoned, you are revisiting some insight or awareness that you have already mined, so look to past wisdom for your answers to today's questions.

Minister: A minister is a religious leader, and as a person who appears in your dream, he or she is a character aspect of your own personality. From a purely archetypal perspective, a minister represents your access to the structure of a spiritual practice. However, your personal association with religion and your life experience with it must be taken into ac-count when you interpret such a figure in a dream.

Mirror: A dream with a mirror in it is asking you to consider what you see in your life. What we experience in our consciousness is reflected back to us based on our inner beliefs, and if a mirror features prominently in a dream, you are contemplating this paradigm. Mirrors can be confounding and confusing. Not only do they reverse everything that they reflect, but their images can give a sense of reality that they do not actually possess. They accurately reflect an image, but are not the image itself. A mirror is comparable to the basic principle of cause and effect. You can use it effectively as a tool to examine the current state of things. However, in order to change what you don't like in the reflection, you must work on the object being reflected rather than alter the mirror itself. Who or what one sees in a mirror in a dream represents that which the unconscious mind is seeing. Consider whether the mirror image is accurate to your self-perspective. Looking straight into the mirror and being comfortable with what you see says that your self-appraisal is honest and real. If what you see seems off-kilter in some way, it could be an invitation to look at where you may be being inauthentic. This could indicate something that you are deliberately hiding from others or something more mundane, such as being more concerned with how others see. The condition of a mirror should also be taken into account. For instance, a cracked mirror may be helping you process a feeling of ominous bad luck due to the old wives' tale common in Western culture that breaking a mirror brings dire consequences to the one who breaks it. A handheld mirror might be offering an intimate glimpse of the self, one that is designed to privately monitor the image you project to the world. A full-length mirror could be pointing toward the need to see more of the whole picture of your current life situations. Someone else's mirror might mean your individual sense of self is being determined at this time based on someone else's values or perceptions. A mirror can possess the magical property of showing the truth about a situation when called upon, such as the Evil Queen's Magic Mirror in *Snow White*. Explore the theme of the dream for its profound truth.

Miscarriage: A pregnancy is a symbolic expression of a new idea, project, direction, or choice to create something that is still in its gestational stage. A miscarriage is simply a change in direction such that you will need to begin again. While such a dream may have emotional connotations to it, the actual meaning connects more to making space for something new to be created.

Mistress: The "other woman" is a staple in many cultures where a man goes outside of his marriage vows in order to have his sexual needs met. At the heart of this structure from an interpretive perspective is the circuitous route that's being used to generate a fundamental human experience that partnership is designed to provide. If someone appears in your dream and is indeed identified as either your or someone else's mistress, that person is a character aspect of your own personality.

The representation here is about the desire to connect to intimacy without emotional risk.

Model: A model embodies a certain aesthetic of beauty and is therefore a symbolic ideal to which many people aspire. The challenge with this image is that there is a great deal of false identification associated with this ideal, and your interpretation must include your personal relationship to beauty and your sense of personal attractiveness. A model as a character aspect in a dream may represent ideals of beauty to which you aspire, but may just as easily connect to the impossibility of such aspirations.

Mold: Mold is a mostly invisible fungus that makes itself known when certain conditions are present, often on food that has been left for long periods of time at certain temperatures. Other molds present a level of toxicity in homes and other buildings. Since molds are essentially unwanted, they have a symbolic meaning associated with disgust and decay. There is a secondary meaning when mold is present that connects with long periods of disregard to matters of cleanliness. If mold appears in a dream, you are being called to take a look at the impact of ignoring certain matters for long periods of time.

Monastery: A monastery is a place of both retreat and extreme spiritual devotion. In a dream, this setting is asking you for a particular increase in your spiritual devotion and self-reflection.

Money: Any dream that involves money is connecting to the principles of abundance, power, and freedom. In a dream, money often represents your inner resources. Your sense of personal value, power, or the ability to make something happen can be expressed by the symbol of money. As a symbol, large amounts of money can represent any sort of achievement or sense of fulfillment as an unconscious expression of desires met. No matter what the financial situation in your waking life, your dream state can find you available for limitless abundance or attached to absolute lack. Since money in life is symbolic in nature, in the dream world it can represent any form of abundance. The appearance of this in a dream could connect to the acquisition of any desire, from a new sense of inner riches to outward expressions of expansion such as a new relationship, job, or other appearance of a heart's desire. On the opposite side of the spectrum, money in a dream could be pointing out feelings of lack that you are experiencing in life. As a wish fulfillment or compensatory dream, connecting to money could be balancing out feelings of limitation. Money that is counterfeit is revealing a relationship to abundance that is false or inauthentic. Though it may look real, it has been manufactured with dubious intentions. In a dream, this might point to ways in which you are (or someone in your life is) trying to get away with presenting yourself as bigger than you really are. Also be willing to look at the various aspects of your current situation; are there circumstances in your life that are costing you more than you can afford? This can apply to both material and emotional conditions. Look at the amount of money or lack of money in the dream as connoting how much or little of some needed

commodity appears in your life. This can be spiritual, emotional, or physical. How abundant do you feel?

Monkey: Whenever an animal is present in a dream, it is pointing to a more instinctual approach to life. You may be obsessed with a pervasive thought pattern that won't let your mind rest. The proverbial "monkey on your back" or the agitation of the "monkey mind" may be what this dream is calling forth. A monkey may also be indicative of the ability to mimic behavior by rote, but without a heartfelt understanding of the deeper meaning associated with the choices you are making. From an aboriginal perspective, the medicine available through the totem of the monkey relates to curiosity and playful energy.

Monuments: This symbol connects to collective expressions of cultural greatness. Structures such as the Statue of Liberty, the Eiffel Tower, the Taj Mahal, and the Great Pyramids are all examples of cultures erecting monuments to their own importance. This has been happening since the beginning of civilization. These enormous expressions of power and technology are designed to celebrate the accomplishments of a society and provide a collective projection of greatness that helps the masses feel safe and protected as well as proud of their accomplishments and feel a connection to their history. Such a dream may be calling you to leave your mark on the world in a very big way.

Moon (Moonlight): Any dream with the moon or moonlight in it relates to the feminine aspect of the life force energy. The moon is a very powerful symbol, just as it is an enormous energetic force in our daily life on Earth. As the heavenly counterpart to the masculine energy of the sun, the moon represents the feminine aspects of life. The primary essence of the moon is its constant changeability. In this regard, the moon symbolizes the ephemeral quality of life and all of the different cycles that human beings experience. If the moon plays a prominent role in your dream, your interpretation should begin with the notion that change is afoot. A distinction should be made about how the moon appears in your dream. If the moon itself is visible to you in the skyscape of your dream, then you are looking at the source of emotional power. If your dream illuminates the light of the moon itself as it falls upon Earth, then you are dreaming of the effect or impact of the moon's magic. If your dream actually takes place on the moon, then you are literally visiting the seat of your unconscious directly; such a dream should be considered as a very deliberate snapshot of your current experience of how the invisible side of life is impacting the visible. The emotional side of life is represented by the moon. This includes all that is changeable and all that responds to the ebb and flow of life. Because of its unquestionable universality to the human race, the moon in dreams should be considered with very broad strokes of interpretation.

Moose: Stately and powerful, the moose is a study in understatement. We rarely see moose in any other posture but stillness, but the amount of brutal strength they possess is astronomical. They are a symbol of restrained power and aggression. They are enormous in size, yet graceful in movement. These contradictions are at the very heart of their medicine as an animal totem. When the moose appears in a dream, you are being introduced to a level of great power that is best understood as a function of that power's potential rather than of actual expressions of violence.

Morning: Daytime represents that which you are conscious of. In the twenty-four-hour cycle, the daylight hours relate to the masculine principle of taking action. Morning is the very beginning of the day and in this way relates to the initial movement in any project or new direction in your waking life. You may have a dream that takes place in the morning when some new cycle is beginning or when you are approaching a new project, relationship, or course of action.

Mosque: You are dreaming of connecting to your spiritual nature in a more conventional way. Churches, temples, and mosques are the center of spiritual life for any community. Just like a house in a dream, any building can be interpreted as representing one's current sense of self. In this way, any place of worship ultimately points to your relationship with spirituality and religion. Because this element of life can be particularly controversial, it is very important that you make a clear distinction between the universal meaning of a mosque as connecting to matters of spirituality and whatever personal feelings you harbor about organized religion. If a mosque is not your typical house of worship, your dream may be asking you to consider the similarities between religious beliefs rather than the differences.

Mosquito: Any flying insect relates to the world of thoughts and the intellect. As a pest, the mosquito connects to patterns of thought that can be both annoying and ultimately harmful. In life, mosquitos carry diseases, and in this way they symbolize the capacity for undesirable thought patterns to cause a great deal of harm if you allow them to land and infect you with their negativity. (See *Insects*.)

Moth: The moth has the same meaning as the butterfly, but it relates to the shadow side of the equation, as it is a nocturnal creature. (See *Butterfly*.)

Mother: See *Parents*.

Mother Mary, Quan Yin: This is an archetypal character aspect that represents the healing that occurs through the principles of love and compassion. While there are many other archetypal representations of the power of love, this entry will limit itself to these two, as they are perhaps the most widely recognized symbols of divine forgiveness in the history of the human race. In dream work, they should be treated symbolically as archetypes, and their appearance in a dream indicates that you are experiencing a high level of self-discovery and integration. Mary, the mother of Jesus, and Quan Yin, Buddhist goddess of mercy and compassion, embody the feminine principle in its highest evolution. The feminine principle connects to the power of love and receptivity. Both of these figures are revered by millions as the purveyors of forgiveness and unconditional love.

Though the traditions that created each of them could not be more different, what they offer to those who turn to them in their hour of need is exactly the same. One of the most difficult challenges that all human beings face is the process of forgiveness, and the ability to forgive one's self is particularly elusive. The human mind is not built for unconditional love, even though it is a concept that many who travel the path of service continually strive to achieve. No matter how she may appear to you, the archetype of the divine mother can help you inch your way out of shame and resentment and move toward the healing that can only come through love and mercy. The appearance of one of these great figures in a dream is to put you on notice that you are in a moment of elevating consciousness and self-integration. It is not uncommon for any archetypal figure to be silent in a dream; it is their mere presence that embodies the impact of the dream. If words and messages are present in the dream, take them to heart and do so literally. However, if this is not the case, your best use of such a dream is silent gratitude for the gift of such a powerful experience of elevated consciousness. (See *Quan Yin*.)

Motorcycle: All vehicles are symbols of how you move about in your life. A motorcycle is very similar to a car in terms of the day-to-day movement through your social and communal experience. However, a motorcycle adds an element of speed, power, and excitement to the interpretation. You may dream of a motorcycle when you crave these elements in your journey.

Mountain: You are dreaming of challenges or obstacles that you must surmount in your life, especially as they might relate to new ideas, constructs, or choices. Mountains are formed when two opposing vectors of movement in the earth's crust push against each other and rise upward to form a new land mass. Therefore, the mountain is symbolic of the newly formed, high vantage place that rises up out of conflict and confrontation. Remember that changes on our planet's surface first begin in the combustible core below. This relates them to the passion, aggression, and other friction-causing emotional states that occur in the lower depths of the unconscious that, in the long run, build new, higher terrain upon which you can see more of your life.

Mountain Lion: All cats relate to the power of the feminine principle. The larger the cat, the greater the power of this totem. The mountain lion is one of the smaller of the great cats, and the association with the terrain on which it is found connects to the ability to traverse higher levels of consciousness.

Mouse: A mouse is a very small animal and thus symbolizes a sense of timidity through phrases such as "timid as a mouse." Mice remain mostly hidden behind walls, and in this way they represent ideas that are mostly hidden but that can be heard, figuratively speaking, scratching away underneath the surface or behind the scenes.

Movies: The creation of your own version of life is featured in this dream. Movies as a symbol connect to our memories and desires as well as a need to control our reality. Movies are so ingrained in Western culture that it is difficult to separate them out from the human experience as something distinct from how we live life day to day. This is especially so with regard to the way in which a film can capture historical events and present altered versions of moments in time that may be seen by future viewers as actual facts. Research has shown that the areas of the brain that are stimulated by the images we see on film are the same as those activated by real events. This blurs the line between fantasy and reality in an alarming way. Movies and dreams are not very different from each other. What is captured on film has a way of becoming real in the imagination of the human race. Even the most unbelievable storyline is made possible through the magic of film. In this way, the symbolic meaning of the movies is the incredible drive the human race has to make our most passionate desires come to life. A common dream that many people report is to have the sense that the dream itself is a movie. The first distinction that should be made when considering the symbolic meaning of a movie in a dream is which side of desire the film is addressing. One connects to manifesting a fantasy into reality and the other embodies rewriting history as you perhaps wish it was. In either case, the presence of a movie in a dream is likely expressing a wish to have more control over how life is being perceived. Ask yourself what area of your life is feeling unreal or that you wish were different.

Moving: A shift in identity or consciousness is at hand. Your home is the strongest symbol connected to your sense of self, and the process of moving indicates that great change is at hand. There is chaos in this transformation, so the dream may be expressing some area in your life where change is happening at such a fast or intense rate that things feel all taken apart. Trust that this is only a process and eventually everything will feel in alignment once again.

Mug: Any container of liquid to be consumed is symbolic of your ability to have immediate access to take in some form of sustenance. A mug is usually associated with a warm beverage, which has connotations of comfort. A mug in your dreams may be expressing a desire to feel nurtured. Many people might associate a mug with drinking coffee, and in this way this image could relate to the need for stimulation.

Muscles: Muscles are a predominantly male image that is symbolically connected to strength, power, and sexual masculinity. Muscles are often hyper-exaggerated and in this way are representative of what can happen when there is too much emphasis put on these qualities. If you have obvious musculature in the dream, you are seeing the evidence of a great deal of effort being put in the doing of some aspect of your life. If someone in the dream is very muscular, use the character-aspect technique and assign that part of your personality an extra dose of strength and power.

Music: Music is the most exalted form of expression and universal communication that the human race has. Any dream that features music is connecting both to a deep passion to express as well as the fundamental structure of life itself. Music is mathematical in nature. This is what makes it perfectly universal. Music might be considered the highest form of creative expression available to the human race. This is evidenced by the importance our society places on music and musicians and the powerful influence that music exerts over people. In all cultures throughout history, the presence of music has created the possibility of people being connected through joy. Not only does music have the capacity to bring human beings together in a shared sense of ecstasy, but it has been shown to exert a powerful influence over animals and plant life as well. When music appears in a dream, your first consideration should be to examine areas in your waking life where you are allowing yourself (or not allowing yourself) to connect to spontaneous self expression. If you are hearing music in your dream, you may be receiving messages from your unconscious to open yourself to a deeper, more joyful sense of life. The degree of pleasantness of the music in your dream may represent your current relationship to your intuitive and emotional nature that goes beyond intellectual understanding. If you are making the music in the dream, you may want to examine areas of your life where creative endeavors are ready to thrive. If background music plays a pivotal role in your dream, you may want to consider this as an underscoring to subtle emotional issues that may be getting ready to emerge into your conscious awareness. In the same way that music deepens the emotional meaning in a film, music may serve to highlight the importance of a dream. If this seems to be the case, remember the manipulative nature of this use of music's power. You may want to examine ways in which your emotions may be influencing your view of some area of your life in ways that may not be authentic. This could show up in the form of drama in a current situation that might be more effectively dealt with using a more pragmatic and less emotional approach.

Nails: A staple in building and construction, the nail is the ultimate tool for keeping the separate pieces of any structure together. A nail is the element that is introduced into an environment in such a way as to join disparate segments together, and herein lies its symbolic meaning. To see or use nails in a dream is to have access to that which will keep the thing you are building together in strength and integrity. The thing you are building represents a new idea in consciousness, and the nails ensure that it will take proper form.

Naked: You are dreaming of vulnerability, and some situation in your life is likely causing you to feel exposed. This is one of the most common dream images experienced by almost everyone at some point or another. It expresses the fear we all have of being vulnerable or exposed in life in a way for which we aren't prepared. In Western culture and especially in the United States, the public is generally not very comfortable with nudity. Given this predisposition to cover up our naked selves, it would be a natural representation in the dream state for nakedness to indicate feeling exposed in some area of life. Where you are naked in a dream and who you are naked in front of will provide you with all the clues you need for an accurate interpretation of such a dream.

Navel: The navel is our original connection to Source. Through it, all needs were met with such immediacy that there was no actual experience of need. This part of the human body also has a connection to the desire for maternal care. In a dream, you may be connecting to either one of these primal sensibilities. The navel is also the seat of the emotional center and is where you connect with your instincts and gut feelings about things. Use the context of the dream to understand how to perceive the meaning of this image.

Nazi: This is a strong image that is ultimately archetypal in nature, but is often difficult to get a grasp on because of the enormous emotional content often associated with it. The Nazi ideology has to do with racial purity, precision, and annihilation. If you dream of a Nazi character, you are dealing with a very deep shadow figure of organized hatred. It is important in shadow work to recognize that all things live within us, even the most deplorable aspects of evil. Such an image in a dream is asking you to step into acceptance of all of your humanity, even that which feels unforgivable.

Neck: The neck is the center of the voice, and as such, any dream image that involves this part of the body is symbolically representing your current relationship with how you are expressing yourself in your life. Any sort of compromise to the neck indicates breakdowns in your communication and challenges in you having a strong connection with your voice. Anything that highlights, adorns, or otherwise calls attention to the neck is asking you to recognize the value of your convictions and to stand up for what you want to say.

Necklace: An adornment worn around the throat, a necklace symbolically highlights the voice and how well you are able to speak your truth and stand powerfully in what you have to say. Dreaming of a necklace indicates that this area of your consciousness needs some attention. Whatever is happening with a necklace in a dream may be a statement of your current relationship with your voice and sense of personal expressiveness.

Needle: The primary use of a needle is to penetrate in an almost invisible way, whether it's a needle for sewing or a hypodermic one for medical reasons. The symbolic meaning therefore connects with this very precise way of penetrating below the surface of something in a way that leaves no evidence of its presence. In a dream, needles connect to this need or desire. The type of needle will figure prominently in your interpretation. A needle that has been used for drug use is an indication that something has happened in the past that is destructive but that has left almost no trace of the original act.

Nephew: A nephew is like the child you can walk away from, giving you a parental sensation without the responsibility. If you have a nephew in waking life, this dream is reflecting the quality of that individual as a character aspect of yourself. Such a dream is asking you to consider these qualities in your own life.

Nest: The primary purpose of a nest connects to giving birth to young, and many creatures in the animal kingdom build nests for this. The implication when a nest is present in a dream is that something has just been or is just about to be created. Since it is likely to be an animal that is using the nest, what is being generated will connect to your instincts, as all animals connect to your instinctive nature.

Net: A net is a structure for gathering some things while letting other elements pass by, such as fish and water. In this way, it is a symbol for distinguishing between an object of your desire and that which is extraneous. What you are grasping for with a net or what the net is designed to capture is an important part of your interpretation. Such an image in a dream indicates the intention to catch a prized object.

Newspaper: Though these are less and less common in our culture, newspapers are a conduit for a person to connect to important current events. As a symbol, a newspaper relates to how well informed you are in your community and your social experience in life. The presence of newspapers in your dream may indicate a desire to be better informed about the world in which you live.

Niece: A niece is like the child you can walk away from, giving you a parental sensation without the responsibility. If you have a niece in waking life, this dream is reflecting the quality of that individual as a character aspect of yourself. Such a dream is asking you to consider these qualities in your own life.

Nightmares: These are the important dreams that help us maintain emotional and psychological balance and equilibrium in the face of stress and fear. Nightmares are those frightening and often very memorable dreams that can wake you up and leave you riddled with anxiety. While there may be underlying neurological causes for nightmares, for the most part they are simply a common experience in the world of dreams; sooner or later, you are likely to have one. There are many emerging theories about the neurological structure of nightmares and what some of the value of having them might be with regard to stress and psychic balance. However, these don't address the question that most people want an answer to, and that is, what causes them? Of course, the answer to that question is that we still don't really know what causes nightmares, or any dreams for that matter. We do know that there are some medications that can impact the quality and intensity of dreams, including the frequency of nightmares. There are plenty of old wives' tales associated with activities that can supposedly bring them on, such as eating red meat or other heavy foods before going to sleep. There are even those who believe the direction you lie in while you sleep can cause bad dreams. These are not, however, proven scientific facts, nor are they validated by my personal experience of interpreting thousands of dreams over many years. Nightmares are not easily forgotten, and the residual emotional reaction they sometimes generate can often linger in our conscious awareness far longer than the fond memories of our more pleasant dreams. However, this inherent capacity to remember them often makes them easy to work with. Additionally, people are sometimes highly motivated to understand them because of the upset they can create. If dreams are indeed messages from the unconscious, a nightmare is one way it has of telling us to pay attention, as there may be shadow material coming up. This always means there is something important to learn.

Nighttime: Nighttime is the feminine side of the day. Because there is darkness at night, any dream that takes place at night is rooted in the shadow and pertains to the hidden aspect of your nature.

Nine: The final number in the system is nine, which represents completion and endings. All things must end in order for the inevitable new beginning to follow. Nine embodies that cycle of existence that demands that change occur and that the old give way to the new. The shadow side to this is the fear of death and the resistance to change that comes with an ending.

Nipples: The nipples provide access to sustenance through breast milk. However, they are also an erogenous zone. In a dream, they may relate to either or both of these fundamental meanings. You may be experiencing maternal instincts and a need to feel more cared for if they appear in a dream. If you are dreaming of a man's nipples, there still may be such a need being expressed to introduce a more feminine-principle approach to your experience.

Noose: A noose is a deadly knot that is designed to end a person's life by cutting off the air supply and also by breaking the neck. Anything that relates to this part of the body is symbolically linked with your relationship with your voice and taking a stand for what you have to say. A noose in a dream is an indication that there may be some strong consequences for either speaking your truth or being unable to do so. The context of the dream and your own personal habits may indicate which is the more likely meaning.

Nose: The nose connects to the sense of smell, the most ancient of the senses and one that is connected to the reptilian brain. Smell is primal in nature and connects you to your fundamental ability to know more about your environment. In this way, the nose in a dream may be expressing your current ability to trust your instincts about where you are in your life. The nose also has connotations about butting into other people's business, with the use of the term "nosy" as indicating someone who pays too much attention to the affairs of others. Such an image in a dream may indicate a crossing of boundaries either by you or by someone else toward you.

Numbers: You are tapping into your structural thinking and getting a glimpse of the building blocks of all reality. Math and numbers are behind all of how life is constructed. The movements of the earth, moon, and other planets are geometrical in nature. Music is simply math expressed as tone. Digital technology reduces various data to numeric sequences and then converts it back to its original form. Our need to describe physical phenomena led us to create nine whole numbers that, in different sequences, can express anything from gravity, to the speed of light, to the way visitors can identify which house on the block is yours. When a number is featured in a dream, there is a rich symbolic meaning hidden in it. You can use the fundamentals of numerology as a way to understand what a dream with numbers might mean. If there is more than one digit involved, add all the values together until you arrive at a final single number. For example, if an address is 115 Main Street, you would add one plus one plus five and get seven. There is an elegant evolution present in the archetypal interpretation of the numerical sequence, which can be considered a sort of journey. We started the journey alone in the infinite (one), discovered opposites and relativity (two), invented creativity (three), built a foundation (four), expressed freedom (five), partnered with another (six), went inward to find spirituality (seven), and expressed and enjoyed the rewards of the outside world (eight), and now we come to a close (nine). Each of these numbers is elaborated upon in the individual entries.

Numbness: There is information in all sensation. To be without sensation is to be blocking some form of nonverbal communication about the potential danger in a situation. You may be blocking painful feelings by making yourself numb to them. This may or may not be a good idea, for sometimes blocking pain is a good way of getting through a very difficult circumstance. Consider where you are feeling numb and ask yourself what you might be feeling or sensing if this part of you weren't numbed off.

Nun: This is an archetypal character aspect connected with extreme devotion to spiritual principles, though often this idea is expressed as the shadow of such devotion because of personal associations with this image. Also because of the media, this symbol carries with it a great number of potential shades of meaning, from an intense level of respect to humorous irreverence. Additionally, especially for those who grew up in parochial school, there is a powerful connection between nuns and strict discipline that is often connected to corporal punishment. On the serious end of the spectrum, the nun is the symbolic bride of Christ and represents a level of dedication that is unparalleled in our modern culture. In this light, the character aspect of a nun in a dream connects to a deeply committed spiritual side of your nature that is willing to sacrifice much for the sake of your beliefs. For those individuals with experience in the Catholic school system, nuns can also connect to a level of strictness that represents obstacles to spiritual connection because of a distaste for the authoritative severity nuns can be known for. Lastly, the figure of the nun in her habit has been incorporated into the world of comedy, and for many people this image sparks feelings of amusement and parody.

Nurse: A nurse is the bringer of care when illness or injury is present. As a character aspect in a dream, it is the part of your personality that can be called upon when a great deal of nurturance is necessary. If you dream of a nurse, you need to cultivate a stronger relationship with your inner caretaker.

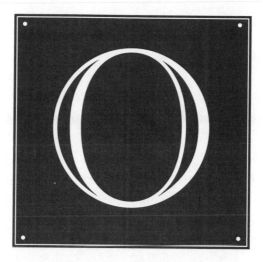

Oasis: A rare area of water in the desert, an oasis is a symbol for anything of sustenance that exists within a great range of that thing's absence. If an oasis appears in a dream, look to where you are feeling an extreme sense of lack in your life. The oasis is an indication that something you desperately need for your journey through life can suddenly appear in order to get you through even the most difficult of times. This could connect to love, money, affection, or rest.

Obelisk: An obelisk is a phallic symbol that is also a spiritual object representing the power of the masculine principle. If there is an obelisk in your dream, you are calling upon this energy to serve you in some area of your life.

Obesity: If you dream of being obese, you are connecting with the consequences of overindulgence in some area of your life. If you have issues of weight in your waking life, such a dream may be more literal. Extra body fat can also be a symbolic expression of protection and avoidance of deeper issues.

Obstacles: Something that gets in your way in a dream is a symbolic block to moving forward in your waking life. This is one of the most frequent dream images and has a very literal meaning associated with it. Life is often experienced as a function of facing the obstacles that we must traverse to get from where we are to where we desire to be. This is a daily struggle. Dreams often help us balance out our sense of frustration and despair as we face this particular challenge, which is an absolutely universal human experience. There are two elements to consider when making an interpretation of a dream of this kind: what is causing the obstacle, and what part of the body or type of movement is being blocked. The more important of the two is how you are stuck. If the feet or legs are involved, this connects to how you are moving through your life. Feet guide us in the direction we choose, so if you cannot walk, your dream is reflecting an inability to make a new choice or find your footing firmly on the ground you desire. If the legs are more prominently blocked, then your direction might be clear, but your ability to move forward is being hindered. If your arms are being impacted the most, such as with netting, webs, or ropes, then issues of capability are probably at play. If this is the case, there may be some area in your life where your effectiveness, strength, or creative power is what is being blocked. Some dreams of this nature involve obstacles to the face where something is blocking your ability to see, hear, or use your voice effectively. When this occurs, look to a situation in your life where you are not able to be as expressive as you need to be. The other crucial element is what is causing the obstacle. Some obstacles that often appear in dreams are nets, quicksand, sticky floors, ground that opens up, and heavy legs or feet. If you can make an association to the stuff that is blocking you, add this to your interpretation.

Ocean: The ocean represents the unconscious mind. It is the much greater presence on our planet, where land covers about one quarter of the total surface area of the earth and ocean makes up three quarters. However, consider the depths of the ocean and you now have a sense of the mysteries of what is contained in the lower kingdom of the unconscious mind. Anytime the ocean is featured in a dream, you are in the realm of the unconscious mind. All water is also connected symbolically to your feelings and your emotional nature. When that water is as vast as the ocean, such a dream may indicate an overwhelming amount of emotional material being expressed.

Octopus: The octopus is the ultimate symbol of flexibility and adaptability. We must add to this the ability to maneuver in the realm of the unconscious, as an octopus's habitat is the ocean, the symbolic environment that connects us to that which is below the surface of awareness. The octopus brings powerful medicine in the experience of exploring the depths of your hidden nature when it appears in a dream.

Office: The office as a setting is a place of work, structure, schedules, rigidity, and all things left-brained. If a dream takes place in an office, you can consider such a dream to be about this part of your consciousness. Anything that happens in your dream office relates to the need for attention to this side of your nature. If you work in an office, the dream may be more literal than symbolic; it is a fairly common stress dream to be constantly at work in your sleeping experience.

Oil: Oil was once plant life; it comes from deep within the earth and holds the ancient energy of the sun in its structure. Oil has an enormous number of uses today, from fueling the modern world to providing the lubricant necessary for machines to run. As a symbol, it may relate to any number of these fundamental uses as the basis for functioning in a more powerful way. Oil is also a symbol for wealth and riches and a measure of abundance. Keep in mind that when oil is used as fuel, it has great consequences for the environment, and this darkness is built into its symbolism as the darker side of abundance.

Oil Spill: Oil itself is a symbol of wealth, abundance, power, and the reserve of riches that has great consequences when it is used or spilled. It is the anti-heroic representation of abundance in a negative form, and we become acutely aware of the danger associated with it when it spills and poisons the environment. An oil spill in your dream is asking you to rethink your true relationship to abundance, wealth, and power.

Old: You are connecting to an archetypal character aspect of yourself who connects with wisdom and guidance. The wise old man and his female counterpart, the crone, are staples in Jungian psychology, as they are the archetypes that represent human wisdom. This is a character aspect shared by every human being on the planet, and it connects us to our inner guidance and our highest thought. We can only connect to this powerful energy when we can learn from our mistakes, a trait often associated with the insight that comes with age and is usually unavailable to us in our youth. An older person whom you know from life may also represent wisdom, but an interpretation of any person must connect to the individual's traits as you experience them in life. When the old man or the crone ap-

pears in archetypal fashion, they will not be known to you personally. They may offer insight, wisdom, or a gift. This archetypal character aspect is often the first one that most people encounter on their inner journey toward integration. This is because all human beings have access to the wisdom that comes with age, making this archetype very accessible within each of us.

Olympics: The Olympics are an opportunity to use healthy athletic competition to replace the aggression of war for dominance and superiority. As a symbol, they represent the highest form of these darker human qualities. If you dream that you are at the Olympics, you are looking to take the higher road around something in your life that is causing you to feel aggressive and competitive.

One: One represents beginnings and is the starting point of existence. In human terms, it is the self alone. It is the idea before any action is taken. As such, it embodies the concept of potential and that which has yet to happen. In fact, the energy of one is limited by its inability to do anything by itself. However, it also connects to stillness and the cultivation of desire that precedes movement. One is the beginning of the journey, which can be a very exciting energy. However, on the shadow side this can bring with it the challenge of loneliness and isolation.

Onions: The onion is known for two things: its ability to induce tears and the many layers that make up its structure. Dreaming of them may indicate one or both of these inherent meanings. You may be expressing a level of emotional expression that is not quite authentic. On the other hand, onions may symbolize the process one must go through to get to the heart of any matter that can only be done layer by layer in a slow, methodical fashion.

Operation: A surgical procedure is a healing proposition designed to correct some malfunction, remove something that is not working properly, or replace something that has ceased to work at all. As a symbol, an operation is evidence that such a healing and transformation is going on in your life that is invasive and frightening and carries with it both a measure of risk as well as a level of profound necessity.

Oral Sex: This dream image connects to the integration of verbal qualities and power and communication issues in general. While some elements of sexual dreams are just that—sexual dreams expressing unrealized desire—there is symbolic meaning to each aspect of this symbol. Sex represents the desire for union, the joining together or integration of separate ways of being or other personality aspects. The oral aspect of this particular act indicates that communication is the area you are investigating. If you are orally pleasuring a penis, you may be appreciating and experiencing a need to take more aggressive power into your speech. To be orally pleasuring a woman's genitalia means that the receptive, sensitive, or creative elements of your personality want to be recognized and embraced. The active position indicates a higher level of urgency than if you are the recipient. If taking on new ways of communicating can be seen as an ongoing process, receiving oral pleasure connects more to the beginning of that process, while giving it might be associated with the end. The object of your affection will give you a great deal of clarity on the matter at hand. This is where many people are disturbed or even horrified by sexual content, for many dreams have us partnering with people from our life with whom we would not ordinarily have sex. However, to the unconscious mind, sex is a symbolic expression of union and has none of the societal or personal stigma we may attach to it. If the person is known to you, use his or her character aspects to indicate what qualities you are integrating into your communication. If the person is a stranger, use whatever information you can recall from the dream to inform your investigation.

Orange: Transformation and change are represented by the color orange. Orange is also related to sexuality, but through the feminine principle of intimacy and transformation. It is the color most associated with creativity.

Oranges: A fruit is essentially a seed and carries with it the potential for something new to be created along with the sustenance needed to feed that new thing. Oranges are this but are also a symbol of sweetness and abundance, as they were once considered a royal fruit available only to those who possessed great wealth. There is a modern association with the orange that connects to its capacity to bring health and vitality with its abundance of vitamin C. Any of these meanings may be present with a dream that features oranges.

Orbs: Orbs are a phenomenon that emerged with digital photography where phenomena of spherical light that elude the human eye are captured by the camera. Orbs are considered by many to be evidence of energy from other dimensions. Spheres of light are powerful representations in the dream world of evidence of the mysterious and unexplainable and should be considered a spiritual symbol of great magnitude.

Orchestra: An orchestra is a group of musicians playing various musical instruments, with each playing something different but connected in one common expression of passion. The symbolic meaning connects with music as a representation of human emotions that are so powerful that they erupt into higher levels of expression. Additionally, an orchestra connects to the power of aligning many different thoughts into one focused intention.

Organ: Any musical instrument relates to a passionate expression of deep emotions. The organ creates a powerful sound that is most associated with religious music, and the presence of one in your dream may be reflecting your views on organized religion.

Organs: Most organs in the body can be understood as being part of the system of processing the life force itself. If you dream of an organ in your body, consider the function of that organ to deepen your interpretation. How well are you meeting life's challenges and handling day-to-day functions?

Orgasm: An orgasm is an explosion of complex activity in the brain and nervous system that stimulates an enormous amount of pleasure through the release of neurotransmitters and the contraction of certain muscles. Of note is that there is a center of the brain that governs behavioral control that is completely shut down for the moments of orgasm that provides a layer of symbolic interpretation connected with total and utter surrender to the bliss and pleasure that life has to offer. It is this spectacular level of bliss that is represented by the orgasm; however, most dreams that involve orgasm often relate to the physiological experience of having one in the sleep state or being unable to achieve one in the dream state. In the former experience, a sleep orgasm may be the body's way of tapping into a natural mechanism for stress relief and sexual expression, and it may be this very physiological need that gives rise to the erotic dreams that create the experience. Many men describe sexual dreams in which they can never achieve the orgasm they desire, and this may have physiological elements as well, but may also represent a level of bliss and ecstasy that they are unable to cultivate in life that may connect to other passions and self-expression that have nothing to do with the sex act. While neuroscience provides a great deal of understanding of how sex, arousal, and orgasm function within the brain, the actual reason for and presence of this phenomenon remains a mystery, and this includes its presence in the dream state.

Orgy: Many sex dreams have a physiological impetus; however, the content can still be interpreted symbolically. All sex acts represent some need or desire for integration and the assimilation of various qualities into your ability to express them. An orgy is a desire to incorporate a number of different modes of expression into one experience of consciousness, like attempting to align various ideas or thoughts into a tangible and organized cultivation of desire. In this way, the sexual element is rendered irrelevant, and you should look to your life to see what is requiring more resources and skill in order to meet the demands of a more passionate expression. With regard to your personal experience of your sexuality, an orgy may be reflecting your ideas around taking risks or trying new things.

Origami: This complex system of folding paper generates an end result of great beauty. Paper is symbolically related to thoughts and ideas in a potential form. The many complex folds of origami represent all of the different and precise thought shifts and changes of mind that may be required in order to achieve some ultimate goal.

Orphan: We experience our identity and sense of self as almost exclusively connected to the parenting we receive. To have no connection to those parents is to have a disconnected sense of identity. This can be either devastating or liberating, and the sensations of the dream will reveal more detail for you. An orphan in a dream may represent an idea, choice, behavior, or pattern that is not connected to the modeling you received from your parents. When a person loses his or her parents to death, the individual becomes an orphan, and such an image in a dream may relate to that fear or the processing of grief after it has occurred.

Ostrich: This bird is known for burying its head in the sand, which is actually a myth. When an ostrich shows up in a dream, look for areas in your life where you might be in denial or practicing avoidance.

Otter: The otter as a symbol is all about joy and playfulness. As a creature that lives in water, the otter connects to the feminine principle and being grounded in the earth. Otters play in the waters of emotion and unconscious expression, and when they appear in a dream, they remind us that the aspects of life that are emotional in nature are to be approached with lightheartedness and reveled in.

Outer Space: All of the solar system and beyond is a symbol for our consciousness, and outer space represents the far reaches of that part of your psyche that you can be aware of but that you can never quite know with a degree of intimacy or clarity. Dreams that take place in outer space have an existential element that may indicate that you are pondering the higher notions of your humanity.

Outlet: An outlet is the structure that gives you access to the constant flow of electricity within the structure of a building. That electrical current represents the creative source that all human beings are plugged into, and an outlet is the symbol of your ability to connect to that power.

Ovaries: These organs of female reproduction are a symbolic representation of the power to create life. Ovaries featured in a dream relate to this creative power. If you are a woman, such a dream may be taken more literally and connect to your relationship with your own reproductive cycle.

Oven: An oven is a heat source that allows you to cook and bake food. Heat is always symbolically connected to change and transformation, and food represents nurturance and self-care. The state of the oven in your dream is reflecting your relationship to your ability to change, transform, and take care of yourself at a fundamental level.

Owl: You are tapping into the shadow side of your wisdom. Owls are nocturnal animals with a great ability to see and hunt in the dark. This makes them symbolically connected to the darker, more hidden sides of human nature. They help us to navigate the more unseen elements of our humanity. Owls have long been associated with intuition and mysticism, and in some traditions they are considered omens. They carry great animal medicine and are to be greatly revered if they come to you in a dream.

Pacifier: A pacifier is a substitute for the nipple used to calm a baby by tricking it into thinking it is receiving milk. As a symbol, it represents the impulse to sedate some irritated aspect of self. Consider who was using the pacifier in your dream and that will give you a clue as to what part of your psyche is screaming at you. If you are struggling to find a pacifier or if it is compromised in some way, you may be dreaming about stress that needs to be soothed. Part of the meaning in this symbol connects to the actual ineffectual nature of a pacifier; it offers the temporary illusion that there is something present that is actually not. In this way, a pacifier in a dream could signal that you are attempting to create something without the authentic power to back up your intentions. If you are the parent of a baby that is of pacifier age, this dream could be more literal.

Package: The real significance of a package is what is inside of it, which is often unknown. In this way, at the heart of this symbol is the excitement of possibilities and the mystery involved. If the package in your dream is meant for you, it represents the acquisition of something new and the expectation that what you are receiving could be beneficial to you. Check the sensation of the dream itself; if there is fear or anxious anticipation about what the package might contain, it could be revealing a level of pessimism and fear-based thinking.

Packing: Packing is about the preparation for something that is in the future and has yet to happen. This is a fairly common recurring dream image that many people report. If this is the case for you, then you may be expressing anxiety about attempting to control that which is ultimately uncontrollable by imagining that you can prepare for any outcome by having the right things with you. The same meaning applies if this is not a recurring dream experience for you, but is likely to be associated with a specific life experience that is causing you anxiety. You can only prepare so much and then you have to let go of the outcome.

Pageant: A pageant is a cultural experience where individuals put certain elements of themselves on display in the spirit of competition. You may dream of a pageant when you feel that your abilities are being scrutinized and objectified. Since a pageant is often associated with the more superficial aspects of a person's value, such a dream may be a response to feeling that some life experience is not allowing you to show the entire picture of who you are.

Paint: You are dreaming of the desire to make changes to some aspect of your life by covering over the past and starting fresh. If the paint in your dream was more artistic in nature, the impulse being expressed may connect to your desire to be creative. Paint itself is the stuff with which this form of alteration is executed. Symbolically, it should be considered as the raw material of change of an expressive nature. The control you are able to exert over this elusive liquid medium will illuminate for you how effectively you may be utilizing your current creative resources. The more control you are able to access, the more effective your expressiveness is likely to be and the more effectively you will be able to manifest your desired intention.

Painting: The action of painting is a creative expression that refreshes and/or rejuvenates. Painting a surface accomplishes several things. First and foremost, it covers whatever is on the receiving surface. It makes a blank canvas come alive with expression. A new image can also cover over an older one. A building or a room can be reinvented with fresh color, or that which was old and dingy can become clean with a fresh coat of paint. Seen in this fashion, painting will always connect on a symbolic level with the emergence of something new and expressive as a replacement of something old or lacking vibrancy. Dreaming of painting a room in your home should be explored through the symbolic meaning of that room. The outside of your home connects to your persona, the part of yourself that you show to the world.

Palace: A palace is the home of royalty or a very high-ranking head of state. All homes in dreams are symbols of your sense of self, and to dream of a palace is to dream of your highest, most aspirational and prosperous sense of self that you can embody. Look to the context of the dream, the people who are present in it, and what is occurring in order to round out your interpretation of your current relationship with abundance.

Panda: The panda is a powerful symbol of abundance and prosperity. Pandas eat bamboo, long a symbol of luck and good fortune; they also eat it slowly and endlessly, connecting the panda to the concept of never-ending prosperity. Compassion and patience are also energies associated with this beautiful, beloved creature. If the panda should visit your dreams, you are being guided by a very powerful totem.

Pants: As an article of clothing, pants relate to both protection for the physical body and personal self-expression. Though this is less so in our modern world, pants are still archetypally a masculine symbol, so wearing pants in a dream connects to where the ability to be decisive, take action, and make things happen is focused. Who is "wearing the pants" has long been an expression to connote the person with the power, and this may be reflected in your dream. The state, style, color, and other elements of the pants must be added to your interpretation.

Paparazzi: Paparazzi take pictures of celebrities with no regard for their personal thoughts and desires about the choice to be photographed, often capturing people in less than ideal situations. In this way, they represent the lack of privacy as well as the notion of modern-day scrutiny. If paparazzi inhabit your dreams, you may be feeling exposed in some way by some circumstance in your life that is robbing you of your privacy and revealing things to the world that you would prefer to keep behind the scenes.

Paper: This is a symbol for the potential for communication, creative expression, the making of plans, or committing an idea to something permanent by putting it on paper. Writing on paper connects to a need to gain clarity with your thoughts. Reading something written on paper is about attempting to absorb some new idea as an intrinsic part of your knowledge base. Folding a piece of paper might reveal a wish to keep something hidden from others or possibly to break something down into more manageable pieces of information. Doing something atypical with paper, such as origami or cutouts, could connect to being creative in a rebellious fashion. Blank paper might point to the requirement of definitive communication that you are not clear about or unwilling to commit to yet. Reams and reams of paper could align with an overwhelming sense of thoughts or feelings that need to be documented in some way. In the business world there is a phrase that something must "look good on paper," referring to the strategic planning that precedes taking action. This highlights the impermanence that exists prior to the permanence that a hard copy of a "paper trail" implies.

Parachute: A parachute is a structure that uses air resistance to slow down the pace at which an object falls to the earth. Falling is a symbol of control, or more accurately the lack of it. A parachute then is the element of safety added so that you can surrender more thoroughly to something of which you have no control.

Parade: A parade is often a symbol for the more celebratory moments of your life moving inextricably forward. You can watch the parade, a symbol of being passive and inactive, as it passes you by. Or you can join the parade and move with the flow of life. Whichever relationship your dream is reflecting, you can think of the parade as the activities that will bring you acclaim and public recognition.

Paralyzed: Many dreams feature a form of paralysis. Part of this is physiological, because the brain paralyzes the body during REM sleep; this is because there is so much brain activity during this type of sleep that you would otherwise move about as if you were wide awake. When this paralysis isn't strong enough, it can result in sleep disturbances such as talking and somnambulism. There is an order to how this process is supposed to work, where the paralysis lifts before consciousness returns. When this doesn't occur properly, you feel awake while your body is still paralyzed. Because you are still in a dream state, you often dream that you are in the very room in which you are sleeping but you can't move and there is often a terrifying sense of a presence in the room. This is what is known as night terrors, which are more common in children and are the origins of the boogeyman and the monster under the bed. There is a heightened sensitivity to energy during this state that may allow an individual to perceive things that are usually hidden from consciousness. Add the terror of being paralyzed to this sense of something in the room and there is often an assumption that whatever is in the room means you great harm. This is not necessarily true, and it is possible to use the mind to alter this experience into something that is very light and beautiful. However, it usually starts with terror. In this way, a dream of paralysis may be connected to this phenomenon and should be thought of as something different from an interpretable dream reflecting unconscious material. If your dream features being paralyzed as a part of a more complex typical dream, then it symbolizes something in your life that is holding you back and keeping you from taking definitive action.

Parents: You are connecting to your inner sense of authority; who you are as a result of the parents you had. The voices of our parents become deeply imbedded in us as parts of our personality. This correlates with whatever information they repeatedly presented to us during our formative years. If their messages were ones of criticism and limitation, they live on within us as those inhibiting parts of our inner monologue. If our parents were supportive and loving, the same would apply. Chances are that they gave us a combination of messages, some positive and others negative. Depending on where you are in your life, you may be more aligned with the challenges your parents presented than the gifts they gave. It is usually most effective to deal with feelings of anger and resentment before authentically moving into forgiveness. The quality of the interaction in the dream will clue you in to where you are in that process. While dreaming of your parents may inform your actual relationship with them, it is important to consider what the dream is saying about how you parent yourself.

Park: A park is a modern-day invention designed to create the illusion of a natural landscape that modern life has all but eradicated. It represents the desire to keep portions of your consciousness clean, pristine, and natural. In the world of symbolism, this relates to being relaxed and free of stress, fear, doubt, and concern for material things. A dream that takes place in a park reminds you of the part of you that is more connected to nature and therefore love.

Parking Lot: Cars and their movement represent the way you progress through your life on a day-to-day basis. Therefore a parking lot symbolizes a temporary stopping of that process either due to a sense of feeling stuck or because of a conscious choice to attend to something before moving on. If a dream has a parking lot in it at any point, consider that as a thematic lens through which to view the entire dream; you are in some sort of holding pattern while an issue is being worked out before you can resume your journey in life.

Parrot: All birds are to be considered messengers of some sort, but the parrot has the distinction of being the one that repeats only what it hears. When this animal appears in a dream, you are being called out on a lack of originality and being called to find your own original voice.

Party: A party is a gathering of celebration. All people in a dream are parts of your own consciousness, and all the people who are at a party can be considered thoughts in your psyche that are coalescing into an idea that it is time to celebrate something or break loose and have some fun. Sometimes a party has the purpose of acknowledging some sort of milestone, and if this is the case in your dream, it is a reminder to consider your accomplishments.

Passport: A passport is first and foremost a form of identification, but it also affords the easy passage to foreign lands. As a symbol in a dream, it represents your ability to extend your consciousness into territory that is far from your comfort zone. Such a dream may also connect with a desire to expand your

life's horizons into something more exciting. To have lost your passport is to feel limited in your ability to accomplish more with your life or problem-solve in a highly creative manner.

Path: A path is a way of moving about some territory that has been traveled before by others such that the way is clear. It is a symbol of your own walk through life that is reflective of making choices that others have made before you. The more wild and remote the path, the more your dream is reflecting territory that is perhaps unique or atypical. A path or any movement along a path in a dream is also a symbol of your private journey through life.

Paycheck: For most people, a paycheck is a symbol of the security of the concept of ongoing prosperity and abundance. The check itself represents the sense that your needs will be met. Anything that is associated with a paycheck in a dream should be focused through this lens. If you cannot find a paycheck, you may feel that your security is threatened somehow. A paycheck that is damaged is also such a threat, but it reflects an incident that happened in the recent past. Finding a paycheck is to be discovering a new source of ongoing security.

Peacock: The male peacock is famous for his beautiful plumage, which has earned him a reputation for being proud. In this way, the symbolic meaning associated with this stunning bird connects with this sensation of being proud of your accomplishments. In a dream, this could be a call to step into such feelings about yourself or a warning that you are being too prideful. Allow the dream context and the feelings within the dream to illuminate which direction to go in.

Peacock Feather: The beautiful plumage of the male peacock contains some of the most startling colors in the natural kingdom and has long been associated with royalty and therefore great abundance. A peacock feather is considered a powerful totem of good fortune and prosperity.

Pearl: A pearl is the calcified product of the oyster that surrounds an irritant with a protective layer of material that humankind has considered precious for thousands of years. At the heart of this beautiful object as a symbol is the grain of sand that must be present in order for this beautiful object to be created. A pearl indicates that some difficult situation has caused a wonderful benefit to be generated.

Pebble: A pebble is the smallest demarcation of rock that we generally refer to. All rocks connect symbolically to the past; they are actually the memory of the earth itself. A pebble can be an irritant or a decoration, depending on the context. If you have a pebble in your shoe in your dream, you are carrying around some old idea or experience that wants to be let go of. If you are using pebbles in a garden or other natural decoration, you are celebrating your past experiences in a healthy and useful way.

Pen: Any writing implement relates to the act of self-expression. A pen is an almost outdated object that harkens back to a slower form of communication from an earlier time. It makes an indelible mark and so relates to the expression of thoughts that you cannot take back.

Pencil: This is a dream about communication that is changeable or impermanent. A pencil symbolically connects with communication issues. The fact that they are erasable adds an element of impermanence to the meaning and therefore a lack of commitment. By varying the pressure applied with a pencil, you can create different shades of gray, which implies a level of subtlety and textural meaning to the communication represented by this symbol in a dream. If you are using a pencil so that errors can be fixed, you may be dreaming about a desire to undo something not aligned with your original intention. Look to areas in your life where you are struggling to be clear and accurate. Also consider your integrity with regard to recent communication. With a pencil, you can erase a statement you wish you hadn't made.

Penis: The penis is the ultimate symbol of the power of the masculine principle of doing and action. This can have sexual connotations as well as an expression of primal productivity. A woman dreaming of having a penis is connecting deeply to her inner masculine on an archetypal level. The same is true for a man, but without the archetypal meaning.

Pentagram: The pentagram is a widely misunderstood symbol; it has its roots in Christianity but is often used in the media in an inverted shape to refer to elements of the evil side of the occult. Its pure meaning connects to the five senses and the experience of the human body. In early Christianity it connects to the five wounds suffered by Christ. In the Tarot, the pentagram connects with money and prosperity. Any of these meanings might be expressed by a dream that features this geometrical image.

Performing on Stage: Life can often feel like a performance. In this way, dreaming of this image indicates that your unconscious is expressing a sense of your current life as being under public scrutiny. This is a common recurring dream, signifying the dreamer's sense of feeling exposed or a fear of performing up to standards. The subtlety here is in whether you are on stage because of heightened vulnerability or because you are hiding your true feelings by "acting" your way through an experience. By considering the timing of the dream with regard to current situations in your life, you can discover your true sense of preparedness for what is being thrown at you at the time of the dream. By examining this thoroughly, you can assess whether this dream means you are feeling incompetent to face a challenge in life or if you are feeling prepared to perform at your peak capability. A highly stylized performance could indicate inauthenticity in some area. Conversely, it could connect to a powerful sense of creative originality. Forgetting your lines may represent your discomfort in some role or false persona you are putting on for the approval of others. Life is often like a performance. How you feel about this dream reveals how you feel about how well you are performing at this moment in time.

Phone: A phone is a symbol of the collective consciousness and the ability to connect to other people in the world instantly. The landline is fast becoming something of the past, and if your dream features such a phone, you may be examining ways in which your communication style is a little outdated.

Phosphorescence: This stunning effect comes from luminescent algae that can light up the ocean. This phenomenon in the animal kingdom is relegated to underwater dwellers and the firefly. The unconscious mind is considered a realm of darkness, and this improbable light represents the mysterious ability to shed light on that which normally cannot receive it. In a dream, it relates to a spiritual presence illuminating normally shadowed corners of the psyche.

Piano: Your creative potential is being expressed. The piano is a feminine image of creative expression. By itself, the piano represents your creative potential, because it must receive the attentions of someone to play it in order to achieve this potential. Since the music that emerges from it can vary from "Chopsticks" to Chopin, its symbolic meaning also connects to mastery. Anyone can cause a piano to sing by striking a key, but only a master can make it truly soar. The essence of music is the magic of joy, and a piano represents this potential lying dormant, waiting patiently to be unleashed. To see a piano and want to play it reveals a desire to tap into your inner creative expression. Actually playing one in your dream may indicate a period of blossoming joy.

Picnic: A symbol of relaxation and escape, a picnic combines the idyllic experience of nature with sustenance and self-care in the form of food. Often a romantic gesture, a picnic in a dream suggests a desire for any one or all of these elements to be added to your life.

Picture Frame: This image is connected to memories of the past and can indicate a desire to compartmentalize feelings. The frame around a picture completes it. We display imagery that reflects parts of who we are through pictures of loved ones and moments in time from our past. A picture is not the thing it represents, but a reflection of it, often imbued with our fantasies and projections. What we place around such captured moments has great significance to explain our feelings about them. This can represent how we have framed them in our minds to make sense of them. If a picture frame is a prominent image from a dream, you may be processing issues represented by the picture in the frame. The frame connects to some explanation, justification, or limitation in thinking about the person or circumstance being displayed.

Piercing: A piercing is a form of adornment through what appears to be painful means. The fact that the adornment itself is a reminder of the breaking of the flesh that it took to create it is a part of the message inherent in this particular brand of self-expression and appeals to young people and a fringe of subculture in society. If you are someone with piercings, such an image in a dream may simply be a reflection of your personal worldview. However, if such a look is outside of your milieu, there may be a call toward attending to something that relates to the area of your body that is being pierced. A tongue relates to your voice and things you would like to say. A navel is more connected to gut

feelings and your instincts. Your ears indicate a need to pay more attention to the messages that are being presented to you.

Pig: Pigs themselves are actually quite smart and relatively clean animals. However, the media and literature have made the pig synonymous with gluttony and avarice. Your dream may be reflecting overindulgence in some area of your life.

Pills: The ability to alter your mind or mood in an instant is reflected in a dream that features pills or any kind of medication. A pharmaceutical medication is a compound that causes the brain to either create or inhibit the creation of certain chemicals that alter an experience in the body. If you are taking a pill in a dream, there may be some area in your life that you wish would transform or go away with relative ease. An overdose might indicate a more extreme search for an easy way out of a challenge or issues of indulgence. If you have health issues in your life, there may be a more literal relationship between the medication in a dream and the desire to get well. Not knowing what kind of pill you're taking or what it might do to you is a possible indication of some ignorance or naiveté in the way you are approaching a situation that needs attention. The specific action of a medication also needs to be taken into account. For example, a pain medication might relate to a desire to escape something difficult. An antibiotic might indicate a reaction to dark, unwanted thoughts. An antidepressant might reveal an avoidance of unpleasant emotions. An antipsychotic medication could connect to feeling a loss of control of your emotions or chaotic thought patterns.

Pink: The color pink is created when red and white are mixed. Red is the color of the root chakra and the slowest vibration of the visible light spectrum. Its qualities are security, groundedness, and the desire to have all your needs met at a very fundamental level. White is representative of purity and spiritual ascension. When these qualities are combined, the resulting sensation is the embodiment of love. Pink is also associated with girls and all things feminine; this may be a consideration for interpreting a dream with this color as a prominent image.

Pipe: A pipe is a conduit for liquid beneath the surface and out of sight. As such, it is a symbol of the capacity to experience flow and easy movement of all kinds. Most pipes are associated with the movement of water and therefore connect symbolically to feelings and emotions. The state of a pipe in a dream may reflect your systems of emotional expression and fluidity. A pipe is also an implement for ingesting tobacco or marijuana and can be a symbol of the relaxation and comfort that smoking one can elicit.

Plastic Surgery: Any alteration to the way your body is shaped is akin to exerting some measure of control over the way you are seen in the world. When this alteration is reflected as surgical in nature, the resulting change is manipulated and inorganic. Plastic surgery is usually chosen in an effort to appear more attractive, desirable, or acceptable than one already feels. Ask yourself how authentic you are being in your interactions with oth-

ers. This dream could point to something out of balance with how you feel and what you project.

Platypus: The platypus is an incongruous creature with the bill of a duck and a mammal's body, and yet it is the only mammal that lays eggs. In this way, its medicine applies to being a total original. Platypuses are semi-aquatic animals and yet close their eyes underwater and use a complex system of electrical impulses generated by muscular contractions to maneuver. This connects them to the power of intuition and guidance; they are the animal totem of clairvoyants and psychic phenomena. When the platypus appears in a dream, you are being called to rely on your intuition and innate guidance system.

Playground: An environment of childlike playfulness, a playground symbolizes the expression of joy. If your dream takes place in a playground, you may be exploring a need to connect more with this part of your nature. If the playground comes from your own childhood, you may be examining specific patterns from your own life about your capacity to embody a lighthearted approach to certain circumstances.

Playing Cards: Dreams that contain cards are related to working with patterns and all the permutations that are possible when you understand the underlying structure of how life works. Cards are numbered and suited, and through working with these categories, an almost infinite number of possibilities exists. This is an analogy for how life itself works. In this way, playing cards are like a testing ground for becoming more skillful in playing the game of life.

Pointing: When someone points, he or she is indicating an object or direction that wants specific attention. It is ultimately a moment of clarity of where to go next. If a character in a dream is pointing at something, the interpretation will need to connect both to what the person is pointing at and who the person represents as part of your personality. Use the context of the dream to gain a deeper understanding of what you are being asked to pay specific attention to.

Poison: A poison is anything that is taken into your body that creates a dangerous or hazardous reaction, from creating illness to potentially death. As a symbol, poison relates to any thoughts, ideas, words, or actions that do the same. In a dream, this image is suggesting that something has recently entered your consciousness that is ultimately unsafe for you to keep inside of you. This may not necessarily come from outside of you, for it is just as easy to have poisonous ideas from within your own consciousness. Such a dream may be a call to find an antidote to any idea that is contrary to your best interests.

Poker: A game of chance and skill, poker has at the heart of it the concept of a bluff, hence the term "poker face," where your true intentions are hidden. The game requires a great deal of patience and strategic waiting in order to accomplish something. If a poker game is featured in your dream, look for ways in which you are hiding what you really have to offer in an effort to gain something that you desire.

Police: The police are ultimately part of the warrior archetype that divides the world into two camps: right and wrong. They are the image that connects to your internal sense of authority as it relates to what is socially acceptable behavior. The presence of the police in any dream suggests that you are weighing a decision or an idea as to its harm or benefit. If the police are interacting with you directly, consider what the context of the dream has to offer about your current life choices.

Pond: Any body of water connects with your emotional experience. A pond is a natural setting, so it relates to your personal experience of your feeling nature. A pond is small and manageable, so it is reflecting a connection with your emotions from an idyllic and resourceful sensibility. Look to the state or condition of the pond in your dream for a glimpse into your emotional makeup at the time of such a dream.

Pool: See *Swimming Pool.*

Pop Quiz: You are being tested on a small amount of knowledge, experience, or wisdom in a very unexpected manner. (See *Taking a Test, Exams*.)

Porch: The house as a symbol is reflecting your sense of self at the time of a dream. The porch is outside of the house, but is still connected to it. In this way, it relates to the part of your consciousness that can maintain a sense of identity but share that identity with others in a social way. This interdependent sensibility is reflected by a dream that involves the porch of a house, so the state and condition of the porch is reflecting how you are maintaining your sense of self, but still interacting with the world.

Porn: Porn is an exaggerated sense of sexuality. It is not real, but often masquerades as such. In a dream, it represents an overvaluing of the lustful elements of your human sexuality and an avoidance of the intimate elements of this experience.

Posture: Your posture is the foundation for all your movement through life. It is an accurate reflection of your underlying mood and expressions of the unconscious. If your dream reflects particularly good posture and an erect spine, you are expressing a profound sense of well-being. This can also be a compensation for neglecting a holistic approach to how you move through life. Bad posture could be a clue that something outside of your conscious awareness is throwing you off entirely; time to check on the foundations of your lifestyle.

Power Lines: Power lines crisscross most of the civilized world, bringing the force of electricity to just about anywhere. In this way, they mimic the idea of the creative power of manifestation that is available to be tapped into at any given moment. They also connect with that instant connectivity through communication technology. If you have power lines present in your dream scenario, then part of what you are connecting to is this force of power that is always available for you to tap into. If the power lines are down, you may be experiencing a temporary disconnect from your source.

Power Plant: A power plant takes some sort of raw material and converts in into usable power. It is a symbol for your own ability to do this, which is part of the human mastery. In a dream, this image is revealing your current relationship to power, energy, and resources. A power plant is used by the larger community, so one in your dream may be reflecting energy that relies on other people in your life. Such a dream is asking you to consider where you are getting your energy from.

Pregnancy: You are formulating a new idea, project, or direction in your life. A pregnancy represents the appearance of something new on the horizon. All ideas, changes in direction, and physical shifts must first be created in the vat of ideas within the mind. Everything that we create in life is first felt as the spark of a new thought. To dream of pregnancy is to be connecting powerfully to this part of the creative process. Consider that something in you or your life is about to change dramatically. Dreaming of pregnancy is not relegated to women alone—men will often dream of being pregnant. Many men report such dreams when their significant other is literally preparing to give birth, and in the dream world, this represents the dramatic change of life that is about to take place as fatherhood descends upon them. Shame or fear of being exposed as pregnant because it is unwanted connects to uncertainty of how the shift in you may be perceived by others in your life. The closer the pregnancy is to birth, the more imminent the change that is germinating. If the pregnancy is experienced by a character within your dream, then consider that it is an element of your personality as represented by that character aspect that is undergoing the change that is afoot. If the term of the pregnancy is clear in the dream, you might want to consider what was going on in your life at the time conception would have been likely. For example, if you were seven months pregnant in your dream, look back seven months in your life for some new element that could be making itself known at this time.

Present: See *Gifts*.

Press: The idea of what the press represents is changing in our world. What used to be a force for the objective presentation of unbiased facts is giving way to manipulative invasion of privacy and the dissemination of controlled information. Your age may factor into how you perceive the press as an image based on this slow cultural change. No matter where you stand on this, the press connects to your public rather than private life and the notion that anything you choose to do may have public consequences.

Priest: This is an archetypal character aspect that represents extreme devotion to spiritual principles. The proliferation of this image in the media makes it a universal symbol for spiritual devotion. Also because of the media, this symbol carries with it a great number of potential shades of meaning, from an intense level of respect to humorous irreverence or even intense antipathy. Your personal associations with priests will therefore play a prominent role in how you interpret a dream with a priest in it. On the serious end of the spectrum, the priest is the symbolic representation of Christ on Earth and signifies a level of dedication that is unparalleled in our modern culture. In this light, the character aspect of a priest in a dream connects to a deeply committed spiritual side of your nature that is willing to sacrifice much for the sake of your beliefs. There is no getting around the current perception that the institution of the priesthood is also embroiled in deep controversy over sexual improprieties. The enforced role of celibacy also plays an important role in interpreting this symbol. If a priest should play a prominent role in a dream, issues of sexuality and sexual expression/freedom may be present.

Prison: There are consequences for the choices you make, and some of those choices bind you in a particular way. When you break the law, you go to prison. And while you have to engage in criminal activity to find yourself in prison in real life, the idea of being imprisoned by something can easily apply to any number of circumstances where you feel bound to some person, place, or thing in a way that feels severely constricting. In fact, the phrase "like a jail sentence" is often used in casual conversation to refer to anything that obligates a person beyond his or her comfort level. There is a difference between jail and prison that may be significant, especially if the dream was clearly taking place in one or the other. While the two have very similar sensibilities, a jail is where people are taken when they are suspected of committing a crime or when the crime is of low severity. Prison is where convicted criminals of more serious crimes are sent to pay their debt to society. If this distinction is made clear in your dream, recognize that jail is a more temporary form of bondage. Prison indicates that a more serious matter is being expressed. At the core of the symbolic meaning of prison is what you did to get there. The inciting incident that ends in jail time is always a choice that may have seemed like a good idea at the time, but has consequences resulting in the removal of freedom and comfort in some area of your life. When this environment plays prominently in a dream, examine your life for where you may be feeling that a decision you made in the past is feeling like something you can't escape in the present.

Prostitute: You may feel as if you are trading on that which is intimate or personal for material gain. They say "money can't buy you love," but it can indeed buy you sex, which can be a substitute for love and intimacy. The challenge with prostitution lies in the judgments we place on selling something as intensely personal as one's body and the act of performing sex for money. This makes prostitution something intensely impersonal. If you dream of being a prostitute, you may be experiencing something in your waking life that is pointing toward a sense of selling out or taking the easier, softer way through some challenge. If you are hiring a prostitute, you may want to look at that part of you that is willing to sell yourself short. If there is prostitution around you in the dream, notice your sense of connection to the concept. If you are in judgment or fear, consider the idea that there is a lack of integrity in the way that you are handling some person or situa-

tion. A more open attitude toward prostitution might point to a need for a more careful appraisal of your self-judgment, whether it be too severe or whether you might benefit from utilizing more discretion with your choices. No matter what your belief system, on some level prostitution leaves a legacy of shame, which is really the essence of this symbol in the dream. Is the price you are paying for your freedom worth it?

Public Speaking: This is a dream about communication on a grand scale, the pressure to get your word out into the world in a bigger way. Speaking in public is challenging for most people. For some, that challenge is so intense that even the idea of it can bring on a terrorizing attack of anxiety. Since there is a literal connotation with this symbol to the act of speaking, a dream that involves this activity will naturally point to an area in your life where your communication is being put on the spot. A person speaking in public is usually a figure of authority on some level. In this way, a dream that includes this as an image is probably expressing some area of your life where you are in your authority or where your authority is being put to the test. This is especially so if you were the one doing the speaking. If you were in the audience and someone else was talking, use that person as a character aspect of yourself to figure out what part of your personality has something to say. It could be that your desire for power and authority in your life is speaking to you through your unconscious in your dream.

Pumpkin: A pumpkin is a seasonal fruit that reminds us the harvest is upon us. There is a strong association with the pumpkin and Halloween, and this may be reflected in your dream. The fairy tale of Cinderella connects the pumpkin with a carriage through the magic of wishing for your heart's desire. Any of these ideas may be expressed by a dream that features a pumpkin.

Puppet: A puppet is usually the figure of a human being that is manipulated by the puppet master to do his or her bidding. In this way, a puppet symbolizes being forced or coerced into choices that may not be authentic or true to you. If you are the puppeteer in your dream, look to where you are using manipulation to get your needs met.

Puppy: A dog represents the masculine principle of unconditional love, loyalty, and unbridled affection. A puppy is this energy in its absolute most exuberant expression. It also represents a less mature approach to love and intimacy, where enthusiasm is greater than the potential authenticity of the love being expressed.

Purple: See *Violet*.

Purse: This image relates to having access to tools for daily living. The key to this symbol is in what is carried inside of it. Whether it's a pocketbook, briefcase, or shoulder bag, the personal carrying case has become a fixture of necessity in our fast-paced world. Purses provide mobile access to important items that may be needed when you are out in the world, such as your wallet, driver's license, credit cards, and all the things that represent your identity. Hence, there is a strong symbolic association with what might be referred to as tools for life on a day-to-day basis. A pocketbook, handbag, or purse is generally carried by women and often contains grooming products. This connects it symbolically to the feminine principle. The items found in a purse will likely be associated with self-care and nurturing. If you have lost your purse and are searching for it, you may be experiencing a momentary obstacle in your life.

Pyramids: A pyramid is a shape found in ancient civilizations that has a great deal of spiritual connotations in today's world. Pyramids represent a connection to ancient principles of aspirational thoughts and ideas. Dreaming of the pyramids may be a call to consider the more esoteric forms of spiritual exploration.

Quan Yin: A goddess of the feminine principle, Quan Yin hears all the cries of despair in the world. She is the embodiment of compassion and relates to the Christian construct of Mother Mary. If this archetypal figure appears in a dream, you are having an experience of heightened spiritual connection to love and compassion. (See *Mother Mary; Quan Yin.*)

Quarry: A quarry is designed to harvest the bounty of what is available just below the surface of the earth in the form of rocks, minerals, and surface metals. In the symbolism of land as representing the conscious mind, these are the symbolic raw materials that are available to you when you are willing to look below the surface of things to find what is valuable. Rocks are also symbolic of memory and the past, so the most prominent interpretation of what a quarry can bring you is value from considering what has already occurred in your life. Of course, you can overdo this process, and a quarry also holds the possible interpretation of the damage that can be done when you obsess over the past and keep digging when perhaps it is time to move on.

Quartet: A quartet specializes in music that can only be made when four different voices come together, whether those voices are human or made by musical instruments. The number four relates to structure and foundation in the realm of numerology. Music connects to passionate expression. Put together, a quartet in your dream signals the creation of the foundations for more passionate expression in your life.

Quartz: The power of crystals is in their capacity to increase vibrational frequencies. Quartz is perhaps the most common and ubiquitous of all minerals that appear in crystalline structure. If you are oriented toward the use of crystals in your waking life, then such a dream may be indicating a need to call upon such energy. If you are someone who is less familiar with their properties, crystals in a dream might be inviting you to explore more esoteric concepts. (See *Stones, Boulders*.)

Queen: In the Tarot, the Queen is a symbol for status, intuition, creativity, and power. If this image should appear in a dream, you may be connecting to the archetypal power offered by this symbol of royalty. The Queen could also be an elevated expression of the maternal instinct. The question of benevolence comes into play with a royal figure in a dream, for when royal strength is used wisely, it indicates being in alignment with an increase in personal power. A dream that features a queen-like figure may, however, be indicating this being out of balance and therefore misused. You may be being asked to consider how well you are wielding power in your life.

Quicksand: This is one of those obstacle symbols that has a shade of meaning connected to emotional overwhelm that is causing you to feel ungrounded. Quicksand is made up of earth and water in a treacherous combination whereby the water is abundant and the makeup of the earth is such that the water is not readily absorbed. Anytime water is present with regard to a symbol, there are issues of emotionality in play. Since quicksand's water content is essentially imperceptible until you find yourself engulfed in it, your interpretation should reflect this sense of being initially unaware of the danger and the astonishment of discovering that you are suddenly in peril.

Quilt: A quilt is a handmade article designed for warmth and comfort and usually has a homey association with it. If it is present in a dream, it may be a call to receive the measure of safety and security such an object can bring with it. If the quilt has a specific association from your life, add that to your interpretation.

Quiz: A quiz is a mini exam where you are being tested on what knowledge you are expected to have integrated at the point at which the quiz is given. Life often confronts you in ways where you must step up and perform based on wisdom you have just acquired, and a quiz in a dream is asking you to perform based on this recent increase in your base of knowledge. (See *Exams, Pop Quiz, Taking a Test*.)

Rabbi: The spiritual leader of a Jewish community, a rabbi in a dream is connecting you to the notion of religion, belief, and faith. All people in your dreams are part of you; the rabbi in your dream is the part of your own personality most connected with matters of spirituality. If you are personally Jewish, this character aspect in a dream is more literally connected to your personal belief system. If you are not, you may be having an experience of looking beyond your typical ideas about faith and God.

Rabbit: A great symbol of luck and abundance, the rabbit in your dream points to great good fortune. Rabbits are traditionally associated with prolific reproductive ability, so they naturally connect us with the concept of never-ending prosperity. Their foot is considered a lucky totem to carry around, so they also bring this to the symbolic table. The Chinese zodiac features the rabbit as a highly peaceful and likeable archetype. If the rabbit appears in your dreams, any of these qualities may be being expressed.

Raccoon: The symbolic meaning associated with the raccoon is based on its markings that look like a mask. In this way, the raccoon as a totem connects to the idea of disguise and secrecy. Its nocturnal mischief further increases the sensibility of this. When the raccoon appears in your dreams, you are being invited to consider what masks you are wearing in your life and where you might be able to deepen your experience of authenticity.

Race Car: A car is a symbol for the quality of the experience you are having of moving through your life, especially as it relates to your social and community experience. A race car has great power and offers a tremendous amount of speed and an escalation of masterful handling. Your dream may suggest a desire to move faster, or if your life is indeed moving at a fast pace, the race car in your dream may be offering you the support you need to handle all that is happening at this time.

Race Track: If a race car implies that your life is speeding up, a race track may indicate that though you are moving very fast, you are actually getting nowhere.

Radiator: An implement for heating an indoor space, a radiator as a symbol in a dream indicates a desire to warm things up in your life. Such warmth can be related to emotional issues, an increase in passion, or anything where an increase in desire is indicated. A car radiator has the opposite implication—that things need to be cooled down in order to run effectively and efficiently.

Radio: A radio pulls invisible waves out of the ethers and turns them into music and news wherever it is located. It is a symbolic representation of the collective consciousness in action, as all people listening to a particular station on a radio hear the same programming. In a dream, a radio relates to collective thought and social agreement. Since there are many stations available on a radio dial, such a dream might be asking you if it is time to change the station.

Railing: A railing is there for protection and safety when an area is open and there is a risk of falling. Fear of falling is always about control and the need to maintain it. A railing as a symbol in a dream is about the built-in protections around staying safe when taking risks. If the railing is broken in your dreams, then you are feeling more unsafe than is comfortable. Grabbing on to a railing may indicate more fear than is necessary.

Railroad: The railroad was once the great leveler that joined the world in ways that dramatically expanded civilization, commerce, and culture. Almost antiquated now, it still has a symbolic meaning connected to ways in which different parts of your consciousness are connected. Any travel in a dream represents the idea of making changes or transformations in your life. When the travel is as slow as railroad travel, the sensation that is present could indicate the notion of considering other possibilities. Railroads in a dream could also symbolize old ways of thinking.

Rain: Rain in a dream connects to emotional expression, as it is the weather system that replicates the falling of tears and water is always a symbolic expression of emotion. As such, rain symbolizes the process of allowing our feelings to flow freely. Rain is cleansing, for it washes away dirt particles and leaves the air clearer, so rain can be a symbol of purification. Rain indicates that an emotional experience is taking place that is ultimately healing. Your reactions to the rain as well as the quality of the rain itself will provide even more information for your exploration. A light, gentle rain could indicate a small disruption in your life that is causing some emotional reactivity. Torrential downpours, such as hurricanes, point to more intense undercurrents of feeling being expressed. The relative intensity of the rain in your dream will mirror the intensity of what your unconscious is trying to express. How you respond to the rain in your dream will illuminate for you the level of resistance you are in. The mightier your attempts to escape the onslaught of the downpour, the more likely you are avoiding the free flow of emotional expression.

Rainbow: Hope, abundance, and the promise of good to come are all wrapped up in the symbol of the rainbow, one of the most magical phenomena that can be found on Earth. Part of the meaning of this symbol can be taken from the emotional reaction a person can have when looking at one. Rainbows are breathtaking and can inspire deep feelings of elation. In this way, a rainbow is almost always going to be thought of as a positive image. There are several major cultural associations to a rainbow. In the Old Testament, God sent the rainbow as a promise to never destroy humanity again, which is the origin of the theme of the promise for the future. The Celtic tradition tells us that at the end of a rainbow is a pot of gold, associating this symbol with the search for abundance. However, both of these time-honored interpretations bring with them darker meanings that bear consideration. The former implies past destruction and the latter is a paradox in that it is impossible to ever actually find the end of a rainbow, as it constantly shifts as you move toward it. However, each of these counterparts is what infuses the rainbow with its most powerful symbolic element: hope. The physical construct of a rainbow is filled with beautiful symbolism. Rainbows contain all the colors of the spectrum and therefore represent a sense of wholeness in a majestic and highly spiritual expression. They appear when the sun and rain are present at the same time. To be able to experience sadness (rain) and joy (sunlight) at the same time is a true sign of consciousness and wisdom.

Rainforest: The lungs and heart of the earth, the rainforest is the birthplace of the oxygen that makes our atmosphere home to life itself. The earth as a whole is a symbol for the self as a combination of the conscious mind as represented by land and the unconscious mind as represented by the ocean. The rainforests of the earth are the symbolic lungs of the planet. A dream about this area is almost archetypal in nature, connecting you to aspirational thoughts about how the breath of life is moving through you. If in your waking life you have a particular affinity for what is happening in the rainforest, this dream may be more literal for your sense of activism.

Ramp: A ramp creates access to something when traversing a certain structure is difficult. As such, the symbolic meaning behind a ramp is the creation of ease and helpfulness in order to get to a particular destination or goal. The way is being made easy for you when a ramp is in your dreams.

Rape: Rape in a dream is a positive symbol even though the association with it is very negative because of its abhorrent nature from waking life. Sex is ultimately about integration and the bringing together of aspects of personality. This is true in the world of symbolism even when the act is forceful and violent. Because rape is an act of violence, this, combined with the absence of consent, puts a very different spin on how to interpret it if it should appear in a dream. When a dream includes something as heinous as rape, it is important to remind yourself that dreams are symbolic, not literal. Rape in a dream is not like rape in life. It simply means that the integration that is occurring within your psyche is being experienced as so abrupt and potentially frightening that the symbolic expression of it appears dramatically. The unconscious will often use nightmares and frightening dreams to get our attention. If you were raped in the dream, consider the rapist. If the person was known to you, then use that individual as a character aspect to see what part of your own personality is demanding to be dealt with. If the person was not known to you, then consider the dream a precursor to a powerful shift that is going on under the surface and is not yet clear. If you cannot glean more helpful insight from this dream, trust that future dreams will inform you of whatever shift is taking place. If you witnessed a rape, you must look inward to see what aspects of your personality are at odds with one another, for they ultimately need to be integrated and made whole. The rapist would be the part of you that is demanding to be recognized, and the victim is the part of you that needs to accept the merging, but may be in resistance to the process. If you were the rapist in your dream, consider the victim as a character aspect that represents the part of you that you wish to subdue. Rape fanta-

sies are common for many people and can be quite erotic and satisfying when handled in an appropriate manner. If the dream of rape was erotic in nature, the meaning is the same, but the integration that is taking place has much lower stakes and may in fact be a source of pleasurable anticipation.

Rapids: Rapids are created when a river is constricted in some way, forcing more flow into less space, thus increasing the intensity of the energy created by the rushing water. Water in dreams represents your feelings, and a river is symbolic of your flowing emotions. In this way, rapids indicate an increased intensity of some emotional experience in your life that not only is causing a rise in how much emotion you are feeling, but also adds an element of overwhelm and sense of potential danger.

Rash: A rash is actually the evidence that something under the surface is not quite right. In this way, it is symbolic of being able to see something that an unseen conflict is causing. Some sort of irritation is troubling you, and it is more visible to the outside world than you may realize. Has something been rubbing you the wrong way?

Rats: Rats are considered pests, as they can overpopulate and bring with them destruction and disease. They are inexorably bound up in our history as the carriers of the Plague. The consequences for not attending to them properly are recorded in our mythology as a loss of innocence, as in the story of the Pied Piper of Hamelin, who, when not paid for his services of ridding the town of its rats, took away the children of the town and led them to their deaths. Rats can be found in sewers, basements, and dark corners. This expands their association with shadow material, which is all the things about ourselves we wish were not true or that we would rather not look at. If rats appear in your dreams in any fashion, there is something to investigate under the surface.

Razor Blades: A razor blade is a very small but very sharp-edged metal tool. The combination of its size and ability to cut very deeply is symbolic of the way in which innocuous moments can hurt without warning, like a sharp tone of voice or sudden action that hurts someone's feelings deeply. If a razor blade appears in a dream, either you may be experiencing such wounds from someone in your life or you may be the one at risk of hurting others without meaning to.

Reality Show: This relatively new form of media has come to dominate the television world, where unscripted life situations with real participants are being presented for your entertainment. At the center of this structure, however, is the fact that all of these experiences are being manipulated, heightened, and edited for certain perspectives to be perceived. The presence of a reality show in your dream world may be an indication that you are manipulating something or over-dramatizing a situation, or you feel that you are being manipulated in some way by some occurrence in your life. If you are dreaming about someone you have watched on a reality show, you may be over-identifying with the drama in your life.

Rearview Mirror: As you drive forward, you can periodically look behind you by virtue of the rearview mirror. In this way, the symbolic meaning of this structure is your ability to consider where you are going by virtue of where you are just coming from. The rearview mirror may be featured in a dream when you are paying too much attention to your past and this is distracting your ability to move gracefully into the future. A broken rearview mirror may indicate a moment when your ability to assess where you are going is inhibited in terms of learning the lessons of your past.

Red: The first color of the spectrum, red is associated with security, grounding, aggression, and passion. This energy is connected with the base of the spine. Often thought of as a color of passion, red aligns with aggression and sexual expression in the masculine principle. We stop at red lights, creating security for ourselves by avoiding the danger of oncoming traffic. Blood is the essence of life force itself and is therefore related to being grounded in the physical body. (See *Colors*.)

Red Carpet: The red carpet is a symbol itself, indicating a special path for people of a certain elevated status. There are two implications when a red carpet is present. One is that there is a special event taking place. The second relates to the exclusivity of passage relegated to only a certain few. This symbol can indicate a sense of aspiration in a dream. If you are witnessing someone else on a red carpet, that person is an aspect of your own personality that has the capability of helping you aspire to greater things. This image in a dream may also point to a desire to be recognized for some special ability or particular accomplishment in your life.

Refrigerator: The primary purpose of a refrigerator is to keep a small amount of space at a cold enough temperature so that anything organic that is placed in it will stay fresher longer. Cold is symbolic of less passion and anger, so one element of this object as a symbol relates to wanting to keep something around for more time by lightening up on how much intensity you allow it to express. The preservation of things that you desire is what is being expressed by the refrigerator in your dream, so pay particular attention to both what is inside of it and the state that the machine itself is in. Both of these will add clues to your interpretation.

Rehearsal: The preparation process for an upcoming performance, a rehearsal is where you get to perfect something that will be presented in the future. To dream of a rehearsal is to be connecting with this desire to be as prepared as possible for some future moment where you want to put your best foot forward. Anything that happens in a rehearsal in a dream is connected to how you are feeling about something that is being created in your consciousness. Use the context of the dream to understand what area of your life is being worked on and how the process is going.

Reporter: A reporter's job is to understand the facts behind some event and communicate those facts to the world at large. As a character aspect of your own personality, the reporter is a witness who is collecting data and attempting to maintain a sense of objectivity

when considering something that is going on in your life.

Reptile: The reptilian brain is something that all animals on the planet share; it governs the most basic functions, such as breathing and survival instincts. If a reptile features in your dreams, you are connecting to this fundamental element of life. There may be additional meaning associated with the specific animal that is present, but certainly the universal meaning of basic instincts is at play when a reptile appears in a dream.

Reservoir: Any water in a dream is symbolic of the emotional side of your nature. In the case of a reservoir, there is the element of storage of the sustenance of life that is represented by this humanmade structure. When a reservoir features in your dream, you are remembering the importance of emotional expression as a natural part of your functioning humanity.

Resort: A resort is a location where you go for relaxation and to escape your daily routine. A dream that takes place at a resort may indicate a need to take a break from the daily grind of your life. Stress may be high, so a dream at a resort may point to a need to relieve that stress.

Restaurant: A dream that takes place in a restaurant has the theme of self-care and the celebration of abundance. Any image that concerns itself with food connects to nurturance. This especially applies to a restaurant, as the ritual of being waited on and served is also a form of self-care. The expense of eating out is always going to be higher than that associated with preparing something at home. The quality of your meal connects with both abundance and the ability to discern excellence. A fine meal could reveal that you are indeed being careful to ensure that your life provides for your needs in a way that reflects a consciousness of deserving abundance. However, a dream in which you are served unacceptable food indicates that there is something out of balance in this area. If the dream includes something as severe as food poisoning, you may want to examine your attitudes more closely.

Resurrection: The idea of resurrection may initially be thought of as a religious symbol, as it has great significance in the world of depth psychology and the concept of the archetypal mind. The idea that something dies in order to be born again is a part of the cycle of consciousness that allows for tremendous growth and transformation throughout a person's life. Any sense of resurrection as a theme or symbol indicates that a time of great change is occurring. What in your life is dying off in order for a new path to be reborn?

Revolution: Change that happens very suddenly can be thought of as revolutionary in nature. Remember that the seeds to such an uprising are sown over a very long time in the form of discontent and dissatisfaction with an old regime before the necessary impetus is present to rise up and demand change. This is the case with internal shifts inside your psyche and the dramatic shifting of habits or patterns that are ready to be changed in a dramatic moment of change. Dreaming of a revolution means that such change is happening in your life.

Rhino: The primary symbolic meaning associated with the rhinoceros is that things may not be as they seem. Though rhinos are enormous in size and move slowly in a way that is deeply connected to what is beneath them, they can run up to thirty miles per hour when charging. Though they can be quite aggressive, they are mostly docile. In this way, rhinos remind us that not everything is as it seems, and if one appears in a dream, you are being called to appreciate the contradictions in your life.

Ribbon: A ribbon is a marker of some kind, designed to draw attention to something in a colorful and playful way. The presence of a ribbon in a dream indicates a desire to highlight something specific. Look to where the ribbon was affixed and if it had any additional sense of purpose to round out your interpretation. A hair ribbon relates to a desire to feel more attractive. A ribbon on a gift is a reflection of a need to have what you offer the world stand out in a dynamic way.

Ring: The circular shape of a ring is a symbol itself for things in life that embody a sense of continuity. An engagement or wedding ring reflects the sense of wholeness and continuity reflected in the choice to partner with another person. In this way, the ring is symbolic of any sort of commitment to something long-term. In a dream, this may not necessarily be to a person in a relationship, but can also reflect a commitment to an idea, a project, a belief system, or some other structure. If a ring is lost, stolen, or broken in some way, consider the ways in which your steadfastness is in question.

Rip: A rip is a break in the integrity of something made out of fabric. The symbolism here is that something has been broken or rendered obsolete because of the loss of structure. If something is already ripped in your dream, the offending moment has occurred in the past. If you are ripping something in the dream, there may be some anger issues that are causing things to break down. If the person doing the ripping in your dream is someone else, consider him or her as a character aspect of yourself and think about what the person is ripping in order to have a sense of what this image means.

Ritual: A ritual is any activity that is imbued with a deep intention and is often a symbol for something in and of itself. If your dream feels like it has a ritualistic sensibility, there may be a call to turn to the more spiritual side of your nature and the part of life that feels mysterious. Some dreams that feature ritual settings feel dark or scary and may reflect feeling overwhelmed by things you don't readily understand.

River: Any dream that involves water connects to emotions. In the case of a river, the essential meaning relates to the expression of feelings and emotional flow. All rivers eventually deposit their contents into the ocean, the symbol of all that is unconscious. This adds the perspective of emotions that move freely across our conscious awareness as they travel back to their ultimate mysterious source. The intensity of the river's flow in a dream is a direct barometer of the level of emotional-

ity in your life that is being expressed by this image. The force of a river can run the gamut from a babbling brook to a torrential powerhouse. The volume of water involved can also vary greatly. A dry or barren riverbed indicates a lack of expression and a desperate need for emotional content. One that is overwhelmed by flooding might point to a situation that may feel dangerous and threatening to the stability of your life. An obstacle that blocks a river, such as a dam, reveals some level of emotional blockage.

Road: The road in your dream is a symbol of your path or direction in life. Your individual path is a combination of past choices you have made and current circumstances and decisions you are about to make that determine the road you're on in any given moment. Such an image in a dream is representative of your current life path. It can be a snapshot of where you are and how you feel about the present moment in your journey. The more isolated the road, the more the dream relates to your private life and personal issues. A public or widely traveled road will likely connect to aspects of your life that are more social in nature.

Roadkill: Finding roadkill in a dream indicates that a violent act has already occurred. An animal killed in this way is reflecting some sense of innocence that has been sacrificed by moving too fast through your life. Consider the animal for additional meaning if it is clear what animal it was.

Robots: You are stuck in a rut of endless productivity and emotionless activity that is robbing you of life force. A robot is a nonhuman entity that is designed to replicate some level of human functioning. Dreaming of one may reveal your own personal relationship to emotional responses with regard to accomplishment. It is important to also ask yourself if there are areas in your life where you might be operating in such an automatic fashion that it might be draining you of vibrancy and joy.

Rocks: See *Boulders/Rocks*.

Roller Coaster: You are dreaming of the up-and-down nature of life, which is often expressed by using the analogy of a roller coaster ride. Just as in life, these extremes can be simultaneously thrilling and terrifying. As a ride in an amusement park, a roller coaster is something that a person chooses to experience, knowing that it will contain surprising twists and turns. If you resist the sensations of the journey, it can be terrifying. If you welcome them, there can be great exhilaration. Which end of that continuum you find yourself on in the dream illuminates your relationship to the ups and downs your life is currently throwing at you. A roller coaster symbolizes one of life's biggest challenges—sudden changes in intensity and direction. These rapid shifts constitute the rhythm of life that we have all come to expect, especially when transition is afoot. Dreaming of such a symbol indicates that life is currently or about to hurl itself up to the heights, plummet into the depths, or both. Remember that if you find yourself riding the roller coaster of life, you have chosen to benefit from all of the possibilities life has to offer. It is through the challenging ups and downs that we are

able to create brilliant manifestations of our heart's desires.

Roller Skates: Roller skates speed up your movement through life and also add an element of playful fun to how you are moving about. If your dream features roller skating, you may want to have things move a little faster and more smoothly. Additionally, if you are not graceful on the skates, such a dream could indicate a moment when you feel out of balance because things are speeding up just a bit.

Roof: The roof is the top of a building; in this way it connects to the mind and thoughts in the consciousness that the building represents. If the roof is not in good shape, then elements from the outside will get in in a way that can be damaging. If this is the case, you may feel that you are not protected from the thoughts of other people interfering with your own ideas about things. If you are standing on the roof in a dream, you desire to get a higher vantage point by connecting to the highest level of thoughts you can have about a situation. This higher vantage point is a powerful place to be, but it also puts you in the position of being able to fall off, so a dream about falling from a roof connects to the risk associated with having vision. If the roof is in disrepair, your thoughts are not in alignment or are out of integrity.

Rooster: All birds are messengers and the rooster has a very specific message that it brings. Its crowing signals that the day has begun. If a rooster appears in your dream, a new cycle is beginning and you are being alerted to this. From Chinese astrology, the rooster is practical and resourceful, but is also the strutting archetype that is filled with confidence. The rooster in your dream may be connecting you to these qualities.

Rope: This symbolizes the potential to do a great variety of structural adjustments in your life by keeping resources close at hand. Rope is a magnificent tool that allows you to do a number of things; the most common is the tying up of objects that would otherwise be separate. In the world of symbols, what you tie together with rope might be anything from ideas to emotions. The rope itself is the potential to execute some measure of control over situations that feel somewhat chaotic. What the rope is doing in the dream will offer deeper meaning. Make sure to pay special attention to how the rope is knotted, as a knot is evidence of past efforts to control things that may not have been as effective as desired. Remember too that any knot can be undone with the right amount of effort.

Roses: Of all the flowers, the rose is the most directly connected to romantic love. Also, flowers represent passionate expression, the desire for forgiveness, and the presence or need for joy in your life. They also connect to the fleeting nature of all such things, as flowers wilt and die before long. The color of the roses has some meaning, where red roses are given to the beloved, white roses indicate pure love on a higher realm, and yellow roses

connote the platonic love of friendship. If the thorns are prominent in your dream, then you are considering the challenges that are associated with love and intimacy. The health of the bloom also has meaning; the fresher the bud, the more hopeful the promise built into the symbol. A wilting rose may point to love that has faded.

Rug: A rug makes the floor feel better to the feet, protects the floor beneath it, and also adds beauty and a sense of décor to a space. There are elements to this symbol that suggest feeling more grounded in a space and adding a sense of abundance and prosperity to your life. The shape that the rug is in may be expressing beliefs you have about such abundance. Something old and worn means your ideas are outdated. Something new and beautiful indicates that you are ushering in a new vision of prosperity and luxury.

Running: Running is walking, only speeded up. On the one hand, it symbolically relates to the desire to move through your life at a faster pace. Running can also connect to a sense of self-care if the act is connected to fitness and exercise. Additionally, running is often present in the nightmare of being chased. You must use the context of the dream to indicate how to interpret this desire to move more rapidly and make sense of the symbol. Ask yourself what are you running from. (See *Slow Motion.*)

Sacrifice: Many ancient cultures used the ritual sacrifice of a life to show devotion to the Divine. In this way, the essence of sacrifice is the exchange that is buried within it. There is a principle in dream work that when a death occurs, it is like a sacrifice, where the old way of being is released in order to birth something new. There is great power in this practice, so if a sacrifice is the scene in a dream, there is a profound level of change going on within your psyche. Something that no longer serves you is being released in order to create something new.

Safari: A safari is a Western-culture attempt to expose an individual to the energy that the African plain has to offer. In this way, it is a symbol of an attempt to cross over into foreign territory in order to be exposed to what that territory has to offer. Such territory can be a new or exotic approach to your current lifestyle. Since animals are the featured attraction of a safari, such a dream may be attempting to express a connection to your more instinctive nature and the spiritual power that the animal kingdom represents.

Safe: A safe is an impenetrable structure designed to keep that which you value safe and free from theft. As a symbol, it represents the desire to protect something you treasure and heighten your sense of defensiveness. You lock anything in a safe that you feel others might want to steal from you, and this can be anything on the symbolic level from love to your opinions and ideas. What are you afraid others will take from you if you are not extremely guarded?

Salesperson: This is the individual who helps when you are looking to make a purchase. As a character aspect, a salesperson is the part of your own personality that is designed to justify and make a case for a choice you are considering. Allow the context of the dream to inform you of whether the intentions of this aspect are to be trusted, for often a salesperson doesn't always have the customer's best interests in mind. Are you trying to convince yourself to make a choice that may not serve you?

Salon: A salon is a gathering of people led by an inspiring host, usually to uplift and inspire those who are in attendance. The concept has been adapted by the beauty industry, where those who gather are uplifting their appearance. As a scene in a dream, a salon connects to the collective ideas of beauty and glamour and the drive to conform to society's ideas about what you should look like.

Sand: Sand is part of the land and as such relates to the conscious mind. The tiny particles that make up sand have an implication of the many thoughts that occupy the mind at any given time. Since sand is so unable to structurally support anything because of its inherent lack of solidity, the symbolic meaning of it relates to the danger of any shifting foundation. How solid is the ground on which you are currently building the structures of your life? Sand is a staple of the beach, where the symbolic consciousness of land meets the symbolic unconsciousness of the ocean. This is the very malleable structure of this ever-changing landscape, and your dream of sand may relate to this.

Sandals: Shoes relate to how grounded you are, what direction you are moving in, and how you'd like to express yourself about how you are going where you are headed. Sandals are the ultimate in casual effortlessness. Their open structure implies a desire to experience freedom.

Sandstorm: Sand represents tiny ideas in consciousness and a sandstorm is the negative consequence of too many chaotic thoughts. Wind is also a symbol that relates to the intellect, and when these two get together in an out-of-balance fashion, you may feel trapped and unable to move with any clarity. A sandstorm combines the power of wind and the structure of small bits of earth. The wind is symbolic of what happens when thoughts are powerfully directed. Sand in this case represents tiny little ideas that taken by themselves have little meaning, but when they are whipped up in a frenzy of directed thought, they can become blinding and destructive.

Santa Claus: This archetypal character connects to the innocent belief in the magical power of love. Christmas comes with the winter solstice, the time when the days are shortest in the Northern Hemisphere. During this darkest time of the year, we reminisce about the bounty of sunshine with a tree that is decorated with the symbolic fruits of spring. Santa Claus is the icon at the foundation of this mythology. He represents the magical power of love to transcend all darkness. This power is associated with the innocence of childhood, for once the belief in it is abandoned, it can be very difficult for people to fully believe in magic again. Somewhere along the line, parents began to use the promise of what Santa might bring to a child in order to manipulate the child toward good behavior. This was popularized by the famous lyric that indicates that Santa sees everything that children do, good and bad. While on the surface this is a charming notion, Santa's voyeurism is a falsehood, so the spirit behind instilling this sort of fear into children is manipulative and judgmental. Look to see where in your life you may be overly concerned with whether you've been bad or good and what the consequences might be.

Satellite: As the human race has moved outward into space, our consciousness has expanded to include objects that orbit Earth. As symbols, these things are part of the global collective consciousness, and the fact that satellites are used for communication of different kinds supports this interpretation. If your dream features a satellite, you are connecting to this expanding sense of the collective. The context of your dream will help you determine what part of your personal life is being affected by global ideas.

Satellite Dish: This object on the ground connects your home to information that is available through the new global consciousness. The satellite dish as a symbol represents your personal ability to stay connected to the world at large. Because the primary focus of the information that comes to you through the satellite dish is entertainment, there is an added element of escapism associated with one.

Saw: A saw is designed primarily to cut through wood in order to create something of struc-

ture. The saw itself represents your ability to change the shape of some form of thought, idea, or consciousness. When put to use, such a tool can be highly constructive but also dangerous. Let your dream indicate which direction to take your interpretation.

Scaffolding: This outer structure is erected alongside a building when repairs are needed. When this exoskeleton appears in a dream, it is an indication that change and transformation are occurring, even though it may be hard to see the direct evidence of that. The change associated with scaffolding is certainly going to be an improvement of some situation in your life.

Scarf: Because a scarf is worn around the neck, as a symbol it relates to issues of communication and having a connection to your voice. One function of a scarf is protection from the cold, and as such, in a dream it may indicate a need to hold back expressions of criticism or disdain. As an adornment, a scarf can also be highlighting a need to become more expressive and free with how you speak. Consider the implications of wrapping the head and face in a scarf as possibly connecting to the religious connotation of humility as part of the interpretation of a dream that features a scarf.

Scars: A scar is evidence of a previous transformation or change that you have already experienced, the pain of which may not yet be healed or forgotten. When a scar is present, it always relates to some previous event that was damaging or otherwise altering. Sometimes the original wound is purposeful and connected to healing, such as with surgery.

Other times it can be the result of an attack of some kind. We use the term "emotional scars" to represent memories of things in our past that stand out as particularly painful and worth avoiding in the present. No matter what the backstory is, the presence of a scar today means something powerful and invasive happened yesterday.

School: School is a place of learning and advancement of intellectual pursuits. In a dream, school represents the need and desire to grow and expand in wisdom. One of the most common recurring dream images involves returning to the school of one's youth, and such a dream relates to anxiety around responsibility and being held accountable for what you know. If your dream does not take you back to your earlier life, a school can be an indication that there are life lessons to be learned.

School Bus: The vehicle that brings people to and from school is the symbol for the access to learning and expansion of consciousness. If you are riding a school bus in your dreams, you may be on your way to learning something new.

Scorpion: The principle of death and rebirth is what is represented by the scorpion. In the astrological zodiac, the scorpion is the only archetype that can kill, so Scorpio relates to death and rebirth, the occult, and the mysterious realms in life. The totem of the scorpion relates to the ability to transform any situation and create great change.

Scrubs: Due to the proliferation of medical dramas in the media, the visual image of scrubs has become part of the modern vernacular. They are the symbol of a character aspect that is connected with healing. If you are wearing scrubs in a dream, you may be taking on a new level of mastery over your health, whether literal physical health or metaphorical health.

Scuba Diving: The ocean represents our deep unconscious mind. Just as with the unconscious, there are realms of the ocean that are available for exploration if you are prepared properly to dive beneath the surface. Scuba diving is the symbolic experience of investigating elements of your own unconscious mind that are generally hidden and out of view, but are accessible through various means of self-investigation.

Sculpture: A sculpture is a three-dimensional piece of art. Part of what is available through such an object is the ability to consider it from all angles. Any work of art is a symbol of your creative expression, and to be able to look at it from all perspectives allows you a greater ability to understand this part of your humanity. If the sculpture in your dream is of a human form, it can also have an additional layer of meaning that relates to the notion of a moment of expression being trapped in one form, revealing a level of limitation and feeling bound.

Sea Lion: The sea lion is a playful and expressive animal and can easily dive in and out of the ocean, the symbolic representation of the unconscious mind. This aquatic mammal reminds us to not take life too seriously and to be willing to go to deeper depths when needed, but remember that the journey is a lighthearted one if we so choose. Sea lions connect us to our emotional life, not with a heavy intensity, but rather with a light and deft ability to move in and out of different emotions with grace and delight.

Sea Monster: Sea monsters are mythical in nature and were created by seafarers of old telling tall tales. Any creature that lives in the deep ocean is a product of the unconscious mind. In the case of a mythological creature that might fall in the category of sea monster, what is being expressed relates to overblown fears of your own creation.

Seagulls: These birds are the guardian messengers of the shoreline, the symbolic realm where the unconscious and the conscious minds meet. As such, seagulls offer a message that important information is about to be revealed to you.

Seatbelt: Cars represent how you are moving down the path of your life. Since a seatbelt is located in a car, there is a direct correlation to this symbolic meaning. This object of restraint increases your safety, which is symbolic of protecting yourself against the challenges and obstacles that you meet on your journey through life.

Security Camera: The essence behind the meaning of the security camera is the discretion with which it captures things that occur; its presence is usually hidden, discreet, or ignored. In this way, security cameras often capture events that people don't intend to make a permanent record of. In a dream, they connect with a sense of being watched and potentially judged for choices you are

making. They loosely relate to a sense of conscience. What would you do or not do if you thought you were being watched? Such a dream may indicate a violation of privacy in some area of your life.

Seeds: This is one of the most potent symbols that represent potential and possibility. From something very small and unremarkable, spectacular expressions of life force can emerge. In and of themselves, seeds are unimpressive. But place them in the right environment and a miracle occurs. One of the most significant things about seeds is their specificity. Each type of seed will transform into one expression only. If you plant a radish seed, you cannot expect a carrot to grow. Every seed has a consciousness about this; as long as it finds itself in the proper conditions, it knows what it is and knows what to do. The essence of the universal meaning of a seed is in its potential, but the less obvious meaning connects to the independence of its development. You could hardly expect your garden to grow if every day you dug up the seeds you had planted to see how they were coming along. Seeds must be left alone to do what is innately inside of them to do. In this way, patience for the possibilities to come is also indicated by this symbol.

Seizure: A dream that features a seizure is an expression of an intense and debilitating confusion about some aspect of life. A seizure is a neurological phenomenon where cells in the brain and the nervous system begin to fire rapidly and out of control. While there are a number of different causes of seizures, the net result is often dangerous. On a symbolic level, anything that involves the brain connects with how we think. The chaotic nature of a seizure represents a kind of thinking that is confounded and confused to an extreme degree. Where in your life are you suffering from confusion, chaos, or anxiety? If you are the one having a seizure in your dream, then look to where confusion may be hurting you on a deep level in your life. If someone else in your dream is the victim, then use that person as a character aspect of the part of your personality that is suffering due to confusion.

Semen: Semen is the fluid that emanates from a man's body in order for him to pass along his sperm in the act of procreation. At the heart of this as a symbol is this connection to the masculine principle around creativity. However, semen itself has many sexual and erotic connotations as well that link it symbolically to virility and the expression of power. The context of the dream and your waking-life gender must factor into how you interpret this image in a dream.

Seminar: A seminar is a gathering designed to disseminate a particular piece of information or knowledge. In a dream, such a setting may indicate a moment in life when you are expanding your understanding of some aspect of your experience. The type of seminar or the content of it can be helpful in your interpretation, if you know it.

Sentencing: The sentencing portion of a trial experience is about consequences. Your dream may be pointing to some experience from your recent past that is requiring you to take responsibility for choices that you have made.

Sequins: A staple for a certain kind of glamour, the sequin is a shiny and reflective object that creates a vibrant effect that is considered slightly vulgar. Wearing sequins or having them available to be worn or affixed to an article of clothing reflects a desire to be noticed for a superficial presentation and a need for attention.

Serial Killer: The serial killer is driven to commit murder over and over again. Consider that in the world of dreams, a death is an act of sacrifice where something that no longer serves you is being released in order to make room for something new. The element of murder means this transformation is happening because of some measure of choice. The serial killer that lives inside your psyche is a beneficial archetype that, though it lives in the shadow, is ultimately a part of your long-range growth and expansion. Such an image might be very frightening in a dream, but it must be examined through the lens of the universal principles it is expressing.

Seven: After all the work in the external world that brought you to the concept of partnership, you are now prepared for a more elevated experience of human expression. Seven is the number of spirituality and higher thought, which are only possible after the basic human needs are met. You are now free to contemplate your existence in a more esoteric manner. Meditation and any consideration of the interior landscape of our humanity is governed by the number seven. This includes thought, contemplation, mysticism, prayer, faith, psychology, and any endeavor that seeks to understand life from a higher perspective. This is a number we are all familiar with as significant: seven days of the week, seven deadly sins, seven notes in the diatonic scale, etc. The shadow challenge associated with this vibration is to get lost in the ethers and lose contact with life on the ground.

Sewer: A sewer is a subterranean construct designed to take waste away. In this way, it symbolically connects to the desire for unwanted material to be easily removed and kept out of sight. A sewer is primarily under the surface and also connects with elements of life that are generally thought of as repulsive, so this is a shadow symbol. If your dream takes place in a sewer, you are exploring the underbelly of your psyche and considering the more disowned parts of yourself. Such a dream may be reflecting a desire to be free of things you prefer not to look at. There is an added meaning to sewers from the notion that through them, you could move from one area to another without being seen, as long as you were willing to navigate the underbelly of your psyche.

Sewing: Sewing joins fabric together with small, delicate yet very strong stitches. It symbolically connects to the precision that is sometimes needed to construct ideas, choices, and the expansion of your consciousness. There is the big-vision part of your experience, but without the tiny incremental steps, nothing will stay cohesive and it is this that any type of sewing connects to. If you are sewing with a machine, there may be more power, force, and conformity associated with what you are up to. Sewing by

hand indicates a moment when there is great individuality being expressed and there may be a need to pay greater attention to the details in something you are creating.

Sex: Perhaps the most misunderstood symbol in dreaming, sex is ultimately about connection and integration. When sex appears in a dream, it is imperative that you put your personal reactions to sex and sexuality aside in order to arrive at an accurate interpretation. Detaching from the thoughts and feelings triggered by the characters involved in the act of sex in your dream is even more crucial to this process. This can be difficult for many people to accomplish. Sex in dreams can be an area of great concern for many people. While some sex dreams are experienced as pleasurable and erotic, more often than not people report dreaming of sexual encounters as troubling because of the nature of the sexual act they dreamed of or the partner with whom they were engaged. However, once examined through the language of symbols, sex loses its potency and charge, while revealing so much more. When two people have sex, on at least some level they are trying to get as close to each other as they possibly can. The act of sex can be defined symbolically as two separate energies attempting to merge into one. Therefore, sex is symbolic of the process of integration. If you remove any personal projections that come up around sex and how it was played out in your dream, the interpretive meaning rises above any potential embarrassment or shame. Though sometimes more difficult to accept, this also applies to sexual encounters that have societal taboos associated with them, such as those involving incestuous relationships or illegal activities. Whoever you are having sex with in your dream represents a character aspect that your unconscious is telling you needs to be integrated into your personality. If you are witnessing a sexual act, then you will need to consider what character aspects of yourself are being expressed by the people having sex. The message of integration still applies, but it will connect more to parts of your personality that need to join forces. Perhaps a life situation is demanding different areas of your skill sets that, if combined, will empower you to be effective in a way that is currently eluding you.

Shadows: The shadow is one of the most powerful elements of depth psychology and dream work. It relates to the parts of your psyche that you wish weren't so, prefer to keep hidden, or feel shame about. If your dream contains the image of a literal shadow, consider the thing that is creating the shadow. Whatever the object is, think of the shadow as the darker side of whatever the thing itself means to you.

Shark: The ultimate predator, this is a very common image in a dream that represents fear and anxiety. As a totem, the power of the shark is phenomenal. Sharks represent our capacity to be single-minded, unstoppable, and driven. And yet, when they appear in a dream, they are often reviled and feared. When the shark appears in your dream, you must ask yourself what you are afraid of. Such a dream may be calling you to step into your personal power in a bigger way. Focus,

self-determinism, and being utterly free of distraction are part of the medicine that the shark has to offer. But first you must get out of the way of your own fears in order to accept such power as your own.

Shaving: Removing unwanted hair is a ritual for both men and woman and is, for some, an essential element of personal grooming. For a man, facial hair is related to masculinity, so there is a symbolic element of softening that when shaving appears in a dream. For many men, the act of shaving is a grooming staple, and in this way shaving may indicate the preparation to present yourself in a way that suggests readiness and competency. For women, shaving the legs and underarms has connotations about the readiness for sexual intimacy, so in a dream such desires may be being expressed.

Sheep: Innocence and vulnerability are the hallmarks of the sheep as a symbol. If the sheep appears in your dream, you are getting in touch with the more tender side of yourself. Be careful, however, of giving up your will, as the sheep is also a symbol of following the herd without individual mindfulness. There is a strong association with sheep and sleep or meditative states with the phrase "counting sheep."

Shelf: The purpose of a shelf is to hold things. Consider the various reasons one might do so. Most objects put on a shelf are for display or to have ready access to. In this way, a shelf in a dream may connect to accomplishments and a sense of pride in things you have done and wish to be able to remember easily or share with others. There is an adage "to put on the shelf," which refers to things you prefer to handle at another time, so such a dream may point to avoidance.

Ship: A ship is a vehicle that travels on the ocean. The ocean represents the unconscious mind, and a ship traverses the very top layer of this mysterious place. In a dream, a ship implies an investigation of matters of an emotional nature. The state of the ship in your dream offers distinctions around this exploration. A sinking ship implies that your feelings are overwhelming you in a profound way. A more powerful ship, such as one that is run by steam or motors, suggests that there is more strength around what you are exploring. A sailing ship implies a simpler or personal search, but also one that relies on things beyond your ability to control. How well the ship you are on is handling the water that surrounds it could point to how well you are managing a difficult emotional situation in your life.

Shipwreck: The implication with a shipwreck is that some difficult experience has already happened. The event is likely to have been emotional in nature and has thrown you off in your daily routine in a considerable way. As a result of emotional turmoil, you are finding yourself in new territory that must be explored.

Shirt: An article of clothing is always connected to self-expression. The torso contains all of the vital organs and therefore relates to the way you process emotions and deal with vulnerability. A shirt is the symbol of protecting yourself while simultaneously expressing your individuality. Consider the phrase "the

shirt off your back" as relating to your personal sense of values that can be changed or exchanged with another's.

Shoes: The feet ground you and also point the direction in which you are moving in life. The shoes in your dreams can illuminate how well you are walking your walk. Since shoes adorn the feet, they represent personal self-expression and choices around where you are headed. The phrase "walk in someone else's shoes" may be important to consider in a dream with shoes in it. Trying on new and different shoes can connect to a need to discover new ways of moving about your life. Different shoes or mismatched pairs are expressing confusion about where your steps may lead you. Lost shoes indicate a need to find ways of grounding yourself and call you to inquire about the ways in which you may not be fully prepared to move in new directions.

Shopping: Shopping is the activity that supports getting your needs met. As a symbol, it relates to being willing to take the actions that will result in self-care, abundance, and sustaining yourself. This can be either in balance and healthy or out of balance and reflecting a level of avoidance and escapism. The nature of what you are shopping for and the sensations around this image in a dream will help clarify your interpretation.

Shopping Cart: The shopping cart is primarily a tool for collecting those things that you are purchasing at a grocery store, and in this way it is a symbol for your ability to contain abundance and make choices that support self-sustenance. Shopping carts have a secondary meaning that is actually more prominent in the collective as an indication of homelessness and the despair that connects with losing everything. If your dream features a shopping cart in this way, then you may be expressing poverty consciousness. A person pushing a shopping cart in your dream is a character aspect of low functioning and a fear that you may lose everything.

Shower: If you are dreaming of taking a shower, then you want to cleanse something in your recent past and let it go. If someone in your dream is taking a shower, consider what aspect of your personality the person represents, as that is the part of your psyche that has something that needs to be released and cleaned up. A cold shower is a symbol for balancing out an overabundant sex drive. A shower that is too hot indicates that the need for purification is at an even higher level.

Shrinking: In the world of symbols, smaller is representative of feeling less than or insignificant. Something that is shrinking and steadily losing size is being diminished in power. Consider what is shrinking in your dream, as that is what is losing its ability to influence you. This may be beneficial or harmful, depending on what is shrinking. If a person is shrinking, then it is a personality trait that is either lessening or needs to be moderated downward. If it is you that is shrinking, look for ways in which you need to hold back or where you may feel disempowered in your life.

Siblings: All people in dreams relate to some aspect of your own personality. If you dream of your actual brothers or sisters from your life, the character aspects that they represent as part of your psyche should be investigated in the same manner as those of any person known to you who appears in a dream. However, because of the powerful dynamic of family systems, the relationships between siblings will connect to various roles that the members of the group often find themselves locked into. When a sibling appears in a dream, there is a great deal of complexity to explore, from your current relationship to your childhood history and even how parenting styles affected each family member. With careful and unbiased investigation, a sibling dream can offer a penetrating snapshot of where you are in your development as an individual, separate from the limitations of your personal history.

Sidewalk: Streets are symbolic of moving through your social and community experience at a fairly fast pace. The sidewalk is a similar symbol for your movement through your community, but at a more intimate level. It also represents the limits placed on you as you move about the world by being told where you must walk, so in this way it is symbolic of social restrictions. What you are doing in relation to the sidewalk in your dream is reflecting your relationship with these limitations and social conventions.

Silver: This secondary precious metal represents wealth, abundance, and prosperity. Because many sacred objects are made of silver, this metal itself connects to the desire to elevate the mundane. Consider the object made of silver in your dream; whatever interpretation you would ascribe to it, the stakes are raised if it is made of silver.

Six

Silverware: Silverware is a symbol of civilization and sophistication. Food is what sustains us and represents nurturing and self-care. By using an implement to connect to our food, we add yet one more separation between ourselves and animals. The meaning attached to silverware must combine the primal instinct to eat for survival with the restraint of social acceptance and grace. Parents struggle to get their children to use silverware for both these reasons, so that they will be able to feed themselves and simultaneously fit in with society. The more sophisticated the circle one travels in, the more silverware there is to contend with. This illuminates the symbolic association of silverware to civilization and cultural hierarchy. Using silverware in a dream connects to your sense of propriety and conformity.

Singing: Singing is an ancient, primal expression of passion. When words are not enough, singing becomes the next heightened form of communication. The ability to sing is so revered that we elevate superior voices to high status in our media and culture. Technically, singing is merely a sustained extension of speaking; the basic principle here is the power and passion of the expression. If someone is singing in your dream, the message that is being communicated is very important—so important that the spoken word was not enough to carry the force of the weight of that message. Therefore, it is important to consider what is being sung and incorporate the message into your interpretation. Losing your voice in a dream might correspond to a feeling of a lack of passion in your waking life or a loss of expression due to some challenging circumstance. If you can sing in your waking life, your personal relationship to your singing is crucial to consider. If you are critical of your singing, you may be connecting to being judgmental of your passion, or lack of it. If you cannot sing as well as you wish you could, you might be longing for more passionate encounters by dreaming of being able to sing in your sleep state. Singing before an audience may connect to a need to rally inner resources behind some common desired aim or goal. If someone else is singing in your dream, use the character-aspect technique to determine what part of you is expressing a passionate need to get your attention.

Sink: The symbolic meaning of a sink relates to its capacity both to draw water to you and to take the waste water away. In this way, a sink is ultimately a reflection of civilized living. The fact that it is a structure that helps move water connects it with the world of feelings and emotions. Consider the type of sink and the state that it is in; both should be utilized in your interpretation. A bathroom sink relates to matters of intimacy and privacy. A kitchen sink connects to how well you are engaged in self-care. An industrial sink has more to do with your social experience.

Sister: See *Siblings*.

Six: Six is the number of partnership, marriage, creative collaboration, and balance. After the freedom of five, there is a need for stability, which is provided by the even number six. This energy can also be seen as a pairing of two threes. If three is about primal creativity at an individual level, then combining two systems of three allows for six to engender worldly partnerships and the concept of marriage and union. The number six represents partnership on every level: business, social, educational, and spiritual. In the personal realm, the number six represents the happy union of opposites within us and the integration of our own opposing forces, such as containing two powerful emotions that contradict each other. The shadow challenge of the six energy connects to responsibility and a sense of burden.

Skateboard: The skateboard puts wheels on your feet and increases your mobility exponentially. In a dream, a skateboard represents a desire to move faster and also to connect to a sense of rebellious youth. If you are someone who skateboards in your waking life, there is less emphasis put on this image in a dream.

Skeleton: You are looking under the surface of things, at the hidden structure of an idea. Skeletons support the physical body and are not readily visible to the outside world. They are the foundation on which everything else is built. In the dream world, they represent this same underlying structure of our bodies and our lives. A skeleton is the invisible underpinning of any physical, conceptual, emotional, or spiritual construct in our waking lives. The skeleton of our lives is the structure of ideas, beliefs, and myths around which we superimpose our sense of self. When you can see the skeleton of something, you have a better idea of what is supporting it or holding it upright. If you dream of this image, you

might be getting a message that something in the structure needs to be examined.

Skin: The largest organ in the human body, the skin is ultimately about protection. It is extremely vulnerable, so a dream that features skin may reflect this sense of vulnerability. The exposure of skin can be very erotic in nature, and this may be reflected if there is this sensibility associated with the imagery in the dream. The skin is very expressive and will reveal things that are going on beneath the surface, so emotional and psychic transparency may be what such a dream is about.

Skunk: The skunk and its odor cannot be separated. When faced with fear, the skunk emits a musk that most predators find objectionable, thus protecting it from danger. In this regard, the symbol of the skunk connects to the ability to keep danger at bay. When the skunk appears in a dream, your mechanisms of self-protection are being stimulated. It is up to you to decide whether this defensive posture is for your own true good or an overreaction.

Sky: The sky is the enormous part of our world that is everything that the earth is not. In this way, the sky is a symbol for the endless capacity of the human imagination. For some, this expansiveness is so enormous that it includes the concept of God. Anything that involves the sky in the landscape of a dream represents this upward-soaring element of the human psyche. Consider what is happening in the sky in your dream, and add that quality, experience, or sensation to your aspirational sensibilities. What is happening in your highest thoughts will be happening in the sky of your dreams, whether positive or negative. Remember that things can "fall out of the sky," which represents sudden, unexpected experiences; again, those can be either positive or negative.

Skydiving: The essence of skydiving is the adrenaline rush associated with the risk of falling to the earth. If you are skydiving in the dream, you may be looking to increase your sense of excitement in your life. The power of this thrill is the relinquishing of control as you descend. In this way, the symbol of skydiving may indicate a need to let go of something you are attempting to control.

Skyscraper: This image indicates expansion to higher levels of conscious awareness. Any building is a reflection of the consciousness of human beings. If a house in a dream symbolizes your personal sense of self, each successively larger building can be thought of as an expansion of this consciousness. In this way, a skyscraper is the ultimate expression of human consciousness, reaching from the ground to the heavens. The skyscraper is also a very American icon and is directly connected to the explosion of urbanization that marked the movement into the current modern era. When steel began to be mass-produced, it paved the way for the bustling city environment to push upward. This ascension then is symbolic of the consciousness of humankind erupting toward higher levels of awareness and intellectual functioning.

Slave: A slave is a character aspect of part of your personality, one that is persecuted and held in bondage. The dream context will help you determine what area of your life has you

in chains. Consider that you may be working too hard and that your life is out of balance because of that. If not work, what are you a slave to?

Slavery: Slavery is a cultural institution, and as such, in a dream it represents a pervasive atmosphere in which one element of your consciousness holds another element of your consciousness back, so much so that you are unable to function properly. Such a dream may be asking you to examine your ideas that are more rigid than is beneficial to you.

Sled: This is a vehicle designed for mobility over frozen ground covered with snow. In this way, there is a primary symbolic meaning associated with a grace and ease of movement in your life when there is a lack of emotional and psychological warmth. If the sled in your dream is more of the childhood variety, the dream may be expressing a desire to release complex emotional challenges in order to experience a moment of relief and playfulness.

Sleeping: Sleep is a state of consciousness that is below the waking state. To be sleeping or to dream of someone being asleep in a dream first and foremost relates to the way in which consciousness is experienced in layers. This is not dissimilar to the notion of a dream within a dream, but it also connects to the idea of "being asleep" as a synonym of being less than consciously aware of things. Where are you missing key things about your life because you are asleep to the awareness you could be having? If someone is sleeping in your dream, there is a part of you that needs to be woken up. If it is you who is asleep, the same applies, only in a more general way—it's time to wake up to more awareness or action.

Slide: A slide is a play structure that offers a short burst of speed and momentum. First you climb and then you drop. In this way, it symbolizes the release that can happen after a small amount of effort as well as the need to return to a more childlike state of mind.

Slippers: Anything connected to the feet has to do with being grounded and the way you would like to express yourself with regard to your walk through life. Slippers are the ultimate in relaxation and retreat from responsibility and effort. Wearing them in a dream represents a desire to feel freer. If someone in your dream is wearing them, then the character aspect in you that the person represents needs a break. Slippers that are not being worn are asking you to consider being more at ease.

Slot Machine: A slot machine is about intermittent variable reward, one of the most addictive systems in life where you may or may not win something so you feel compelled to continue trying. In what ways are you continuing to focus on something because there is a very slight chance of a big payoff? This dream may be pointing to a way in which you are tied to the habit of hope at the detriment of other aspects of your life. Of course, some gambles do pay off, so such an image in a dream may also be asking you to take a risk.

Slow Motion: You may be dreaming about a desire to slow things down a bit in your life. This could be to reduce stress, but also to be able to look at something more closely. Consider what was occurring in your dream during what felt like slow motion. The context will offer you insight on how to interpret such an image. (See *Running*.)

Slum: The geography of a slum is about the desire to keep certain unsavory elements of the social strata in a separate area, away from the mainstream. The same is true of a slum in a dream, only now the geography is a symbol for some area of your consciousness. To visit a slum in your dream is to be exploring the parts of your life that aren't being tended to and need some loving attention.

Smells: There are dreams in which the sense of smell is activated. Smell is the most primitive of all of the senses, and there are powerful sense memories that are evoked when certain smells are present. This type of deep memory-response may be what is triggering a dream in which smell plays a role. If there is something specific that is being smelled in the dream, use that to inform your interpretation.

Smile: A smile is a reflex that is connected directly to feeling a sense of joy. Sporting one is a contagious experience, and when one person smiles, it often sparks a smile in another. In this way, the symbolism of smiling relates to both of these notions: that joy is present in abundance and that when it is felt and processed, it can spread with ease. If you are smiling in a dream, then you are expressing an overflow of joy or the need and desire for more of it. If someone in your dream is smiling, consider the character aspect of your personality that the person represents and understand that that area of your personality has the capacity to increase your joy quotient.

Smoke: Something is changing but is currently obscured or unclear. As the saying goes, "Where there's smoke, there's fire." Since fire represents drastic change, smoke is an indication of the occurrence of transformation without necessarily having the ability to see the actual source of the shift. Smoke can cause asphyxiation by blocking the lungs from receiving oxygen, so dream smoke may indicate a suffocating life situation about which your unconscious is sending you an alarm. A smoke screen is a mechanism for keeping something hidden. It is a battle technique that was developed in World War One, associating it with danger and violence. It has entered our language as something that indicates a deliberate desire to obscure a person's true intentions or create a diversion in order to perpetrate some act of betrayal. If your dream smoke obstructs your sight in any way, you may want to consider what current difficulty in your life may be blocking your view of things as they really are. Ask yourself if you are focusing on what's really important and not being distracted in some way.

Smoking: Cigarette smoking is a hotbed of controversy in today's society, such that the symbolic meaning attached to it can be complicated. The media has always portrayed smoking as glamorous and sexy, though that is changing. Those who smoke may have a relationship with their smoking that runs the gamut from frustratingly addictive to apathetically indifferent to the consequences. Health-conscious nonsmoking individuals can be quite virulent in their objections, and many states and cities have banned smoking in public places altogether. Given these radically different perspectives, if a cigarette features prominently in your dream, you must use your own associations with smoking to arrive at an accurate interpretation. No matter what your personal focus is, the health risks associated with smoking make the symbolic meaning connect to making choices that are not impacted by your knowledge of the consequences. The factor of addiction is an important element to consider. Smoking can represent any choice in life that is not healthy, but is difficult to avoid.

Snail: The general association that most people have with the snail has to do with its very slow pace. A snail in a dream may be asking you to consider the value of moving slowly.

Snake: There is a significant amount of change or transformation in your life if you dream of snakes. Snakes can inspire great and varied personal emotions and therefore can ultimately connect to very different shades of meaning based on your associations. But first and foremost, snakes represent change and transformation. This connects to the fact that they shed their skin in their growth process and that many of them are capable of causing fatality to their predators, implying the symbolic rebirth that follows any death experience. There is a healing element to this, as many snake venoms can also be used as curatives. This may connect to the two snakes that appear on the physician's caduceus, representing the challenge to life and the response of the healer to match it. In the

Judeo-Christian tradition, the snake bears the responsibility for tempting Adam and Eve. As such, a snake can represent a confrontation with a change in your value system. It is important to remember that Adam and Eve's yielding introduced the human race to the knowledge of mortality and the birth of consciousness. A serpent in your dream may actually represent a major shift in your awareness that may bring about the death of an old paradigm that brings you into a whole new world. In Eastern cultures, the awakening of spiritual power is often referred to as a snake. Known as kundalini, it is experienced as an incredible energy that undulates up the spine. Stimulating this can induce a tremendous healing force that has the ability to purify the nervous and glandular systems. The practice of yoga is designed to awaken the snake that lies dormant at the base of the spine. As a dream symbol, a snake could represent the potential for power and energy if properly channeled.

Sneakers: All shoes relate to how grounded you are feeling in your life and also the choices you are making about where you are walking metaphorically. Sneakers imply a readiness for effort and exertion and a need to be grounded enough to work hard. There may be a literal call toward physical exercise in a dream that features sneakers in it.

Snow: You may be experiencing some emotional disconnect around some area where you are lacking warmth. Snow is frozen water. Water represents emotions. Emotions that are frozen imply a disconnection from authentically experiencing them in their raw, wet form. When

snowfall is particularly heavy, it can impede visibility and render you immobile or housebound. When seen through the perspective of emotional avoidance, it is easy to see that a large dose of emotional expression that is not being dealt with can seriously limit any forward movement in your life. Since snow melts, facing the underlying issue is inevitable. The snow just postpones the confrontation and does so with beauty and the promise of temporary peace.

Soap: You may feel a need to cleanse yourself of some troubling thought, idea, pattern, habit, relationship, or experience. If you are using the soap in your dream, you may get a clue as to what is troubling you by virtue of what part of your body you are washing. Soap cleans things up in the present; that which you want to clean up was created in the past. Therefore, soap in a dream may be responding to a desire to take care of some shame or regret from your past.

Solar Power: To dream of tapping into the technology of solar power may allow you to recognize that every human being has a birthright to an endless supply of abundance and limitless life force.

Soldier: An archetypal character aspect, the soldier resonates with the warrior. The job of this particular archetype is protection and aggression, but primarily through the ability to divide all things into the two categories of either right or wrong. A dream with a soldier in it may be asking you to tap into this inner wisdom to face a life circumstance in a very black and white way. Since we live in a time in which war is a very present reality, a soldier also connects to sacrifice at the community and global levels, as they are the individuals in society who are willing to risk their lives to fight for high ideals. If there is someone in your life who is a member of the armed services, such a dream image may be more personal.

Soul Mate: A soul mate is the embodiment of an idea that there is a very particular person you are fated to connect with in intimacy and partnership. As a symbol, this is really an inevitable expansion of your total self, and the kernel of the meaning to soul mating is in its feeling that it was destined that the two of you meet. While such a dream may feel like it is connected to this search in your waking life, on a certain level such a dream is part of your journey toward integration. Searching for your soul mate indicates that wholeness and/or the blocks to wholeness have not yet been identified. A successful connection with your soul mate may mean that integration is at hand. If there are challenges to connecting with your soul mate in your dream, those challenges represent the obstacles to wholeness in your current life.

Soup: The original comfort food, soup in a dream may be expressing a desire to nurture yourself at a fundamental level. Since the making of soup can be improvised with whatever ingredients are available, this dream may also connect to a spontaneous need for sustenance that goes beyond planning or preparation.

Spark: Fire is a symbol of great change and transformation. Since a spark is essentially a tiny amount of fire, the spark is a symbol

for the impetus for change to take place. This may take the form of the initial idea that indicates that a sense of great vision is to follow. It sometimes takes many sparks before an actual fire starts, so such a dream may be an indication of the current availability of inspiration in your life.

Special Powers: This symbolizes a desire to increase your confidence through enhanced abilities. Most special powers can be related to one of the four elements of fire, air, water, and earth. A power associated with heat or flames should be considered as a function of combustion and the transformation that fire can generate. Any power associated with water connects to emotions; the use and manipulation of water relates to channeling the power of emotion, whereas transmuting water to either steam or ice has the impact of altering emotional energy for one's use. The grounded element of earth is represented by anything rock-like or by strength-oriented power. Air is the element in question when powers such as invisibility or flight are concerned. If your special power does not conform to one of the elements, the key to your interpretation will lie in discovering the underlying use and essence of the power you possessed in the dream. Ask yourself what area of your life needs amplification based on the area of your skills and abilities that was amplified by the increased power.

Speech: Making a speech has two perspectives, because on the one hand it has a universal meaning that connects to the projecting of a single focused thought in an effort to create mental agreement. The person making the speech is a part of your consciousness that has the main idea. Those listening represent other thought patterns that are being exposed to the singular idea. What are you trying to convince yourself of? On the other hand, since many people have strong feelings about public speaking, a dream about a speech could indicate that you are preparing to face something in a public way that frightens you.

Speeding: The speed limit is a set of suggestions that are based primarily on community safety. Driving represents the movement through life, and speeding suggests that you are moving fast and taking risks in order to do so. Consider the sensation of the dream to inform your interpretation. If you feel euphoric, you may desire to increase the exhilaration in your life. If the speed frightens you, the speed of things in your life is overwhelming. If you are being pulled over for speeding, you are paying the consequences for risky behavior.

Speeding Ticket: A speeding ticket is a symbol of the consequences around choices you have made with regard to behavior that is risky or dangerous. Since driving is a public experience, the part of your life that such a symbol relates to is your social life or community experience.

Speedometer: Anything that relates to a driving experience is symbolic of how you are moving through your life. The speedometer is your mechanism for managing the speed with which you are moving in order to allow you some measure of control. A broken speedometer indicates a loss of your ability to regulate some aspect of how something is unfolding.

Sperm: Sperm is the male side to the ultimate in human creativity. As a symbol, sperm is the most fundamental element of the creative process from the perspective of the masculine principle. The masculine principle is the realm of action and decisiveness. If sperm features in your dream, you are looking to increase your own power to create through doing.

Spider: The spider spins a web and then waits patiently for its prey, trusting that all it needs and desires will come to it. In this way, the medicine that the spider carries is of creativity and patience. This is a powerfully feminine symbol. Many, if not most, people have an aversion to spiders, which makes them a creature of the shadow. A spider bite may indicate that an infusion of the feminine principle may be in order for your current dealings to succeed. The irritation, illness, or death that is possible from a spider bite indicates the level of sacrifice that will be required of you on an emotional level at this time.

Spider Web: Profound abilities in the area of creativity are represented by the spider web. A spider's webbing is a miraculous feat of engineering and unparalleled beauty. Its purpose is twofold. On the side of nurturing, it is a home. However, it is also a weapon of prey—a trap set to capture, kill, and eat. A spider web may point to creative ideas that are currently being spun. This also indicates that a period of waiting must follow in order for success to be achieved.

Spine: The spine is the center of the physical structure of any mammalian body, and as such, it is symbolic of the core around which all else is organized. When the spine is in alignment, all movement works well, and when it is not, breakdown begins to occur. In this way, anything that is happening with your spine or the spine of a person or animal in your dream is asking you to consider what is at the very center of your thinking about something and how well it is supporting you. Look at your beliefs. To be spineless is to lack all conviction, so if this is featured in your dream, you may want to consider that your belief system is in serious question.

Spiral: The spiral is actually the truest shape with regard to the movement of all life. Plants, flowers, and even the solar system itself move in a spiral-like direction. If you are dreaming of the shape of a spiral or movement that appears to be unfolding in a spiral, you may be dreaming of the sacred geometry of life itself. A new level of psychic energy may be being released in your experience. The context of the dream will indicate whether you are feeling in control of this burst of energy or overwhelmed by it.

Splinter: A splinter is a very small object that causes a great deal of discomfort. In this way, it is a symbol of something innocuous that is bothering you in a constant and irritating manner. What annoyance needs to be plucked out of your life?

Sponge: The essence of a sponge is its ability to absorb. We use this simple plant life as a metaphor for learning at an aggressive rate, as in soaking something up like a sponge. In a dream, a sponge may indicate a desire or present circumstance in which there is a lot for you to take in. The context in which the sponge appears in the dream should offer some clues about what area of your consciousness is currently expanding.

Spoon: A spoon is an implement that assists in taking in nourishment through eating. In this regard, there is an implication that such an image in a dream may point to needing to sustain yourself more efficiently. Spooning also has a strong identification with its use as a euphemism for a particular kind of physical intimacy where two people fit together in a very comforting way. If this is the image in your dream, this need may be expressing itself. Both uses imply taking in certain sustaining ideas; where in your life do you need more care?

Sports Car: A car in a dream is a symbol for the way in which you move through your life. In the case of a sports car, your dream may be expressing a desire to increase the speed and exhilaration with which you create your life. A sports car is an indication that more power is needed in order to fulfill the needs your journey is presenting you with.

Spotlight: A spotlight in a theatrical setting is designed to pull focus on a particular point, usually a person. In this way, it connects to the desire to be noticed and highlighted out in the world for some particular accomplishment or a need to prove yourself in some way. What do you want other people to know about what you are doing?

Spray Paint: A staple in the graffiti art world, spray paint allows the immediate and portable use of the paint that is inside the can. As a form of expression, spray paint may highlight a desire to be more creative in a rebellious fashion.

Sprinklers: Controlled dissemination of water is what sprinklers offer. If the sprinklers in your dreams were for the purpose of gardening, your dream is reflecting a desire to make sure that something you are in the process of creating will get a consistent amount of the attention necessary to complete the project or idea. A sprinkler system that is designed to help put out fires is about the desire to keep sudden and unexpected changes at bay. Change can be overwhelming, and the presence of a sprinkler system in a dream indicates precautions against too much change too fast.

Squirrel: The squirrel knows how to prepare for the future by putting aside abundance today. In this way, the squirrel relates to practicality and prudence. However, this is not to be mistaken for a fear-based sense of hoarding. The squirrel is extremely playful and carefree, reminding us that we can prepare for the future without fearing that our needs will not be met.

Stabbing: Something is making a deep and penetrating impact on you, perhaps a betrayal of some sort. The act of stabbing creates a very narrow, deeply penetrating wound that can do a surprising amount of damage by compromising a fairly small amount of flesh. In other words, a little goes a long way. Harsh or sharp words can have the same effect.

The right phrase, delivered with the proper tone, can cut very deeply and wound a person at a surprisingly deep level. In fact, any penetrating action that occurs suddenly and contains a touch of violent intention could be represented by stabbing in a dream. A sudden change in loyalty is often referred to as a stab in the back. Unexpected news can feel like a stab in the heart. The nature of a small wound that produces a great deal of blood symbolizes the devastation that can follow even the smallest of hurts.

Stadium: The power behind the stadium in both waking life and as a symbol is the sheer number of people it can hold. First and foremost, people in dreams represent thoughts and ideas. When thousands of these are gathered, it is a symbolic representation of agreement and the momentum that is created when great enthusiasm is put behind a single notion. What are you gearing up for in your life that requires an intense focus?

Stage: A stage is a structure for presentation. As a symbol in a dream, the stage suggests a moment in your life when you either desire to or are being required to present a certain idea, concept, or new direction in your life in a very public way. Because what is presented on a stage is a manufactured reality, this image in a dream may be asking you to consider how authentic you are being in your life right now.

Stain: A stain is evidence of some sort of accident or unintended occurrence that has happened in the past and has shifted or altered how you think about a person, place, or thing. In this way, a stain connects to regret or shame about something you cannot undo that is having a residual impact on your memory.

Stairs: You are in the midst of a transition in life, perhaps directly connected to personal growth or assessment. Climbing up stairs should be interpreted as ascending to higher levels of consciousness. Going down stairs connects to revisiting places or moving into lower levels of thought, such as anger and envy, or facing your own emotional development by revisiting old issues. Where the stairs are is important to consider. A stairway in a home is about personal transitions, whereas stairs in public environments reveal issues around how you operate out in the world, in full view of others. There may be literal elements of this image in a dream, as a dream that takes place on a stairway at your workplace will likely connect to issues that are work-related. A stairway in a public park may reveal shifts that involve issues of relaxation and leisure.

Stars: Stars are the tiny impressions made by gigantic objects of great magnitude that are vast distances away from us. They are the constant reminders of the enormity of the universe in which we find ourselves. In a dream, stars may be expressing your highest, most aspirational consciousness. Stars often remind people of the concept of fate, that certain experiences are "in the stars." If this feels in alignment with the context of your dream, you may be experiencing a powerful sense of inevitability about something that is unfolding.

Statue: The power of a statue is in the stillness of the object itself. Many statues are works of art that depict the human form. In this way, a statue can represent the sensation of feeling stuck in one particular form of expression.

Stealing: You may be expressing a desire for things that are not rightfully yours. The objects of theft are often things of value. Therefore, the symbolic meaning implies resources or levels of abundance that are being coveted and then taken without permission or regard for consequences. The reverse side to stealing is being stolen from. This interpretation features the same themes and adds the elements of violation and loss.

Stepfamily: The stepfamily has the same meaning as a family of origin with the added element of fate thrown into the mix, as a secondary family by marriage indicates a choice that brings with it a multitude of relationships. If you have a stepfamily in your waking life, the people who make up that family represent character aspects of your personality and also reflect the primary relationship that connects that stepfamily to you. Such a dream may be reflecting both your own consciousness as well as the waking-life interactions of the individuals involved. (See *Family Members*.)

Stepsiblings: If your waking life includes a stepfamily, your dreams may reflect this by those individuals showing up as characters. If this is the case, the stepsiblings in your dreams are acting as both character aspects of your personality as well as reflections of your archetypal consciousness as defined by the family. (See *Family Members, Siblings*.)

Stepparents: If your waking life includes a stepfamily, your dreams may reflect this by those individuals showing up as characters. If this is the case, the stepparents in your dreams are acting as both character aspects of your personality as well as reflections of your archetypal consciousness as defined by the family. (See *Family Members, Parents*.)

Stigmata: A mystical expression of the Christ consciousness, stigmata replicate the bleeding at the hands and feet of the crucifixion wounds. If they appear in a dream, they may be a symbolic expression of a powerful initiation and you may be moving to a higher level of your spiritual awareness. If you are a Catholic, there may be a more personal association with the stigmata as an outward sign of your inner devotion.

Stock Market: At the heart of the stock market as a symbol is the notion of taking enormous risks with the possibility of a high return on investment. The very essence of speculation is the notion that nothing in life is certain, and if the stock market is featured in your dream, some element of your life is feeling the acute challenges of the nature of life to move up and down in quick succession. What are you willing to risk?

Stockings: Though stockings are a little out of fashion at the moment, their primary purpose is to give the illusion of beauty and glamour to a woman's legs. In this way, they also have a measure of eroticism associated with them. The legs do the walking, so consider how you

are walking the walk in your life when stockings are featured in a dream. The context of the dream will offer distinctions for your interpretation.

Stones: A stone is a small piece of rock. Rocks are connected to memory and things that are part of the past. A stone in a dream is like an old idea that you either have been carrying around with you or are being invited to pick up and take with you from a current experience. (See *Diamond, Emerald,* and other specific stones.)

Store: A store is a place where a specific need is met. Consider the type of store as part of your interpretation and understand that this symbol indicates your ability to get that need met. (See *Market, Hardware Store, Groceries*.)

Storm: A storm is a symbol of an emotional disturbance, since in most cases water is involved, and water is the ultimate symbol of emotions. Rain symbolizes tears and grief, and wind connects to thoughts and intellect. When these two elements of the human condition combine in very violent ways, a storm is born. A storm in your dream is evidence that some challenging situation in your life is either coming soon or just about to pass, as all storms move on eventually.

Stove: The implication behind the stove as a symbol is that something may soon be cooked. Since cooking food is directly connected to sustenance and nurturance, the stove in your dreams relates directly to the shape of your relationship to self-care. A working stove indicates that all is functional, whereas a stove that is broken or otherwise compromised is indicating that something about how you are providing for yourself needs to be examined.

Stranger: A person unknown to you is still representing a character aspect of your personality, even if his or her identity is concealed or the person is a stranger. When making an interpretation about a person you don't know, you must focus on what you actually do know. What the person is doing in your dream and how you feel about that will give you the essence of your interpretation. Whatever message your dream is presenting you with, the fact that it comes from a stranger or a person with a concealed identity indicates that the unconscious is not quite ready to reveal what is being called into action in your current situation. More will be revealed; we learn in stages and increments and often resist change, so be prepared for initial levels of fear to come up around this type of imagery. The unknown assailant who chases us may simply be trying to give us our forgotten lunch money or an umbrella because it is raining. When there are clear personality traits apparent and the person's identity is unknown to you, it likely points to an area of development within your own personal makeup. An angry or aggressive stranger may point to an integration of that energy into consciousness. A more helpful or gentle stranger indicates that softer elements are being called into prominence. Whatever end of the continuum your dream stranger is on, be prepared to consider the necessity and power of the energy he or she is embodying in the dream. A deliberate concealment of identity can also indicate a matter of the unconscious tricking the conscious into hearing a difficult piece of information; for just as in life, it is sometimes easier to hear impactful news from a stranger than from someone we love.

Strangling: You are feeling constricted in areas of communication. Since strangling involves cutting off the air supply at the neck, communication is the focus of the interpretation of any dream with this image in it. It is important to recognize that there is a specific intention associated with strangling, which is to cause death. Any death in a dream should be considered a transformation of such magnitude that an inevitable rebirth must surely follow. Strangling necessitates that two people are involved, which means that you should consider the other person as a character aspect of yourself. If you are the aggressor, then the person you are choking is a part of your personality that you are attempting to or needing to stifle.

Street: A street is part of the construct of a city or town where there are buildings on either side, as opposed to a road, which can be more rural in nature. All roads are symbols of your movement through life, so a street in a dream is more about places where you may actually stop and create some lasting element of your social experience. Consider the phrase "on the street where you live" as an indication of this symbol connecting to home or your community.

Strip Club: A strip club is an interesting location for a dream because it simultaneously represents elements of both the masculine and the feminine principle in action. It is a place that celebrates the female body and in this way expresses the power of the feminine. The objectification that goes on there indicates elements of the masculine principle in an undeveloped form. Issues of sexuality, seduction, and eroticism are the focus of such a dream setting; however, be willing to also consider that this energy is not in alignment or true integration. Sexual feelings may be pulling at you in an unbalanced way.

Stripper Pole: The pole around which a stripper dances is a symbol itself for the penis, and the dance itself is a seduction of the feminine principle interacting with the masculine principle. This dance can be symbolic of an erotic or sexual desire, but it can also be a symbol for stimulating the life force and creative impulses within you.

Stroke: You may be harboring destructive, negative thoughts, and they are having a dangerous impact on you. A stroke is caused by some sort of disturbance in the integrity of the brain. Caused by a blood clot or the eruption of a blood vessel, the damage that results from a stroke can range from innocuous discomfort to death. The brain is the symbolic center of the intellect and thoughts. When thoughts are compromised by some sudden challenge, a symbolic dream-stroke may occur if the cause is severe enough.

Stuffed Animal: One of the first staples of childhood comfort, a stuffed animal is primarily a symbol for affection and warmth. Your personal relationships with stuffed animals from your childhood should feature into your interpretation, as a person with a deep

connection to such things may be activating a sense memory of such comfort. Also consider the animal itself; there may be a connection to the power that the animal represents and the need to have a portable availability to such nurturing energy.

Submarine: A submarine is capable of diving to extreme depths and navigating the world far below the surface of the ocean. As the ocean represents the unconscious mind, the places where a submarine can go are akin to parts of the psyche that are absolutely down in the depths of the unconscious, but that ultimately can be explored in a limited fashion—like the thoughts, memories, and material that are usually buried but occasionally are investigated and made known. A submarine in a dream indicates that a deep investigation is underway, and anything else that such a dream expresses could be important information.

Subway: An underground world of its own, the subway system in any city can get you from one place to another without seeing the light of day. Any travel from one place to another in a dream represents a change or transformation. Since a subway ride is relatively short, the scope of the change it represents is also relatively minor. The idea that is being represented the most by this image in a dream has to do with being just under the surface of your consciousness. Such a dream indicates that you can learn something by doing a little investigation of what is lurking below and find yourself in some new territory as a result.

Succubus: The succubus is a mythological creature that is itself a feature of dreams. The succubus is the female version of this mythological creature, and it is thought to be a phantom that removes life force from its victim and is often a feature of night terrors. If you are visited by a succubus in your dream, look to where in your life some woman or other experience is draining you of passion and power. (See *Incubus*.)

Suit: Any article of clothing relates to your personal expression and the persona you are choosing to present to the world. Wearing a suit indicates a connection to more formal activities as well as to the workplace for many people. If you are wearing a suit in a dream, you may be calling upon a more serious aspect of your expression.

Suitcase: See *Bag, Luggage*.

Sun: The sun is the source of almost all life on Earth. The power contained within the sun is so enormous, it is almost unfathomable. To dream about the sun is to connect to this level of power within you.

Sunrise/Sunset: A sunrise may point to a new beginning, just as a sunset may indicate an ending of some sort. If your dream-sun is blocked by clouds, you may want to consider where in your life your personal power is being limited or held back.

Surgery: A healing is underway, though it is potentially disruptive and violent in nature. Surgery is usually thought of as a painful and invasive procedure undertaken when some form of healing needs to take place. In its essence, healing is a process that fundamentally alters the structure of some part of the body. All surgeries can be categorized as either removing or adding something to the body. If something is being removed, begin your investigation in areas of your life where you are facing loss or release. If you are being surgically enhanced with new material, such as replacement joints or a pacemaker, look to ways in which you are currently taking on new paths or ways of being that are foreign to you. No matter what the surgery is, there is an implication that some area in your consciousness requires dramatic healing.

Sweat: This is evidence of some underlying fear, shame, guilt, or stress. On a social level, sweat is sometimes evidence of inner stress. This can reveal the presence of guilt or panic that betrays the person. If you feel this may be the case in your dream, your interpretation should involve investigating secrets or issues in your waking life that you would rather keep hidden.

Sweating: You are working to restore balance because of stress, fear, or guilt. There are both emotional and physical correlations to sweating and the appearance of sweat. However, the essential meaning assigned to sweat must connect with its most basic and primal function: to regulate the temperature of the body. We would die if this process did not operate effectively. If you are sweating in your dream, your interpretation may uncover an unconscious message that some life experience is posing a threat to your equilibrium and balance. Heat represents a visceral reaction to perceived danger in the form of anger or aggression. Sweating represents your desire to restore balance from whatever might be the cause of those feelings of threat. Sweating also serves to rid the body of toxins, so dream-sweat may point to the presence of underlying thoughts, ideas, or behaviors that are ultimately poisoning your sense of well-being.

Swimming: You are navigating the waters of your own emotional journey. Water represents the emotional realm of our feelings, both conscious and unconscious. Swimming is specifically about progress and making your way through the emotional territory in your life. The effort of propelling yourself forward is completely self-motivated and generated exclusively by your own body. This reveals how effectively or ineffectively you are pushing yourself through an emotional challenge in your life. The ease, pace, and depth of your swim offer a great deal of texture for you to investigate. The harder you have to work, the more effort is required to arrive at your destination of emotional growth. How fast you are moving will inform you of the speed of the process you are undergoing. The level of immersion communicates the emotional territory through which you are traveling; being on the surface reflects the emotions you are aware of, whereas swimming underwater implies deeper feelings that reside in your unconscious mind.

Swimming Pool: Water connects to emotional issues. A swimming pool is a humanmade construction that contains a small amount of water that is used for recreation and relaxation. In this way, a swimming pool in a dream relates to a manageable amount of emotional expression that feels beneficial and not overwhelming. Swimming in a pool might relate to being in a comfortable emotional state or a need to control your emotions. To avoid jumping into a pool reflects a desire to rise above emotional issues. Drowning in a pool is to be overwhelmed by emotional issues of your own making.

Swimsuit: A bathing suit implies that the act of swimming has recently or will soon occur. Any image involving water in a dream relates to your feelings and emotions. Taking a swim is an act of immersing yourself in your emotional nature, so the bathing suit in your dream indicates a readiness to explore your emotional nature more deeply. There may also be an aspect of experiencing your feelings in a more playful and restorative manner indicated by such a dream.

Swings: Swinging is one of the first ways in which a child feels a sense of freedom and exhilaration. In this way, a swing is a symbol of both this sensation as well as the childlike innocence that allows for such easy access to those feelings. In a dream, a swing set indicates a longing for this aspect of your consciousness. If the swings in your dreams feel dangerous or are connected to an injury, then you are processing some stress around needing more freedom in your life.

Swing Set: A childlike sense of play is what is reflected in this image. The idea that something so simple can generate an enormous amount of joy is presented by a dream with a swing set in it. If you have personal associations with a swing set from your childhood, those should feature in your interpretation. Sometimes the most joyful images can show up with a sense of distortion in a nightmare. A nightmare simply means the stakes are higher; such a dream may be calling for more of this playfulness in your life as something more important than you might think.

Table: Since the primary cultural association with a table is eating meals, the symbolic nature of this object is about groups and connections, with a potential emphasis on the family. As such, a table in your dreams may be pointing to the quality of this construct within your own life. If there is a gathering around a table in a dream, look to those gathered for clues as to the qualities and skills you need to feed and therefore nurture at this time. The shape of the table has some significance as well. A round table harkens back to the mythology of King Arthur, where this shape was the first representation of democracy within leadership. A table that is broken or otherwise impaired signals an inability to gather inner strength.

Tadpoles: The frog is amphibious and can dwell in both the realms of the conscious and the unconscious, as represented by land and water. This intermediary state of tadpole signifies the natural order of things to begin in the inner realms before venturing out into the air. There is a connection to the tadpole and the notion of ideas that must swim around in the nurturing ponds of your mind before they are ready to spring forth into action.

Tail: Tails in the animal kingdom have a number of functions, from expressiveness to movement and balance. Since our most consistent relationship with this body part is through domesticated pets, it is the tail's ability to express anxiety and joy that is most likely the meaning of a tail in a dream. If you have a tail in a dream, it relates to both a return to primitive instincts as well as the transparency that comes when you can't hide your true feelings.

Taking a Test: You are having anxiety around being held accountable in some aspect of your life. Quizzes, tests, and exams are part of the structure of education that most people in the West first experience in childhood. This is imprinted in the brain as a permanent memory, associating the sensation of performance anxiety with images of being tested in school. In dreams, these become a metaphor for the ways in which we are tested by challenges in life. We only pass such tests if we have gained a sufficient level of knowledge from past lessons learned. When you dream of taking a test, your unconscious is letting you know that there is underlying anxiety around how prepared you feel to face your life. Examine your life for areas where you feel you are being held accountable, even if the only person holding you accountable is yourself. This is often a recurring dream for people who experience high levels of performance anxiety, a fear of failure, or frequent feelings of judgment from others. It can also indicate a hidden need to be acknowledged by those in authority in your life and to feel validated for your accomplishments. In this way, a test dream can be a compensation for feeling undervalued. (See *Exams, Pop Quiz, Quiz.*)

Talent Show: Two themes are involved in a talent show. The first is a public display of gifts and abilities. The second is the competition for the top spot. Such a dream may indicate a sense of a strong desire to have your gifts and talents recognized in the world. A secondary meaning may connect with feeling a sense of competition for such recognition—that there is only room for a limited amount of appreciation.

Tampon: A tampon is used to stop the flow of blood that connects with menstruation and reflects a desire for certain natural experiences to be tidier and cleaner than they naturally are. What flow in your life are you trying to stop from moving naturally because of some sense of shame or inhibition? There is an interesting use here of something phallic to alter something vaginal; look for where you are switching out a masculine approach when a feminine one would be more authentic.

Tape: There are many different kinds of tape, but the premise is the same: repairing some sort of damage to a flat surface by bonding to that surface, creating adhesion that keeps what had been torn apart in one piece. Tape is easy to use and ubiquitous, and herein lies the symbolic meaning: something needs a minor repair and there is a simple solution. Look to something in your life that can be easily mended.

Tapestry: A tapestry is a large, magnificent image created by the knitting together of thousands of different colored threads and yarns. This is a metaphor for life itself, a beautiful creation that can only be constructed one thread at a time. Look to the tapestry of your dreams to reflect how you are feeling about the overall arc of your life so far.

Tar: Tar is an organic petroleum substance that is very sticky. When it is put to good use, it can help make roads more durable and waterproof a roof. However, in its natural state tar has been known to lead to the demise of any animal unfortunate enough to get stuck in it. In this way, its dark and smelly quality represents elements of life that can be frightening, coarse, or unfortunate when ignored, but can turn into productive aspects when used properly. What challenge in your life are you not recognizing as an opportunity?

Tarot: The Tarot is a powerful community of archetypes that can be examined for their own individual meanings. If you are familiar with this divining tool, look to the specific images that arise in a dream as guidance coming from your inner wisdom. If you are not familiar with it, a visit from the Tarot may be your soul asking you to look to more esoteric means of spiritual expression.

Tattoo: The desire to ink your skin runs the gamut from a powerful need for self-expression or a tribal sense of symbolic presentation all the way to drunken regret. As such, in a dream you must consider your personal relationship with body ink before you arrive at a satisfying interpretation. Understand that on a universal level, there is a very rich tradition of adorning the skin this way in the development of human history across the ages.

Taxes: The inevitability of paying taxes evokes a great emotional response from most people. At the heart of this act are the principles of accountability and responsibility. If tax issues are part of your dream, this symbol may be reflecting a reaction to elements of your life that are asking you to be accountable in some way. To whom much is given, much is required. Additionally, the word "taxing" can indicate something that is burdensome or onerous.

Taxi: You may need to improvise in order to get your ideas into action. A taxi takes us from one place to a desired destination, and this is symbolic of a change or transformation that is brief or small in nature. The fact that you can get a taxi with ease by waving your hand or making a phone call speaks to the improvisational nature of how to get that change to manifest.

Tea: There is a great deal of ritual associated with tea, and despite the caffeine that some teas contain, the act of drinking tea is often associated with relaxation, civility, and calm. To be making tea in a dream is an indication of a desire to incorporate more of these gentle qualities into your life.

Teacher: A teacher in a dream is part archetype and part character aspect. The teacher is the one with the knowledge, and to dream of one is to be tapping into the part of you that knows. If the teacher is someone known to you, add the element of that person's personal qualities to your interpretation. The less you know of the teacher in a dream, the more you may be experiencing wisdom at an archetypal level. No matter how the teacher appears, consider that there may be something for you to learn. Learning occurs by accumulating small amounts of data that build upon each other. Teachers know what piece of information needs to be added next in order for learning to take place. A figure of authority, the teacher is the one person at school who knows what the lesson plan is. Teachers have both the questions and the answers. Not only do they control what happens in the classroom, but they also know why things are ordered in a particular way. Each of our teachers presents us with the specific information needed to master a particular level of our functioning. Any teacher in a dream represents the part of you that understands this concept of step-by-step mastery and provides the mental environment in which learning occurs, or is blocked. There is great patience built into this process, even though many of your teachers in life may have lacked this quality. When a teacher appears in your dream, examine the person as a character aspect of yourself. The teacher's behavior toward you in the dream and your resulting feelings will offer insight as to how well your inner guidance system is operating and to what degree you are showing yourself patience with the pace of your growth. A kindly teacher will result in a very different interpretation from one who is abusive or frightening.

Teeth: Teeth connect to abundance and prosperity. When interpreting this symbol, please understand that money is only one form of abundance and prosperity. Teeth attract love by revealing themselves in a smile. They can protect you by exposing themselves through a frown as an aggressive snarl. They also assist in the body's ability to take in sustenance. It is in this way that teeth symbolize prosperity by virtue of being the arbiter of love, protection, and nurturance.

Teeth Falling Out: You are feeling insecure about some area of your life. Teeth serve three primary functions. They allow us to process our food so we can nurture ourselves. They express joy when revealed in a smile, and they can indicate aggression when exposed in a snarl. All of these things—nurturance, joy, and protection—connect directly to security and well-being. If individuals cannot nurture themselves, attract loving connections, and protect themselves from danger, the basic constructs of a secure life are not likely to be available to them. Without these three important parts of life, fear will prevail. Therefore, when this dream image appears, issues of personal security are at the forefront of your unconscious expression. There are various levels of intensity associated with this symbol. It can fluctuate from a slightly loose tooth to having all your teeth crumble out of your mouth in a bloody mess. The scale of intensity of the dream will indicate the amount of fear being expressed. Whether it is a general fear of being out of control, looking bad, aging, or some other issue of unmet needs, the appearance of this dream indicates underlying insecurity in some area of your waking life. The teeth are used for chewing, and this association can indicate a need to "chew on something for a while," as in mulling over a choice or course of action. "Sinking your teeth into something" refers to taking on life wholeheartedly. Losing your teeth in a dream could indicate an inability or unwillingness to do so. Losing our teeth as children is such a powerful rite of passage. On some level, losing your teeth in a dream will connect to the process of growing up, even in adulthood.

Telephone: Staying connected with others is at the heart of this symbol, which is rapidly becoming an obsolete item as more and more people abandon their telephones for the portable benefit of the cell phone as their only means of connection. No matter what form the phone takes, the meaning of communication and instant gratification applies. If every person in a dream is a reflection of the dreamer, the phone is the power of the connectedness of thought. (See *Cell Phone*.)

Television: The collective consciousness and the concept of manufactured truth are represented by a television in a dream. Television represents this collective thought in action. Through programming, especially the news, there is an almost hypnotic experience in the Western world that makes the general population accept what is seen in TV as the truth about life, whether or not that is actually so. The line between what is truth and what is fiction is continually blurred, and this has increased with the advent of so-called reality television. The proximity between yourself and the television in your dream should be considered to represent your current relationship to the impact that television and its content is having on your life. Some people never watch TV, while others are addicted. Where you fit on this continuum will affect how you view this symbol in a dream. First examine the landscape of the dream for an accurate, contextual theme of what messages the dream might be offering you. Then filter this through the perspective that television always presents manufactured truth. Ask yourself how you might be being manipulated by what other people think as opposed to your own authentic notions about life. It may be time to turn the television off and start living life in real time.

Temple: You are dreaming of connecting to your spiritual nature in a more conventional way. Churches, temples, and mosques are the center of spiritual life for any community. Just like a house in a dream, any building can be interpreted as representing one's current sense of self. In this way, any place of worship ultimately points to your relationship with spirituality and religion. Because this element of life can be particularly controversial, it is very important that you make a clear distinction between the universal meaning of a temple as connecting to matters of spirituality and whatever personal feelings you harbor about organized religion. If a temple is not your typical house of worship, your dream may be asking you to consider the similarities and not the differences between different sets of religious dogma. (See *Church, Mosque*.)

Termite: The primary element of the termite's existence that illumines its symbolic meaning is its destructive powers. Hidden from view, termites can completely destroy the structural integrity of a building and are a homeowner's worst nightmare. If you see a few termites, there may be hundreds unseen eroding the foundation of something you hold dear. When termites appear in a dream, be prepared to look beneath the surface for evidence that some structure in your life may be being eaten away.

Terrorist: Terrorists create an enormous amount of death and destruction based on the fundamental belief that they are doing the right thing, usually out of a profound sense of spiritual faith. If you are feeling disenfranchised, such strong urges can erupt into a violent reaction. If a terrorist is featured in a dream, be on the lookout for misdirected passions.

Test: See *Exams, Pop Quiz, Quiz, Taking a Test*.

Testicles: The testicles are the source of power in the masculine principle. Testicles featured in a dream relate to connecting with male fertility and the capacity to disseminate great amounts of creative energy. There may or may not be a sexual element involved.

Texting: Texting relates to the notion of instantaneous communication and the desire to get your thoughts connected to another person with a sense of immediacy. Texting has become such a standard part of modern society that it may have very little symbolic meaning beyond this desire to make an instant connection.

Theater: A place devoted to the presentation of created stories, a theater in a dream is a place where people gather to share a common experience. Any building in a dream is symbolic of an idea or a belief system that you have. This particular one is about themes that occur in the collective and have to do with social conformity or community agreement. If your dream takes place in a theater, you may be exploring ways in which your community or social experience is playing out the story of your life.

Therapist: A therapist is a symbol for a character aspect that relates to the part of you that is wise and helpful. It is common to dream of your therapist when you are actively in therapy. This indicates that an internalization of the therapeutic process is occurring. If the therapist is not someone known to you, then you are activating the part of you that can guide you with wisdom and clarity.

Three: When two are gathered, eventually their energy will create a new element, and a third is born. Three is the number of creativity and is a powerful energy. There are many examples of the concept of three: mother, father, and child is perhaps the most universal. The Holy Trinity in Catholicism is another instance. The artist, the paint, and the finished work is just one case that can be applied to any creative endeavor. In music, a triad is the simplest and perhaps most pleasing harmony. In the world of geometry, it is only when you have three points to work with that you can create an actual shape. The shadow challenge of three is a lack of grounding and separation from reality. This is because three relates so strongly to the drive to create that feeling unable to do so would be the fear-based side of this energy.

Throat: The throat is the seat of all communication, and anything that occurs in this area of the body in a dream relates to issues you are having around your voice, such as owning it and communicating from an authentic and strong perspective. Many dreams that involve the throat include challenges and compromise, from violent attacks to permutations of the body. Whatever is happening in the dream with your throat, consider it a description of how you are using your voice in your current life circumstances and relationships.

Thunder: You are seeing evidence of dramatic moments of enlightenment. Thunder is the auditory evidence of the presence of lightning. If lightning is to be understood as a sudden burst of enlightenment and awareness that appears in an instant and changes things forever, thunder is the booming announcement that comes along with the moment. There is an old method of determining one's distance from lightning strikes by counting the number of seconds between the lightning strike and the clap of thunder that follows. If thunder and lightning are both present in the dream, it raises the stakes of the dream. It can also point to the distinction between a moment of awareness and the secondary impact of the change it initiates.

Tick: You are feeling pestered by nagging thoughts that are slowly draining your motivation and life force. A tick is an insect that grabs on to flesh and sucks blood for its own sustenance. Blood is symbolic of passion and life force, and to lose even a little bit can represent the small ways in which annoying thoughts of negativity can slowly deplete your sense of well-being. To be infested with ticks is to recognize that the tipping point has come and your negativity is beginning to overwhelm you.

Ticket: A ticket is a symbol for the power and right to enter. What the ticket is for adds an important distinction to how to interpret it as an image in a dream. At the heart of it, the ticket represents the possibility of some sort of an adventure. A theater or movie ticket connects to a desire to see your life a certain way. A ticket for any sort of transportation reflects the need to make a more drastic change. Losing a ticket symbolizes that you feel that the opportunity for something has potentially passed you by.

Tie: The tie is an adornment and in this way connects to personal self-expression. Because it is worn around the neck, it highlights issues of communication and speaking with a powerful ownership of your voice. A tie can represent a sense of restriction where responsibility is concerned.

Tiger: The tiger is the ultimate animal symbol for strength and sensuality and is also connected to vitality and health. When a tiger appears in a dream, you are being acquainted with a powerful totem to guide you through any difficulty. Tiger medicine is the perfect antidote to fear and aversion, for the courage, strength, and cunning associated with this animal are without parallel.

Tightrope: Originally part of a circus act, the tightrope is an extremely narrow path for a person to traverse as an act of thrill. If you are walking a tightrope in a dream, you may feel as if some circumstance in your life has you in a very precarious situation. Something may be asking you to move very, very slowly and constantly check in for a sense of balance.

Time Travel: The ability to move through time is a fascinating dream symbol, for in dreams time has no limitation whatsoever. In this way, if you are dreaming of time travel as a concept, it is the desire to shift time perspectives in your waking life that may be inspiring such a dream. To go back in time relates to altering an error or regrettable choice. To move forward implies a desire to escape present circumstances.

Tiptoe: A more delicate approach to something may be required. When you walk on the tips of your toes, you reduce the evidence of your presence by making less noise and impact. This is beneficial when you desire to make less of an impression. However, there is a consequence to this, as you relinquish power and a sense of being grounded. The context of the dream in which you are walking on tiptoe will give you more insight as to whether this act is beneficial or inhibiting. If a character in your dream is walking on tiptoe, then the aspect of yourself that the person represents is looking to remain less visible.

Tires: The tires of any vehicle are what give it traction and allow it to move with relative ease. The state of the tires in a dream relates to your journey on the path through your life as well as how grounded that journey is. A flat tire indicates a temporary obstacle that halts your movement. Missing tires are the same, only the challenge is greater and the delay longer.

Toes: The toes are about balance and finesse with regard to your movement through life. They can also be a source of adornment and self-expression. Something happening to the toes in a dream may indicate that there are some obstacles impeding you. A stubbed toe is an error in judgment that gets your immediate attention.

Toilet: See *Bathroom*.

Tomb: A tomb is a building that houses the dead. A building in a dream represents some construct of your thought process or your consciousness. A tomb, therefore, is elements of your consciousness that are no longer active and considered dead and buried. A tomb in a dream may relate to the past.

Tombstone: A tombstone marks a place where someone is buried. In the world of dreams, the death of a person is usually a sign that some way of being in the world is no longer serving you and needs to be sacrificed in order for growth and expansion to occur. A tombstone indicates a need or desire to stay somewhat connected to that part of your psyche. For more layers of an interpretation, consider who the tombstone is representing; whoever the person is, it is the qualities that he or she possesses that have been released. The tombstone indicates that the process has already occurred.

Tongue: Anything involving the tongue relates to your ability to articulate in the world of communication. Conversely, the tongue could also relate to the sense of taste and the quality of life that taste brings to the experience of eating. The tongue is symbolic of our innate human desire to be understood and relates to issues around communication. This can reflect everything from being soft-spoken to possessing a sharp tongue. If communication is too passive, the speaker may be rendered ineffective. If it is too pointed or overly direct, wounding can occur, often in opposition to the communicator's intention. A damaged tongue could indicate a need for you to examine how effective you are in this area. If your tongue is paralyzed, you may not be speaking powerfully enough to achieve your intentions in your waking life.

Tool Belt: If you dream of a tool belt, you may be faced with a time in your life when you need ready access to various problem-solving approaches. Tools connect with the masculine principle of doing things, and having such choices at hand is what a tool belt signifies.

Tools: Tools are for fixing and building, and as such, they relate to a masculine approach to problem-solving. If you dream of tools, there may be some obstacle or challenge in your life that requires a hands-on approach to be solved. Consider the type of tool. A hammer indicates that a strong and definitive step should be taken. A screwdriver may imply the need to work your way slowly into the meaning of a problem. More complex tools may relate to the need to approach a situation with a level of finesse and sophistication.

Toothbrush: The teeth are directly connected to the security that comes when you can nurture and protect yourself and attract love. The toothbrush is a symbol of the ongoing care needed to sustain these security-building abilities.

Toothpaste: Similar to a toothbrush, toothpaste is a tool that connects to caring for the teeth, the symbol of security and the ability to attract love and take in sustenance. Toothpaste is more in alignment with keeping the teeth attractive and healthy, and so in a dream it represents having this ability at hand. However, like many elements of self-care, you have to use it for it to do any good.

Top: You are stuck thinking the same thoughts repeatedly. A spinning top represents the way in which something repeating over and over again has the power to keep you stuck in one place.

Torch: Flames are always a symbol of great change and transformation. A torch is often used to light dark places, and as such, it is a symbol of being able to see just enough of what is usually hidden to make your way through a period of change. Also consider that "carrying a torch" is a common phrase for maintaining a pervasive connection to someone you no longer are connected to in a romantic fashion.

Tornado: There may be destructive forces brewing in your consciousness that are emerging out of opposing energies. These weather phenomena are incredibly destructive and completely unpredictable in their movement. The devastation that they leave in their wake is almost unfathomable, but there is also an element of creation present, as their symbolic meaning lies in their formation. A tornado is the result of two air masses of very different temperatures colliding with each other. Under the right conditions, these two systems meet up with each other and each tries to force the other to submit to their direction of movement. As a result of this conflict, the two form a third energetic system that combines the force of both, creating a tornado. Resistance is at the essence of the interpretation of this image, so when a tornado appears in a dream, look for areas in your life where you may be in resistance. In addition, the chaotic nature of a tornado's path makes this a perfect expression of waking-life chaos. This dream may be indicating an unconscious reaction to the unpredictable nature of how things are unfolding around you, especially in areas where you are facing direct opposition to your desires.

Torture: At the heart of torture is the desire for information to be revealed; the moment the torturer is satisfied, there is freedom. Are you harboring secrets or a hidden agenda that has you suffering in some way? There may be some secret truth that you are holding back when torture appears in a dream.

Tour: A tour is a safe and contained way to explore a foreign landscape. If that foreign landscape is a symbol for some unknown territory in your own consciousness, then the meaning of a tour in a dream is the assistance desired when exploring deeper realms of parts of you that you have yet to meet. Consider the location of the tour in your dream and add any personal associations you have with it to your interpretation.

Tow Truck: A car is a symbol for how you are moving along your path in life. A tow truck implies that the car is not working for some reason, and the tow truck is your symbolic access to being able to make the proper repairs and be on your way. If you are feeling stuck in your life, the tow truck indicates that you will soon be moving again.

Tower: A tower offers a vantage point in the defending of a fortress, and in this way the symbolic meaning of a tower connects with con-

sciousness that is higher. You may be seeking higher ground in terms of your aspirations. However, the tower is also synonymous with a prison, and as such, you can be locked in the tower if your thinking is too myopic. How has a particular idea about something in your life imprisoned you?

Toys: If you dream of toys, you may be expressing an impulse and a desire to return to the playfulness of childhood and a more innocent time in your development. You must decide if the toys in your dream indicate that this impulse is a supportive and creative move toward incorporating more childlike qualities into your daytime life in a productive way, or if you are expressing a desire to escape your adult responsibilities.

Tractor: The tractor is a staple in farming, increasing the level of productivity exponentially by dramatically increasing the workload potential in the field. Farming becomes a symbol for all creativity, and the tractor is the symbolic tool for increasing your efficacy in creating abundance. Part of what a tractor accomplishes is digging deeper into the earth, so a tractor in a dream may also symbolize the desire to become more grounded and dig deeper into your consciousness.

Traffic: Vehicles are so much a part of modern life that as a symbol in a dream they can represent the ways in which your outer or social experience in the world is constantly moving and results in a sense of chaos. In this way, a traffic jam is a symbol of when there is too much of this attempted movement and things get backed up. Are you attempting to do too much at once? Are there things you would like to accomplish, but other things, such as responsibilities or obligations, are getting in the way?

Traffic Light: A traffic light manages the flow of vehicles on the road. In the world of symbolism, traffic represents the myriad thoughts that are constantly rushing through your mind. The traffic light is a symbol of control and restraint and represents an attempt to minimize chaos in your life. If the light was red, you may need to stop and pause in some undertaking that is currently unfolding. A green light suggests that it's time to take action. A yellow light is asking you to bring some caution to how you are moving about in your current circumstances. A broken traffic light indicates that your ability to control the movement of your thoughts is not working properly and may be causing some anxiety, stress, or depression.

Trail: A trail is symbolic of being on some sort of a journey. Since a trail is usually related to something that is found in a more natural setting, the journey that is being expressed in this dream is more closely related to something personal about your nature—an inner journey as opposed to your public life. The quality of the trail and the things that happen while you are on this trail will give you more insight into what this dream means.

Trailer: A trailer is a home and in this way is ultimately a symbol of your sense of self at the time of the dream. The function of a trailer is to allow such a home to be mobile and easily moved from one place to another. This movement is symbolic of change and transformation such that the essential self as rep-

resented by the trailer is unchanged. Such an image in a dream might indicate that outside circumstances are shifting in your life and there is a desire to maintain a connection to your essential self as you allow those changes to unfold.

Trailer Park: A community of mobile homes, a trailer park may be a literal representation of your world if you actually live in one. If you think of each separate home as a thought or an idea, then the symbol of a trailer park is about many congruent ideas gathered together. But though there are many thoughts that are in agreement in this symbolic homestead, they also represent ideas about which you have some flexibility or willingness to easily change. What areas of your life seem permanent but ultimately are not?

Train: You are undergoing a pretty significant change or transformation. Any vehicle that moves you from one location to another signifies that big shifts are occurring. A train is much faster than a car but slower than a plane. In this way, being on a train in your dream means that there is a medium amount of transformation going on in your life. A train is a type of public transportation, so the changes that are taking place are more likely to relate to your public rather than your private life. The state of the train, such as its age and the shape it is in, will offer you more distinctions to add to your interpretation.

Train Station: A train is a vehicle of transportation and as such represents a change or transformation in your life. The station is the waiting spot that implies that such a change either has just been completed or is just about to begin.

Train Tracks: Train tracks symbolize a desire for change or the imminent sense of danger that upcoming change portends. If the train represents change itself, then the tracks connect to the possibility of shift and change that could be occurring but at present is not yet happening. Train tracks have a measure of danger connected to them because a train could come along at any moment, putting you in peril. In this way, a dream that takes place on train tracks could be pointing to the possibility that some dramatic change is on its way and, when it arrives, has the potential for causing fear or destruction. The tracks that carry a train indicate all the places a train might go. One interpretation relates to the potential for movement and travel. There is a very powerful association with train tracks as a dividing line between classes, as in the "other side of the tracks." Which side of the tracks are you on in your dream?

Transsexual: The expression of gender in our culture is very complex and ultimately misunderstood by most people, making this image in a dream equally complex. If the transsexual experience is something you are familiar with, your dream may simply be an exploration of the different ways in which roles in the world are much more fluid than most people imagine. At the heart of this symbol is the switching between the masculine and feminine principles, between doing and being. The presence of a transsexual character in a dream may be asking you to consider the opposite point of view in some

situation in your current life. When you imagine that taking action is best, perhaps being still is what is called for. When you have traditionally been slow to move, taking bold action may be a more powerful choice.

Trap Door: You may be harboring some secrets. A trap door indicates that there is a landscape below that is separated from the rest of your current consciousness. This can imply something that is being kept hidden. Your job is to determine what, if anything, is below you; do you know what it is, and how do you feel about the possibilities inherent in this structure? A trap door may suddenly swing open and capture someone, adding an element of risk and deceit to the mix.

Traveling: Travel is a common dream theme that relates to how you are moving through life. It is best to break this symbol down into very basic segments. The location you are leaving is likely tied in with your past and elements of your life that you are letting go of and moving away from. Your destination, if there is one, may offer clues to where you are heading or desire to be. An unknown destination can point to a need to move your life into new territory, even though you may not currently be aware of what that might look like. The emotional qualities of the traveling can provide a good snapshot of how your unconscious is responding to your current life path and the movement inherent on your journey. The mode of travel will reveal issues around the way your life is supporting the desires you have. The effectiveness of your vehicle and the control you are able to exert over your direction may be a reflection of how these themes are playing out in your waking life. The obstacles that present themselves are to be considered as a barometer for challenges you are facing that may be impeding your progress. Being stuck or unable to control where you are going might connect to some element of your life that is stagnant. The speed of travel is important to determine how fast an area of life is moving. A train might indicate things speeding out of control, whereas a cruise ship could feel impossibly slow. Very often, only a small part of a journey is what appears in a dream. In this case, the context and location will help identify what specific path of life needs to be examined by stopping and paying closer attention.

Treadmill: Though there is great benefit to be gained from using a treadmill during waking life as a way to exercise, as a symbol one must consider the futility of running but staying in the same place. If a treadmill is featured in a dream, you may be feeling that your actions are getting you nowhere.

Tree: Trees can represent your growth through life, with the roots connecting to where you come from and how you are grounded in your experience. The trunk is the part of the tree that most relates to your personal life and your physical body. The branches of the tree connect to the different choices you make during the course of your life—your relationships, your interactions with family, and the different modes of expression you choose. Trees also connect with your family of origin and your ancestry through the image of the family tree. Trees are deeply

grounded in the earth but also reach into the sky, so in a dream landscape they connect to the balance between your instincts and your intellect.

Trial: At the heart of a trial is the principle of right and wrong, and the process of deciding what is true. You may dream about a trial when you are feeling guilty about something or when you are being accused of something you are innocent of. The word "trial" is synonymous with any very challenging situation, and such a dream image may appear when you are facing anything in life that feels onerous and difficult.

Truck: This is a practical symbol that relates to how you are moving through your life. As with any mode of transportation, a truck connects symbolically with the movement on one's path through life. A vehicle that is not your usual mode of transportation points to an underlying shift in perspective of where your life is heading. A truck is a utility vehicle that is used when there is a need to move heavy cargo with ease. When one appears in a dream, the need being expressed connects to traveling into new territory that may require a considerable inventory of resources. The size, structure, and purpose of the truck in your dream will give you the most informative clues for your interpretation. In identifying the truck's specific use, you will have a better sense of the shift that is underlying this symbol's meaning. A moving van has implications that are far greater than a pickup truck might have, as one indicates the need for a complete reorganization of some aspect of your unconscious while the other implies only a minor alteration. A truck with towing capacity points to the need to carry something old and broken into the new landscape that is emerging. A more specialized vehicle, such as a cement truck or a construction vehicle, might lead you to consider what structural or foundational changes in your life may have sparked this image. The body type, age, and color of the vehicle can also be considered for shades of meaning. An older truck could mean that you've made this change before, whereas something new could be commenting on the newness of what you are going through.

Tsunami: The ocean is a symbol for the unconscious mind and the overwhelming emotions that can emerge from such a deep place. A tsunami results from an earthquake, which is a symbol for a great disruption that happens after a great buildup of pressure. A tsunami is a symbol for the unavoidable emotional upheaval that can result from unexpected changes in your current landscape. This is a common recurring dream image that relates to the ways in which the emotional cycles of life can be challenging and overwhelming.

Tumor: A tumor forms when cells divide faster than is considered normal. In this way, a tumor is a symbolic representation of the damage that can occur when things are allowed to get so chaotic as to be completely out of control. Over time, such chaos can lead to drastic consequences, and the damage may be done long before it is discovered. A tumor in a dream represents something that has been going on under the surface for a while but that is now demanding attention to be healed.

Tunnel: You are making a transition through lower levels of consciousness. A tunnel allows for movement underground and safe passage underneath a body of water or other above-ground landscape. Being inside of a tunnel connects to a transition into new territory in your life. The part of this transition represented by the tunnel itself is the most difficult part, often characterized by a sense of loss and lack of direction. Very often when you are inside a tunnel that is symbolic of a transition, you may not know where you are coming from and, even more frightening, where you are going to wind up. The thing most often looked for while in a tunnel is the light at the end, so there can be a sense of hope in uncertainty.

Turkey: Though a turkey is a bird and therefore merits some attention as an animal totem, in the United States it is almost entirely synonymous with the Thanksgiving holiday.

Turtle: "Slow and steady wins the race" is the credo of the turtle. Patience and fortitude are the hallmarks of the medicine associated with this animal totem. When a turtle appears in your dream, you are being gifted with the patience you may need for any endeavor. Since turtles are also symbolic of self-protection, due to the fact that they carry their homes on their backs and can retreat at any moment, their appearance in a dream may be reminding you that no matter what the circumstances are, you are always safe.

Two: When a second joins the one and two is formed, a partnership is created. The concept of relativity evolves out of the energy of two, as the one has something to which it experiences itself as relative to. The one can now know itself as self, because there is that which is "other." All of the elements of two are embodied in this idea: partnership, duality, opposites, yin/yang, balance, and sharing, to name just a few. The shadow side of two is the potential for collapsing into one another and losing the sense of self.

UFO: This is a dream that includes the exploration of very high levels of consciousness. Much time has passed since the UFO craze swept into our consciousness. Since then, the term "unidentified flying object" has permanently entered our cosmopolitan vocabulary. For the sake of defining this term, a UFO is referring to any extraterrestrial mechanism of travel as it may appear in a dream, no matter how fantastic or out of the realm of possibility it may appear to be. As with any mode of transportation, the essential meaning must connect to your path in life. Clearly, if you are traveling through outer space or being visited by beings from outer space, you are dreaming of some deviation from your more grounded life on Earth, and your interpretation should incorporate some sense of this atypical, expansive exploration. Typically, this image in a dream will spark either fear or fascination, or some combination of both. Your reaction to your UFO dream experience will inform you of your emotional relationship with esoteric elements of spirituality that the dream is trying to express. Being abducted adds a shade of meaning that connects to expanding processes of thought that may be occurring in your unconscious, whether you want them to or not. If this is the case, look to your present circumstances to where you may be feeling forced to think way outside of your usual thought paradigms. If you were not abducted but were actually proactive and perhaps even motivated to go with the aliens, this may indicate a readiness to explore new intellectual territory in some area of your waking life. Seeing a UFO from the ground could be a precursor to new, higher levels of consciousness that are making themselves known to you before they fully arrive. Your emotional reaction to what you are seeing in your dream will illuminate for you how open or resistant you are at this time to the inevitable expansion of consciousness that comes when you step onto any path of self-investigation.

Ukulele: Any dream with a musical instrument may be a call to being more creatively expressive. However, a ukulele is a fairly obscure instrument, and the call here may be to explore something that is off the beaten path or truly unique. A ukulele is extremely portable as well, so the need to have ready access to your unique sense of creative expression may be what this dream means.

Umbilical Cord: This is the first place where your needs get met as a human being. In fact, with an umbilical cord, there is no distance between a need and its immediate fulfillment. In this lies the symbolic meaning of the notion that all needs get met. There can be a hidden meaning in a dream that features this symbol of wishing to return to a time when you did not have to work for what you desire.

Umbrella: When an umbrella appears in your dream, you feel you need protection from emotional experiences or unwanted expression of emotion. Water relates to emotions, and of all the ways in which we experience water in nature, rain is the most like crying. An umbrella is the standard-issue object designed to keep you dry in what ought to be a very wet experience. In this way, an umbrella in a dream connects to a desire to stay as unaffected by some emotional outpouring as you possibly can. This could be your own feelings or the emotional expressions of others in your life.

Uncle: All people in your dream represent aspects of yourself. An uncle connects to family history as it relates to the previous generation, so he will have a loose connection to a life view generated by your parents. The fact that he is a sibling to one of your parents allows you to see the influence of the generational dynamic without the direct challenges of the child/parent relationship. An uncle of yours appearing in a dream is asking you to consider how some waking-life issue relates to family history and patterns. (See *Family*.)

Undertow: Water is the symbol for emotions and that which is in the unconscious mind. The waves at the beach represent the way in which material from this hidden and mysterious place constantly interacts with our conscious mind as represented by land. The undertow is a profound place where the interplay of simultaneous movement toward and away from the shore is dynamic and powerful. It is the unseen force that can drag you away if you are not careful in your explorations of this potentially dangerous realm. It represents the fear of being overwhelmed by what is in your unconscious mind.

Underwater: Water is symbolic of the emotional side of the human experience. To dream of being underwater is about being immersed in the nature of your feelings. A common dream is to be able to breathe and move with ease underwater; this represents a level of grace and ease with a current emotional situation. Fear of being underwater reflects the opposite. If it is you that is underwater, then it is your own life experience that is being expressed. If someone else is underwater, then the aspect of your character that the person represents may be key to what is creating an upheaval of feelings.

Underwear: All clothing represents our self-expression on some level. Additionally, clothing can be thought of as protection against the elements. Both of these concepts are reflected in the symbolic meaning of clothing. Underwear takes these concepts to a level of privacy and intimacy because they are worn under your outer clothes, make direct contact with your body, and act primarily as covering for the sexual areas. In this way, underwear represents your desire to keep a lid on your sexuality. Also to be considered is the layered desire to protect yourself from being completely vulnerable; if you are in your underwear in your dream, you are certainly exposed, but are not as vulnerable as you might otherwise be. Your mother always warned you to wear clean underwear in case you got into an accident and had to be taken to the hospital. This element of being prepared for exposure also relates to the shame associated with our most private experiences of being human.

Undress: The act of undressing is about exposure and vulnerability. This can be either terrifying or erotic, or somewhere in between. No matter what the circumstances or sensations around undressing or being undressed in a dream, consider your interpretation as ultimately about being willing to expose your most private and vulnerable self. If you are being undressed or undressing in the dream,

it is you who is experimenting with being more open. If other people are involved, consider the character aspects of you that they may be representing and you will see that there is some area of your life that needs a more vulnerable approach. Such a dream may also be expressing a feeling of invasiveness from a relationship or experience in your life where your boundaries are being invaded.

Unicorn: This magical creature is a powerful symbol of magic and spiritual purity. It is an ancient symbol that has permeated modern media more than any other creature. The unicorn is a white creature and in this way connects to purity and the highest vibration of life. It can fly, which increases this ascension sensibility. In some ways, its very name contains some of its power as a totem; the unicorn has a single horn, which means it is free from duality and recognizes the oneness of all. A visit from a unicorn in a dream is to be connected to some very powerful medicine, and you can consider yourself to be guided by strong spiritual forces.

Uniform: A uniform is a symbol itself; the nature of the outfit defines the wearer very specifically in a particular role, as uniforms are designed to be instantly recognizable for the discipline they relate to. In order to understand such a dream, you must first identify the uniform itself and the qualities associated with someone who might wear it. In most cases, the archetype most associated with a uniform falls in the warrior category, which relates to the principle of dividing everything into either right or wrong. To dream of wearing a uniform is to desire to connect to the energy that the uniform represents. If someone in your dream is wearing a uniform, there is a part of your personality that is needed to face some current life circumstance.

United Nations: This is a symbol for world peace. If the United Nations features prominently in your dream, you may be connecting to a collective energy around issues that are currently affecting the planet as a whole. This image can also be interpreted on a more personal level as representing the possibility that various ideas and beliefs within you that are ultimately contradictory may be able to be integrated, turning dissonance into harmony within yourself.

UPC Code: This invention of the modern world is a complex identification system. It features several sets of codes within a large string of numbers that relates to a manufacturer and all of its available products. This code is used to track movement and profit. In a dream, it relates to the desire to stay connected to all of your thoughts and ideas in order to be able to take advantage of the opportunities within your mind.

Uphill: This is symbolic of exertion in your current life's journey. Any path in a dream, such as a road, trail, or walkway, connects to your journey through life. The degree of inclination is key to understanding how your unconscious is experiencing the current level of stress involved. This should be applied literally to the interpretation of how you are experiencing some life experience. While going uphill can be exhausting and debilitating, a modicum of exertion can also be very stimulating and the accomplishment of the climb can be very satisfying. If you are debilitated in life in some way, challenged movement in your dream could be an expression of frustration with your limitations. If the uphill journey in your dream stops your ability to move at all, you may be working out feelings of inadequacy and may be shut down in the face of a life challenge. If there is a view at the top of the hill, you may be looking at the motivating forces that underlie your current choices.

Upstairs: The level or floor in a building is directly related to various levels of thought and consciousness. Higher levels are connected to more conscious awareness and that to which we aspire. Anything connected to the ability to move upward is a symbolic representation of this desire to ascend.

Urinal: Urination connects to toxicity or anger that needs to be released. As a receptor for urine, a urinal relates to the consciousness of releasing this toxicity in a neat and ordered manner.

Urination: The release of toxicity is the primary meaning of this symbol. Urination in a dream may be pointing to a buildup of negative thoughts or unexpressed anger, hence the phrase "pissed off." There is a sexual subculture in which urinating on someone or being urinated on by another is considered highly erotic. It is also a symbol of the hierarchy of power between two individuals. In sexual role play, while it may appear that the dominant party holds more power by virtue of the act itself, in actuality the receiver, or "bottom," is the one with the control in any interaction. Therefore, in any dream involving this sort of activity, consider that if you are the giver, you may be experiencing toxic backlash in some area in life where you are being insensitive or lacking compassion. If you are on the receiving end of urination, then you may want to consider where in your life you may be compromising yourself through manipulation or some other hidden motivation. There can be a physiological function involved in this dream image, and the body may assist in the unconscious process: if you have to pee, you just might dream about it first. This does not alter the interpretive meaning, and such a dream deserves investigation of its imagery as much as any other.

Usher: An usher's ultimate job is to offer assistance in a setting where finding a seat is paramount. The idea of sitting for an event has to do with being grounded, safe, and available for whatever is being presented. If you dream of an usher, you are tapping into the part of you that can assist in your readiness to receive something of significance, such as new information, or to witness an important shift in your life.

U-turn: Inherent in this maneuver is the option at any moment to reverse your direction and choose to go back the way you came. This is different from a standard turn because it implies returning to some point of origination. Look to see where in your life a choice that you made in your past is one that you wish you could unmake.

Uvula: The uvula is the thing that hangs down in the back of your throat. Its function is primarily related to the articulation of certain sounds within the range of human speech. It can often swell when there is an infection being fought by the body and, when stimulated, can cause a gag or retching reflex. If something is occurring with the uvula in a dream, it should be considered as describing in symbolic terms your ability to fully express yourself.

Vacation: The essence of any vacation is the change in routine. In a dream, to be on a vacation is to be feeling a call to change the elements of your life that feel tedious and repetitive.

Vaccine: A vaccine protects from certain diseases by introducing a small and manageable amount of the infectious agent into the system, creating an immune response that is ultimately protective. In this way, the sensibility being expressed by a vaccine connects to moving toward something in order to build up an ability to tolerate it. In a dream, this symbol suggests that your fears would be best conquered by facing them a little at a time.

Vacuum: A vacuum is the absence of everything we experience as air and atmosphere, so at the heart of this symbol is emptiness. Through this emptiness, the technology of a vacuum cleaner is helpful at removing unwanted dirt and debris. In this way, a vacuum cleaner symbolizes this desire. However, there is a more sinister meaning that could be present when this shows up in a dream in that a pervasive feeling of emptiness can suck the life force out of you if you are not mindful.

Vagina: The vagina is the ultimate symbol of the power of the feminine principle of creativity and receptivity. This can have sexual connotations and also be an expression of primal productivity. A man dreaming of having a vagina is connecting deeply to his inner feminine on an archetypal level. The same is true for a woman, but without the archetypal meaning.

Valentine: A modern-day symbol for romantic love, Valentine's Day offers some people a connection to romance and inspires cynicism in others. Both perspectives exist in the collective consciousness. If the physical structure of a valentine features in your dream, you are likely expressing a wish to connect in a romantic way, either with a specific person or with the nature of romantic love in general. If it is the day itself that features in your dream, examine your personal associations with this holiday for a more accurate interpretation.

Valet: The valet is the intermediary between driving and a particular destination. If driving connects to your movement through your life and a destination is the consciousness of something to be expressed, then the valet is the representation of the part of you that makes sure your access to your movement through life (your car) is well cared for when you are having an experience. Your relationship and sensation around what happens with the valet in your dream will inform your interpretation.

Valley: Anything that is part of the land is symbolically connected to your conscious mind. A valley can be thought of as a beautiful expanse of land nestled within the higher elevation that surrounds it. Often idyllic in nature, a valley represents the part of your awareness that is protected by the higher levels of thought that surround it. You cannot have the sense of a valley without having the sense of the mountains or hills that create it, so the valley becomes the representation of what can be appreciated when higher levels of thought have been acknowledged. A valley also connects to the protection and shelter created by such higher aspirations.

Vampire: When a vampire appears in your dream, someone or something is draining you of life force. Vampires are creatures of death that survive by drinking the blood of the living. Blood represents passion and life force. A vampire in your dreams represents some aspect of your personality or way of being that has the potential to drain you of your vibrancy and energy. Because vampires can only move about freely at night, they are in the symbolic realm of the shadow. This indicates that whatever issues are robbing you of your vitality are hidden from your conscious awareness and must be examined with this in mind. What we keep in the shadow are parts of ourselves that we can't accept and have difficulty integrating into our personal identity. Not doing so can suck the life force out of us until we face what we are resisting. As vampires are often portrayed as sexy or seductive, consider that the vampire may represent a situation or person in your life that seemed alluring at first but is now exhausting or depleting. There may be some habit, behavior, or emotional trait that is sucking you dry. Since vampires cast no reflection in a mirror, this may be a part of you that you are unable or unwilling to see directly. We often feel drained by responsibilities and the things we think we should be doing. You may want to become more aware of those things you are attached to in a negative way. Holding on to old attitudes and beliefs can be draining. Consider that it can be just as draining to avoid responsibilities that are legitimately yours. It is the ignorant victim who foolishly leaves the window open and unwittingly invites the vampire to visit. Other internal vampires include neediness, self-doubt, lack of forgiveness, and judgments. All of these kill passion for life. Commit to emotional healing and your vampires will return to the grave where they belong.

Van: Any mode of transportation connects to how you are moving through the journey of your life. A van has several connotations that must be taken into consideration. A minivan brings with it the connotations of a family and maternal instincts. For some older generations, a van is a symbol of youthful excess. The media has portrayed the van as a dark and ominous element associated with the predatory nature of rape and pedophilia. The context of the dream and your personal associations with this type of vehicle will illuminate how to interpret a dream that features a van.

Vase: A primary use for a vase is to hold cut flowers, a symbol of beholding beauty for beauty's sake. Therefore, a vase is symbolic of your own ability to contain this principle. The state of a vase in your dream will reflect the state of your ability to attract and express love.

Vault: The height of protection, a vault symbolizes an exaggerated need to protect your assets. This can be a positive image for guarding against loss, but can just as easily be an indication that you are hoarding due to a fear that what you have will be taken away from you. The resources that you keep hidden and locked away cannot do you any good unless they are flowing and moving in the world.

Vegetables: "Eat your vegetables; they're good for you" is one of the most prolific adages of parenting in the Western world. In this way, as a symbol, vegetables represent taking responsibility for doing what is good for you. In the same vein, the presence of vegetables in a dream may point to the potential for healthier choices in your life, and the way vegetables appear in the context of the dream may point to your relationship with such choices.

Veil: A veil obscures the object it covers, and in a dream, it connects to anything that is partially hidden. A veil as connected to a marriage ceremony has the added connotation of the separation between two things that are about to merge and integrate, and when the veil is lifted, that process has occurred. The lifting of the veil is also a New Age expression for accelerating consciousness. What confusion in your life needs to be or is about to be cleared up?

Vending Machine: Vending machines are primarily about convenient access to the idea of snacking. As such, both concepts must be applied to the symbolic meaning in a dream. The convenience factor relates to fulfilling an immediate need. However, the materials found in most vending machines have very little nutritional value, so the meaning is expanded to include the immediate fulfillment of a need through a low-consciousness choice. How are you feeding yourself?

Venereal Disease: Shame toward sexuality and negative consequences due to poor choices are at the center of this symbol. Take a look at the darker side of your feelings about sex if venereal disease is a part of your dream. The person who has symptoms in the dream should feature prominently in your interpretation. If it is you, then a general sense of sexual shame is being explored. If the person in your dream is someone other than you, use the character-aspect concept to associate what part of your own personality or decision-making process is emanating out of a shameful place.

Ventriloquist: The notion of speaking without detection and bringing a voice to an inanimate object is ultimately about inauthenticity and deception around your true voice. In what ways are you not speaking your truth?

Vest: A vest is an article of clothing that completely covers the most vulnerable part of the body, underneath which all of the vital organs are located. In this way, anything that relates to a vest in a dream connects to this center of your life force and the risks therein. How may you need to protect yourself right now? Also, playing things "close to the vest" implies some measure of restraint around revealing your desires and plans. A dream that features a vest may be asking you to hesitate before sharing your goals.

Veterinarian: A veterinarian is a doctor and as such connects to the archetype of healing. Veterinarians specialize in animals and therefore also relate to the wisdom available from the archetypes of the animal kingdom. As you heal certain wounds and limitations, you may be drawn closer to the power of animal medicine.

Video: This modern-day invention of moving pictures captured through a portable and ubiquitously accessible format pervades our culture in such an enormous way that there are literally dozens of ways in which the concept of "video" connects to other elements of symbolism. At the heart of it, video relates to our ability to create in our own image the experience of being human. We make movies and those movies become a permanent record of our journey. Once the lofty realm of only a privileged few, the technology of video has been made accessible to the masses. There are two sensibilities that must be considered when this symbol appears in a dream. The first is the creative impulse to capture an element of life unfolding. The ability to record, pause, fast-forward, and watch at your leisure instills a sense of control in the meaning of video in a dream.

Video Games: Video games are symbolic of total and utter escapism and mindless thought. They are a modern phenomenon that will have very different symbolic meaning based on your personal relationship to them. The diehard gamer will have a joyous experience of that escapism, while a critic might hold a more judgmental perspective. Where you stand on this continuum will provide the full picture for your interpretation. There is a perspective of video games that connects to a type of skill building; however, those skills have very little practical value outside of the realm of playing the game repeatedly. This is where the element of mindless thought enters into the symbolic meaning of video games. The presence of a video game in a dream is an ironic appearance of detachment and should be considered as a possible defense against whatever the unconscious mind may be attempting to express. If someone in your dream is playing a video game, understanding the character aspect in you that the person represents will identify what area of your consciousness is avoiding reality.

Viking: You are dreaming about a deep-rooted sense of archetypal power. The Vikings were a fearsome nation of traders and explorers who crossed the expanse of the Atlantic Ocean and Northern Europe early in the last millennium. We still connect to their powerful mythology led by the Norse god Odin through the collective unconscious. In modern media mythology, Vikings are ferocious warriors and conquerors. A dream about a Viking is to be calling upon this masculine-principle form of power to enter your life in some circumstance that is asking you to be more decisive and action-oriented. The most universal image of a Viking for people today is of a rugged sea traveler who is large in stature and strong in every way. If a Viking character appears in a dream, you may be being called by something from this mythology through the power of the collective.

Vineyard: A vineyard yields the fruit of the vine, and the symbolic meaning of this in a dream connects directly to the power of the grape. Wine is an ancient beverage that connects to celebration and ritual as well as a desire to escape and revel in excess. The vineyard is the source of all these elements of life.

Violet: Violet is the final color of the spectrum and is considered the most spiritual. It is connected to the crown of the head and therefore is not encumbered by the demands of the body. In this way, it is the vibration that is connected to us, but reaches upward into higher realms of energy. There are many examples of violet (more commonly referred to as purple) being associated with spirituality and high levels of consciousness. Merlin, the wizard from the King Arthur tales, is often depicted as wearing a purple hat. The Purple Heart medal represents the ultimate in bravery. In Catholicism during the holiday of Lent, all images of Christ are covered with purple. People who meditate with discipline report seeing violet light as part of the trance experience.

Virgin Mary: This is one of the most profoundly powerful archetypes of love and compassion. To be visited by Mother Mary is to be comforted at a deep level, as she has the ability to take away any pain, no matter how devastating that pain may be. Such a dream image is powerful indeed, even if you do not resonate with this image from a religious perspective.

Vitamins: When vitamins appear in a dream, you are concerned about your health and are looking for quick answers to whatever ails you. A supplement promises to make up for things that may be lacking elsewhere, so consider this dream as possibly pointing to a need for more balance.

Volcano: A volcano is symbolic of the possibility for a rageful, destructive expression after prolonged constraint or restraint. The outer image of the volcano reveals the aftermath of the essence of this symbol: constraint or restraint. The earth's crust can only hold back the brewing force of heat and combustion for so long before the buildup of pressure generates an explosive eruption that permanently changes the landscape. The intense heat and molten lava connect to feelings of rage, anger, and any other suppressed emotions of great power. The eruption is the breaking point that is either imminent or close at hand. A dormant volcano connects to past issues of pent-up stressors that no longer threaten your comfort and safety. An active volcano indicates an ongoing, volatile situation that is still emitting steam and could erupt again at any moment.

Vomiting: A dream that features vomiting reflects a need to reject and expel harmful emotions or ideas. The body possesses a natural reflex for getting rid of something harmful that has entered the digestive system. This regulatory impulse senses the presence of toxins or poisons and triggers a muscular contraction to expel the unwanted material. While vomiting can be caused by different stimuli, from tainted food to a viral infection to self-inducement, the symbolic meaning is the same: getting rid of something that is perceived to be bad. Because of the connection between vomit and food, this image will always have something to do with nurtur-

ance and self-care. If it shows up in a dream, there is something amiss in how you are being nurtured. (See *Gagging*.)

Voodoo: Voodoo is a fairly misunderstood religion that is pagan in nature and is often thought of as being connected to evil intentions. The common perspective about voodoo is that the practitioners of it have the power to control and manipulate human experience through magical interventions. To dream of this may connect to fears of things of a mystical nature and an expression of the shadowy side of the mysteries of life.

Voting: The ultimate act in the principle of democracy in action, voting connects to the power of the collective consciousness in action. If you are voting in a dream, you are exploring the ways in which small ideas or thoughts have the capacity to be gathered in great number in order to create change. There is also an element around voting that creates a boundary separation between sides, and you are either voting for or against something or someone. Such a dream may be asking you to take a stand in your life: yes or no.

Vulture: The vulture is a scavenger bird and is therefore a harbinger of death. All birds are messengers of some kind, and the vulture's presence is a signal that some negative experience has occurred.

Wading: Any image that involves water is connecting to your emotional experience. When you wade through water, you are generally up to waist-high, which is a definite commitment to being wet but still a manageable amount to navigate by virtue of walking. To understand this symbol in a dream, apply this same sensibility to your emotional experience: enough feeling to be considerably felt, but not so much that you can't continue to walk through the feelings.

Wagon: This very slow and archaic mode of transportation is most associated with the settlement of the United States by virtue of pioneers moving westward. In this way, the wagon is intrinsically bound up with the idea of taking great risks, eschewing the comforts of stability, and moving into new territory. Look to where in your life you are branching out into the unknown.

Waiter: As a person in your dream, the person bringing you your food is a character aspect of your personality. Since a waiter is the direct line of access to sustenance, this person's symbolic meaning connects to your ability to nurture and provide self-care. Consider the behavior and effects of the waiter in your dream as reflecting your own relationship with how well you are taking care of your needs.

Waiting Room: The implication of a waiting room is that something important is about to happen. If your dream takes place in such an environment, look to where in your life you may be anticipating an event or a change in direction. If you know what you are waiting for in your dream, add that to your interpretation.

Wake: A significant part of the grieving ritual in many traditions, a wake is where we gather around the body of someone who has just passed in order to pay our respects and mark the beginning of the process of letting go. In this way, a wake in a dream signifies that something has been sacrificed that will undoubtedly need to be processed in some way, and you are put on notice that a cycle of change is just around the corner.

Wall: Walls are boundaries that turn what would otherwise be an open space into something specific and functional. By compartmentalizing thoughts and ideas in our minds, we are able to manage our thoughts and feelings more effectively, and walls are symbolic of the structure that allows us to function in this way. The walls in your dreams represent this ability; the condition of these walls is to be interpreted as either helping this process or an indication that this process is being challenged.

Wallet: A wallet is a container for your money and identification. This makes it a symbol for your easy access to prosperity and self-awareness. If you have lost your wallet or it has been stolen in a dream, you are feeling separated from your ability to feel abundant and confident in who you are. If the wallet in your dreams belongs to someone else, you may need to examine new ways of connecting to prosperity and identity.

Wallpaper: Wallpaper is a covering that makes a room more pleasing in an aesthetic way, but as a symbol it is more connected to that which it is covering up. If there is wallpaper featured in your dream, take a look at what you are hiding or wanting to be kept out of view in your life.

Wand: The primary tool for the wizard or witch, the wand is a focal point for the energy to manifest your heart's desire. Connected to the principles of alchemy, the wand is a symbol for your ability to make radical changes in your life and to exert control over things that may not be controllable. An instrument of the wizard, the wand is the tool that allows this magical archetype to wield his or her power. The presence of Harry Potter in the zeitgeist has normalized this image as something accessible to all individuals. A wand in a dream is asking you to consider your own power to create anything you desire.

War: War in a dream indicates that shifting boundaries are causing enormous upheaval. The object of war is for one entity to obtain the land and/or resources of another. Therefore, war in a dream indicates change on such a large scale that it can only be accomplished by the use of major force. Our world is a set of organized boundaries that we know as countries. Our psyches are divided in a similar way. These boundaries are, ultimately, fluid. Things change—sometimes dramatically—which leaves us feeling vulnerable. When the change is sudden and violent, the unconscious may use a dream of war to express the enormity of the internal shift that's occurring.

Warehouse: You have some unfinished business or may be trying to postpone something. You also may be preparing to take action on something soon, but it is not yet time. Warehouses are places where we gather and store items that will later be distributed for their intended use. What is key to this symbol is that the storage is temporary—what is kept in a warehouse is eventually going to be moved somewhere else. In a dream, a warehouse is a symbol of change. In the arc of any transformation, a warehouse points to the middle of a greater shift—a point at which resources are gathered but have not quite yet arrived at their final destination.

Warts: Warts are unsightly growths that are created by a virus. They have long been associated with witches in fairy tales as evidence of their evil or bad intentions. If you have a wart or warts in your dream, you may be seeing the visible results of resentments and anger issues that have been previously hidden.

Washing: When some type of washing occurs in a dream, you are cleansing or clearing out something that no longer serves you. The primary symbolic meaning for any kind of bathing connects to this desire to be clean and available for social interaction with others. This can connect to unconscious feelings of dirtiness that are both literal and metaphorical. There may be ways in which you are feeling unclean and in need of purification. Anything that involves water in a dream is going to connect somehow to issues of emotions. Using water to bathe might point to a need or desire to immerse yourself in the realm of your feelings in order to cleanse yourself of the pain that life sometimes brings.

Washing Machine: As a function of routine, clothes are kept clean in this mechanism. In this way, a washing machine is a symbol of this impulse to keep elements of your life at a certain level of condition. You may be expressing a need to clear off thoughts or feelings that are unwanted.

Wasp: Like bees and ants, wasps have an overall totem energy that connects with community regulation and interdependent structure. Wasps are predators by nature, and lower forms of insects are their prey. Therefore, in the higher order of things, wasps regulate the population of the insect world by virtue of their predation instincts. If you are dreaming of wasps, you are looking to tap into your instinctive ability to manage large structures of thought and imagination. Consider that a wasp dream may indicate that this instinct is overworking itself and that you are being called to relinquish an obsessive need to control things that are really beyond your ability to control.

Watch: While this is soon becoming an archaic object in the realm of keeping time, the watch is a symbol of measurement and staying connected to the rhythm of life. More importantly, any mechanism of keeping time is about connecting with the world in agreement so that things can unfold simultaneously. If there is a watch in your dream, you may need to be more connected to the movement of your life and schedule and how that relates to the pace that other people are operating at.

Water: Water is the ultimate symbol of emotions in a dream. It also connects to things that rise up out of the unconscious mind. In fact, it could be said that emotions themselves are evidence of something that is occurring in the unconscious mind. In this way, water connects to both emotions and the unconscious. Human beings are made up of a great deal of water, and the welling up of feelings can cause this precious liquid to leak inexplicably out of your eyes in the form of tears. In this way, the presence of any water in a dream is asking you to consider the emotional side of your nature. The larger the body of water, the more feelings the dream is expressing. If the water is potentially overwhelming or dangerous, as in a tidal wave or waterfall, then the sense of danger must be added to your interpretation, as we are often afraid of feelings when they are greater than we think we can handle. Feelings flow and so does water, so the quality of movement of the water in your dream is pointing out the way in which you are experiencing your emotions. A slow creek is like a small amount of emotional flow that is significant but sustaining and calming. A raging river is more like the force of feelings that are much more intense and, if not navigated well, can be dangerous to your sense of well-being. Rain is the most like tears, and weather patterns in dreams that involve water may be pointing out the way you are experiencing or avoiding the easy flow of emotions associated with some current life experience.

Water Heater: Any image that relates to water is about your emotional experience. Hot water implies the addition of anger or other passionate sensibilities. Keep in mind that a water heater has the function of providing comfort and sanitization to your life. A healthy relationship to your emotional expression does the same. Look to how well you are connected to fluctuations in your emotional expression of water-heater features in your dream.

Waves: Energy moves in waves, and any dream that features this motion is connected to the fundamental structure behind all movement. Waves in water are about emotional fluctuations. Waves that are more related to the physical laws of the universe are similar, but are more about thoughts and shifts of intellect. When waves are easy to navigate, all is well, as you can easily allow yourself to move with them. However, they can suddenly become overwhelming in the dream world, and if this occurs, you are examining your relationship to things beyond your ability to control.

Web Cam: This relatively new invention allows more direct connectivity in the world through the Internet. As this way of connection expands through technology, it creates a new level of consciousness. The web cam is the new "eyes" of this consciousness. How are you allowing yourself to be seen in this new world that is being created? What is it that you wish to explore in others? These are the questions that a dream that features a web cam is asking you.

Wedding: A wedding is the ceremonial joining of two aspects of character in a commitment to work together in order to create a new way of being in the world that the relationship represents. The ritual of a wedding is the declaration of your intention to have a significant shift of perspective. If your life is calling forth a transformation, a dream about a wedding is significant evidence that the change is at hand.

Weeds: Your random thoughts of worry, doubt, and anxiety may be crowding out your ability to feel joy. Weeds are the unwanted plants that disrupt our sense of harmony created by the lovely flowers or vegetables we would rather have growing in our gardens. If allowed to, weeds would overtake what we are cultivating and strangle the life out of what we have chosen to plant. In a dream, weeds represent these ubiquitous thoughts, habits, and patterns.

Weights: Weights are used to counterbalance the muscles in the body in order to help them expand and grow. Weights connect to the principle that controlled effort is a part of the idea of change. If weights appear in your dream, you desire to increase and expand certain aspects of your identity and are willing to make the effort to create that change. Such a dream may also point to resistance to the work associated with facing change. Look to the context of the dream to illuminate which sensibility is being expressed.

Well: The availability of emotional sustenance from deep places is what this dream is expressing. Anytime water is featured in a dream, what is being expressed is the state of your emotional life. Water is the necessary ingredient to sustaining life. A well is dug to provide consistent access to this lifegiving elixir. In the symbolic world, there is a correlation between water as emotion and water as life-sustaining substance. We need water to live, and our souls need emotional balance to thrive. A well is often a community resource, so the state of the well in your dream may be revealing your current life's relationship to your own feelings and how much you may have to give to oth-ers. If your well is running dry, you may need to consider your own needs first. If it is over-flowing, take a look at how your emotional life may be more than you can contain.

Welts: A welt is evidence of wrongs done, the aftermath of attack, or an underlying problem that is now beginning to become notice-able. Your interpretation will vary depending on the part of the body that is affected. The arms relate to strength and action, and the legs connect to movement and motiva-tion. The hands represent creativity, and the face connects to the persona you show to the world. Additionally, consider that a welt on an exposed part of the body means your wound is visible to others. An area that is generally covered by clothing may connect to the ability or desire to hide your wounds.

Werewolf: The beast lives within all human be-ings, but when bit by the werewolf, the beast unleashes the shadow in relationship to the cycle of the moon. The moon represents all that is unconscious, and when it is full, we are able to see more of what is usually hid-den. The werewolf is one of the most power-ful symbols of the dark parts of human na-ture that must be faced when looking at the unknown.

Whale: To understand the symbolic meaning of this majestic animal, consider its habitat. The ocean represents our deep unconscious mind, and the whale is the animal that breathes air, but can dive to the depths and explore what is under the surface. In this way, the whale is a powerful representation of our ability to connect to emotions and currents that run very deep and are typically hidden from our conscious awareness. When a whale appears in your dreams, the medicine that is present is this ability to dive below the surface to gain great wisdom.

Whale Song: You are being called to dive deep and explore emotions and patterns that are hidden just below the surface of your consciousness. (See *Whale*.)

Wheel: The circle is the most pure and perfect shape in geometry. The functionality of the wheel is thought to have changed civilization more dramatically than any other invention. Through the wheel, travel and connectivity are increased exponentially. In this way, a wheel is the fundamental structure that allows powerful movement through life. The state of a wheel in a dream is a reflection of how well you are able to progress on the path of creating what you desire.

Wheelchair: The wheelchair eradicates a level of disability by providing movement where movement is challenged. In this way, it is a symbol of triumph over adversity. Additionally, a wheelchair may appear in a dream when you feel a need or desire to continue moving through your life while expending less effort.

Whirlpool: Any image involving water relates to an experience of your emotions. In the case of a whirlpool, the implication is that there is a circling back over some focused point again and again until the momentum created pulls you down to your ultimate demise. This is what happens when you perseverate over some challenge that is causing an emotional reaction as a persistent thought or feeling. The whirlpool in your dream is asking you to consider what you can't let go of.

Whisper: You are receiving a message of heightened importance; pay close attention to what your dreams are telling you. Even if you cannot understand what is being whispered in your dream, trust that the information is being received at the deepest level, at the level of the whisper itself. A whisper in a dream may also imply that the message that is on its way to you is not yet ready to be heard and understood or ready for public dissemination. A process may be incomplete.

White: Purity and wholeness are represented by white, as this is the unification of all the colors of light that are visible to the human eye. For some, white is the color of highest spirituality. For others, it connects to the perfection that arises out of the absence of contamination, as in virginity and chastity. An object that appears white reflects the light outward, absorbing none of the individual colors of the spectrum. It is this concept of reflecting the light that shines onto you back out into the world that embodies the high consciousness associated with the color white. (See *Colors*.)

White Animals: There is a rich history in many aboriginal cultures that is still part of the collective consciousness around the purity of the color white in the realm of animal totems. Most commonly associated with the buffalo, the wolf, and large cats, the elevation of an animal's power is what is being expressed when that animal appears as white. In the color spectrum, white is perceived when all the vibrations of light are combined, so the symbolic meaning of white relates to complete integration and wholeness. It is a holy color (pun intended). Any animal that appears in your dream as white is a very sacred visitation indeed.

White House: This building is itself a symbol for the United States, modern democracy, and the American Dream. To be dreaming of the White House may be a reflection of your desire to achieve higher levels of expression in your community. Also, such a dream image may appear when your association with the state of affairs in politics is either inspiring you or causing you to despair. As the home of the president, the White House represents the personal consciousness of the freedoms that are fundamental to the way of life in the United States. A dream that features this image is first and foremost an expression of the collective consciousness of the United States as a great world power. Additionally, the dreamer's personal associations with government and politics must be added for a satisfying interpretation.

Wig: Anything that covers the head relates to your thoughts and intellect. A wig covers the head and is primarily a symbol that relates to wanting to hide your true thoughts and present something more to your liking to the world. There may also be elements of attractiveness and feeling deserving of attention that are highlighted if a wig appears in your dream.

Will: The implication with a will is that someone has died. In the world of symbolism and dreams, this means that there has recently been a change where you have allowed some aspect of your personality to be sacrificed so that change could take place, like letting go of an old habit, belief, or way of behaving. The will is then a symbol for the gift and benefit that such an aspect has left behind. There is always value to a challenging situation, and a will in a dream is pointing that out.

Wind: Things may be changing rapidly. Your thoughts may be increasing in their intensity. These two notions may or may not be related, as wind has several connotations in symbolism. Anything connected to the air or sky correlates with the intellect and the realm of thoughts. Wind is an increase in the movement of this area of consciousness and therefore will always relate to how you are thinking about your world. The phrase "the winds of change" will also feature strongly in any dream that has wind in it, as increased gustiness has the capacity to alter things quite dramatically.

Window: You may want to see more deeply into some situation in your life. If you are inside a space and looking out through a window, the dream may be expressing a desire to move into new territory and free yourself from current restrictions. You may be experiencing a new opening of perspective in some area of your life.

Wine: Wine is known as the fruit of the vine and is one of the world's oldest fermented beverages. The alcohol in wine connects it symbolically with escapism and overindulgence. However, there is great reverence associated with wine, as it is often featured in rituals that celebrate spiritual perspectives. The context of your dream will inform you of which direction to take your interpretation. (See *Vineyard*.)

Wings: Flying implies an ability to defy gravity, which is one of the most powerful symbols in the human experience. Wings are the agents of flight, and in this way they are evidence of your own power to elevate your experience up from any depths. Consider what the wings in your dream are attached to. Once you have a satisfying interpretation of that symbol, add the element of rising to higher consciousness through the presence of wings.

Wisdom Teeth: These teeth are so named because they usually come in later in life when a person has gained more wisdom through age. They are often the cause of discomfort, from blockage to generating abscesses, and need to be removed. To dream of them is to be recognizing a shift in your development to a higher level of wisdom and the discomfort that comes from growth.

Witch: This is an archetypal character aspect that connects you to magic, the occult, and the mysteries of life. The witch is a creature of relatively modern invention with little, if any, presence in the older mythologies that have shaped Western culture. Today, the witch figures prominently in contemporary fairy tale folklore and is a staple character of Halloween. The witch no longer heals and ministers to people—now she casts evil spells and eats children. Since this is an archetype, how the witch appears in your dream is important to your understanding of your own personal development. The areas of life ruled by this archetype are mysticism, healing, and magic, primarily in the feminine principle, which relates to creativity, receptivity, nurturance, and caretaking. Examine your witch for character, skill, and motivation. Her character will inform you of the level of good versus evil within your psyche. The power of her skills will inform you of your personal access to the magic in the universe. Understanding what inspires her will get you in touch with your own movement toward integration and away from manipulation. Any number of haglike female characters could be considered the witch archetype. Some may in fact be evil, while others may be disenfranchised healers. Given the witch's origins in mysticism and the history of misunderstandings over the centuries, it is important to consider this duality when interpreting this symbol. Though she may inspire fear and dread, the witch has powerful magic that, if understood and properly used, can be invaluable to the human experience.

Wizard: This very powerful archetype has taken on new meaning in the past few decades because of the presence of the wizard in film, television, and video games. The wizard is the arbiter of magic, which in human development relates to the ability to create drastic change in an instant. In Jungian psychology, this archetype is known as the magus, or magician, and he brings with him the capacity to alter your perspective of life in miraculous ways through the power of increased wisdom. In a dream, the wizard is a harbinger and bringer of great and important information, so pay attention. The wizard has a lot in common with the witch.

Wolf: One of the most powerful totems associated with the feminine principle, the wolf is a pack animal that is most active at night. This nocturnal behavior connects the wolf symbolically with the shadow and your ability to maneuver in the darker territories of your nature. The wolf's strong association with the moon also cements the relationship between the wolf as a symbol and the moon's connection to cycles, changeability, and all things that relate to the movement of the unconscious mind. When the wolf appears in a dream, you are being guided by very strong forces that know their way around the darker recesses of the psyche.

Womb: The womb is where all life is created and prepared for birth. This is a powerful symbol of gestation, whether what is about to be born is a life, an idea, a creative impulse, or anything that you desire to manifest. An empty womb indicates a sense of loss or lack around your power to create something new. If there is indeed something growing in the womb of your dream, patience will be required to allow the process that you are engaged in to run its course.

Wood: Wood is one of the mainstays of our existence and is even considered an element in some of the elemental systems in various cultures. It was not that long ago in human history that everything of strength and fortitude was created out of wood. While today wood is no longer the strongest material we work with, it symbolically represents a desire to create something of substance that simultaneously connects us to the earth in a grounded fashion. Anything made out of wood in a dream is asking you to connect more to nature and your earthly origins.

Work: You are dreaming of your daytime obligations and responsibilities. We are a society centered around jobs and work. Most people relate to their jobs as something that they have to do in order to make ends meet. In this way, your job and your workplace are symbolic representations of all of the responsibilities and obligations that life presents you with. Very often, dreams about your work are to be taken very literally. You spend a great deal of time there, and your dreams may be filled with images from your day. A dream taking place where you work may very well be a compensatory dream helping you cope with the stress and wake up the next day to face it all over again. However, such a dream could also be a convenient way for your unconscious to express feelings surrounding other responsibilities and obligations that need attention. Not all dreams taking place at work are stressful. If this is the case, use your feelings about your job, the environment at work, and your coworkers to help you identify what elements of your own personality are being expressed in your dream. Many people have a very different sense of self in the workplace than in other parts of life. Consider your relationship to your work carefully when examining a dream that took place there.

World Trade Center: A global symbol for the power of the United States of America, the World Trade Center entered the permanent collective consciousness as a symbol of indomitable spirit and the fundamental human capacity to withstand change at a terrible and dramatic level. No attack can actually touch you at the level of your soul, and the presence of the World Trade Center in a dream may be reminding you of the bigger picture of your very existence as a spiritual journey. This may be most needed when facing the collapse of things in your life that you hold dear.

Wound(s): This evidence of a past experience is revealing current levels of vulnerability. A wound is an indication that something dramatic and dangerous has already occurred. It not only is evidence of the event itself, but also symbolizes the residual damage that the wounding event may have left you vulnerable to. While wounds to the body are physical in nature, they can symbolically represent emotional, psychological, and spiritual wounds as well. The most important thing to con-

sider about a wound in a dream is the state that it has left you in. The greater the risk, the higher the stakes of the life situation that the dream is expressing. The presence of infection may be revealing that an old hurt left unattended is festering and causing you pain and discomfort. Anything that results in a loss of blood relates to passion and life force being leaked out or dissipated.

Wreath: The wreath itself is a symbol with origins in pagan cultures where branches of trees were fashioned into circles to symbolize the continuity of the seasons. If you dream of a wreath, you may be being inspired by the holiday season, but what is being expressed is the deeper connection to the original meaning of honoring the constant cycle of the dying off in winter so that spring will come again.

X-ray: When an x-ray appears in a dream, you wish you could see through an obstacle to perceive something more clearly. The radioactive nature of an x-ray is a health risk, so something in a dream that involves an x-ray may be expressing the dangers inherent in looking too deeply into something.

Yard: A house represents your sense of self, and the yard is the part of the house that bridges the gap between your personal identity and your public persona. A yard is connected to the house itself, so that it is directly expressing part of who you are. It is outside and therefore is also related to the public part of yourself that you allow people to see. Since people have a lot invested in how they present their yards for public scrutiny, the yard in your dream is a symbol for this very same kind of attention toward superficial details that project a desired identity that may or may not be true to what is happening on the inside. A front yard is more public, and the back or side yard to a house relates to the same general interpretation, with the caveat that a deeper sense of privacy or an invitation is required in order for that part of your nature to be visible.

Yard Sale: One has a yard sale to get rid of stuff that is no longer wanted but could be beneficial to others in exchange for money. In this way, the symbolic meaning of a yard sale connects to this desire to transform the past into a sense of abundance now. A desire to clear things out and make space for something new could also connect to this image in a dream.

Yarmulke: The yarmulke is a sign of devotion and respect in the Jewish tradition, where keeping one's head covered at all times is a symbol of reverence to God. It is also a visible identifier for the outside world to recognize a person of the Jewish faith. In this way, a yarmulke symbolizes both this inner sense of devotion and this outer sense of identity. Your interpretation will depend largely on your personal relationship to this particular religion.

Yelling: We raise our voices in volume when what we are expressing is fueled by anger or a sense of higher stakes with regard to what we want to express. In this way, yelling in a dream is an indication that whatever is going on has a heightened level of importance. This is also a typical dream image when the dreamer is processing deep-seated rage. Often, the desire to yell is present but the voice is unable to respond, and the dreamer is left feeling shut down by the overwhelming experience. This image in a dream is a reflection of the overwhelming way in which rage can be crippling and must therefore be examined, processed, and released. Examine who you are yelling at for more details about where in your psyche the breakdown is occurring. If you are being yelled at by a character within your dream, who that person is will offer you clues to where in your life the rage is originating.

Yellow: Yellow is the color of emotions and gut feelings and is appropriately centered in the solar plexus, creating a relationship with this area of the body and the color of the sun. The solar plexus is where we experience our feelings and the rapid shift from one state to another. Associated with the adrenal glands, yellow connects to adrenaline, the chemical manufactured by the brain that creates anxiety, sudden bursts of energy, and the fight-or-flight response. This is reflected in the use of yellow to indicate caution in signage and traffic management. Of course, many emotional states are very pleasant, which is embodied by our experience of sunlight as warm and comforting. (See *Colors*.)

Yin/Yang: This symbol from the Hindu tradition represents balance, wholeness, and integration. In a dream, it is a powerful expression of these principles calling to you from a higher realm of consciousness.

Yoga: The practice of yoga is one of the most ancient disciplines on the planet. It is based on the principle of moving the body through space and holding particular poses for long periods of time to stimulate organs and the glandular system. The fortitude required to hold the poses long past what is comfortable is the foundation of a successful practice. When yoga appears in a dream, you are being pushed past your comfort zone in some area of your life.

Yogurt: This delicious food is created when a bacteria is introduced into a dairy product. This contradiction is what is at the heart of yogurt as a symbol, for it reminds us that sometimes that which is sour can add to your experience when you remove the judgment from the mix. This symbol in a dream may be asking you to accept some distasteful elements and trust that there is good in everything.

Zebra: One of the most remarkable visual creations in the animal kingdom, the zebra reminds you to stand out from the crowd. The medicine of this animal totem is originality and whimsy. The zebra's power lies in its unique stripes. When a zebra appears in a dream, you are being called upon to appreciate your individuality without compromise.

Zero: This number symbolizes an absence of information; the beginning before the beginning.

Zip Code: The zip code system is designed to catalog and organize an enormous amount of data. If a dream features this as a prominent image, the need to codify your sense of direction or bring clarity to otherwise chaotic thoughts is being highlighted. The expansion of digital communication is slowly making snail mail all but obsolete, so such a dream may harken back to old ways of establishing boundaries.

Zip Line: A dream with a zip line in it may be expressing a desire for a certain amount of freedom or risk-taking that is safe and contained.

Zipper: Something needs to be either contained or released. A zipper that is broken may point to an inability to control whether you let something be revealed or not. Being unable to open a zipper may point to some level of frustration around feeling confined or controlled.

Zodiac: The zodiac is a system of archetypes that together describe the human experience as a function of twelve different styles or sensibilities. While not everyone believes in the validity of astrology, these archetypes are embedded in the collective consciousness of the Western world.

If you dream about any aspect of the zodiac, you are being invited to consider archetypal thinking.

Zombie: You may be lacking passion or life force when a zombie appears in a dream. The definition of a zombie is one who is no longer alive but rises to walk again, seeking human flesh to eat. The walking dead are a symbolic representation for those moments in life when the very process of living is devoid of any joy or vibrant energy. A zombie in a dream may signal a period of very low energy or a depletion of energy by some situation in your life. The real danger of zombies is their ability to transform their victims into zombies as well. In this way, they represent the cumulative effects of depression, fatigue, and a sedentary lifestyle. Additionally, zombies can also be an image inspired by a person or persons in your life who rob you of joy by virtue of their negative disposition.

Zoo: This symbol relates to the repression of deep, primal urges and instincts. No matter how humane the conditions of a zoo are, there is the inescapable fact that the animals are out of their natural environments and on display. Whether done for amusement or educational value, the restraint of an animal is symbolic of the restraint of primal instincts. In a dream, this connects to those urges that our thinking, rational mind keeps beneath the surface of our consciousness. We project onto caged animals qualities that live inside of us and ponder them from a distance through the bars. The more dangerous the animal, the more primal the urge being repressed. A more docile creature on display might connect to lost innocence. Whatever qualities you ascribe to the zoo animal, it is those qualities that live in yourself that are being compartmentalized by your psyche and exhibited in your dream.

INDEX

TO WRITE TO THE AUTHOR

If you wish to contact the author or would like more information about this book, please write to the author in care of Llewellyn Worldwide Ltd. and we will forward your request. Both the author and the publisher appreciate hearing from you and learning of your enjoyment of this book and how it has helped you. Llewellyn Worldwide Ltd. cannot guarantee that every letter written to the author can be answered, but all will be forwarded. Please write to:

Dr. Michael Lennox
℅ Llewellyn Worldwide
2143 Wooddale Drive
Woodbury, MN 55125-2989
Please enclose a self-addressed stamped envelope for reply,
or $1.00 to cover costs. If outside the USA, enclose
an international postal reply coupon.

Many of Llewellyn's authors have websites with additional information and resources.

For more information, please visit our website at www.llewellyn.com.

GET MORE AT LLEWELLYN.COM

Visit us online to browse hundreds of our books and decks, plus sign up to receive our e-newsletters and exclusive online offers.

- • Free tarot readings • Spell-a-Day • Moon phases
- • Recipes, spells, and tips • Blogs • Encyclopedia
- • Author interviews, articles, and upcoming events

GET SOCIAL WITH LLEWELLYN

Find us on

www.Facebook.com/LlewellynBooks

Follow us on

www.Twitter.com/Llewellynbooks

GET BOOKS AT LLEWELLYN

LLEWELLYN ORDERING INFORMATION

 Order online: Visit our website at www.llewellyn.com to select your books and place an order on our secure server.

 Order by phone:
- • Call toll free within the U.S. at 1-877-NEW-WRLD (1-877-639-9753)
- • Call toll free within Canada at 1-866-NEW-WRLD (1-866-639-9753)
- • We accept VISA, MasterCard, and American Express

 Order by mail:
Send the full price of your order (MN residents add 6.875% sales tax) in U.S. funds, plus postage and handling to: Llewellyn Worldwide, 2143 Wooddale Drive Woodbury, MN 55125-2989

POSTAGE AND HANDLING:

STANDARD: (U.S. & Canada)
(Please allow 12 business days)
$25.00 and under, add $4.00.
$25.01 and over, FREE SHIPPING.

INTERNATIONAL ORDERS (airmail only):
$16.00 for one book, plus $3.00 for each additional book.

Visit us online for more shipping options. Prices subject to change.

FREE CATALOG!

To order, call
1-877-
NEW-WRLD
ext. 8236
or visit our
website

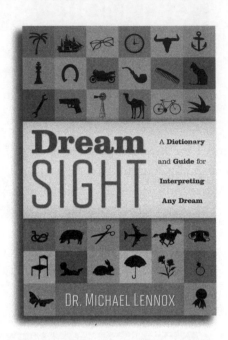

Dream Sight
A Dictionary and Guide for Interpreting Any Dream
DR. MICHAEL LENNOX

Most dream dictionaries contain brief, overly generic meanings of the universal symbols that appear in our dreams. *Dream Sight* is different. With in-depth, classic meanings and an empowering technique for personalized interpretation, *Dream Sight* is the most complete and balanced guide to understanding your dreams.

Based on twenty years of experience, psychologist and renowned dream expert Dr. Michael Lennox presents his easy and practical three-step approach. Begin by reading the universal symbols in your dreams, then consider the context, and finally pinpoint your unique personal associations. This method leads to deeper, more profound interpretations that will unlock the mysteries of your unconscious mind. You'll also get insight into common types of dreams—recurring, precognitive, nightmares, and more—plus advice for remembering your dreams and looking at them objectively.

Combining warmth and a touch of irreverence, *Dream Sight* is both a unique teaching tool and a fun reference guide that gives you everything you need to understand your dreams and your innermost self.

Features an alphabetized list of over 300 dream symbols and images with classic meanings.

978-0-7387-2602-1, 408 pp., 6 x 9   **$19.95**

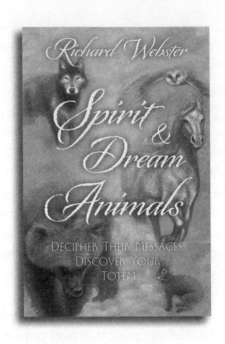

Spirit & Dream Animals
Decipher Their Messages, Discover Your Totem
RICHARD WEBSTER

Have you ever dreamt about a bird, wolf, lion, or some other creature and wondered what it meant? From the cheerful bluebird to the courageous tiger, the animals in our dreams often have specific messages that can guide us on our life paths. Once you know your totem animal, you can call upon it for healing, protection, strength, wisdom, and spiritual guidance.

In *Spirit & Dream Animals*, bestselling author Richard Webster will teach you simple and fun techniques to identify and connect with your spirit animal.

- Lucid Dreaming
- Astrology
- Numerology
- Pendulum divination
- Meditation
- Dancing

You'll also learn about animal symbolism in various cultures, the shamanic tradition, and how to recall your dreams more easily and vividly. This handy book also features an alphabetical dream-animal dictionary. With it, you can quickly look up the symbolic meanings of more than 150 creatures—including pets and domestic, wild, and legendary animals.

978-0-7387-2770-7, 264 pp., 5 ³⁄₁₆ x 8   **$14.95**

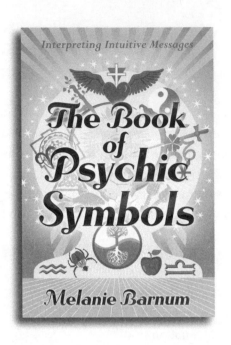

The Book of Psychic Symbols
Interpreting Intuitive Messages
Melanie Barnum

A strong feeling, a remarkable coincidence, a strange dream … What may seem ordinary could actually be an important message: a helpful hint or a warning from a deceased love one or spirit guide. Open yourself to a wealth of guidance and opportunities by learning how to recognize and interpret the signs and synchronicities all around us. *The Book of Psychic Symbols* can help you decode dreams, intuitive flashes, and all psychic impressions. Intuitive counselor Melanie Barnum explains what psychic symbols are, how we receive them, and where they come from. She also shares amazing stories from her life that clarify how the wondrous intuitive process works. In addition to a comprehensive dictionary of 500 symbols, there are many practical exercises for exploring symbols in your life, fortifying your natural intuition, and using psychic symbols to manifest your desires.

978-0-7387-2303-7, 288 pp., 6 x 9   **$15.95**

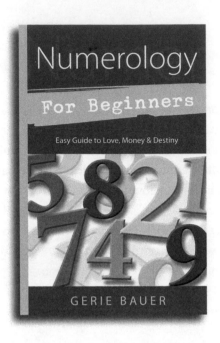

Numerology for Beginners
Easy Guide to Love, Money & Destiny
GERIE BAUER

Get fresh new insight into your personality, energy cycles, and future with numerology. Numerology can answer dozens of questions about character traits, upcoming opportunities, careers, and relationships—all you need is a name, a birth date, and this book! Within minutes, you can learn how to use the numbers 1 through 9 to calculate the energy vibrations around almost anything in your life—from love to the lottery. You can also determine in advance what sort of opportunities are in your future.

978-1-56718-057-2, 336 pp., 5 ³⁄₁₆ x 8 $13.95

Discover *your*
Psychic Type

Developing and Using Your Natural Intuition

SHERRIE DILLARD

Discover Your Psychic Type
Developing and Using Your Natural Intuition
Sherrie Dillard

Intuition and spiritual growth are indelibly linked, according to professional psychic and therapist Sherrie Dillard. Offering a personalized approach to psychic development, this breakthrough guide introduces four different psychic types and explains how to develop the unique spiritual capabilities of each.

Are you a physical, mental, emotional, or spiritual intuitive? Take Dillard's insightful quiz to find out. Discover more about each type's intuitive nature, personality, potential physical weaknesses, and more. There are guided meditations for each kind of intuitive, as well as exercises to hone your psychic skills. Remarkable stories from the author's professional life illustrate the incredible power of intuition and its connection to the spirit world, inner wisdom, and your higher self.

From psychic protection to spirit guides to mystical states, Dillard offers guidance as you evolve toward the final destination of every psychic type: union with the divine.

978-0-7387-1278-9, 288 pp., 5 ³⁄₁₆ x 8   **$15.99**

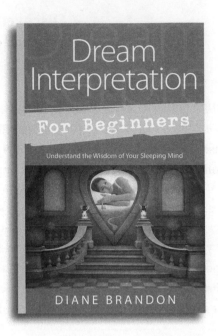

Dream Interpretation
For Beginners

Understand the Wisdom of Your Sleeping Mind

DIANE BRANDON

Dream Interpretation for Beginners
Understand the Wisdom of Your Sleeping Mind
Diane Brandon

Decode the messages that your dreams may be trying to give you. Exploring your world of dreams, as well as your world of sleep, can enrich your life, improve your relationships, and help you achieve a sense of personal unfolding. *Dream Interpretation for Beginners* shows you how to use dreams for personal and spiritual growth, as well as improved problem-solving and deeper insight into your life.

978-0-7387-4191-8, 312 pp., 5 ³⁄₁₆ x 8   **$15.99**

Psychic Development for Beginners
An Easy Guide to Developing and Releasing Your Psychic Abilities
William W. Hewitt

Psychic Development for Beginners provides detailed instruction on developing your sixth sense, or psychic ability. Improve your sense of worth, your sense of responsibility, and therefore your ability to make a difference in the world. Innovative exercises like "The Skyscraper" allow beginning students of psychic development to quickly realize personal and material gain through their own natural talent.

Benefits range from the practical to spiritual. Find a parking space anywhere, handle a difficult salesperson, choose a compatible partner, and even access different time periods! Practice psychic healing on pets or humans—and be pleasantly surprised by your results. Use psychic commands to prevent dozing while driving. Preview out-of-body travel, cosmic consciousness, and other alternative realities. Instruction in *Psychic Development for Beginners* is supported by personal anecdotes, 44 psychic development exercises, and 28 related psychic case studies to help students gain a comprehensive understanding of the psychic realm.

978-1-56718-360-3, 216 pp., 5 ³⁄₁₆ x 8   **$13.99**

Melissa Alvarez

Your Psychic Self

A Quick and Easy Guide to
Discovering Your Intuitive Talents

Your Psychic Self
A Quick and Easy Guide to Discovering Your Intuitive Talents
Melissa Alvarez

Ever wondered if you were psychic? *Your Psychic Self* is designed to help you recognize your natural intuitive abilities and strengthen them to enhance your daily life.

In an easy, conversational tone, professional intuitive Melissa Alvarez shares her own experiences and offers direction for discovering where your skills and interests lie within the psychic and metaphysical worlds.

Good for beginners or as an all-around reference, this guide gives you an overview of the signs of intuition, different kinds of abilities, psychic experiences, and forms of intuitive communication. Understand the types of readers—from psychic detectives to animal communicators—and explore your own connection with spirit beings. Use the practice exercises to develop your abilities and learn how to protect yourself from negative influences.

978-0-7387-3189-6, 264 pp., 5 ³⁄₁₆ x 8   **$14.99**

You Are Clairvoyant
Simple Ways to Develop Your Psychic Gifts
BelindaGrace

Clairvoyance is a gateway to unimagined possibilities—and it's within us all. Learn how to activate this powerful skill and use it to find greater happiness and fulfillment.

Anyone can connect with inner wisdom and divine guidance by following these simple techniques and easy exercises. On this enlightening path, you'll meet and talk to angels and spirit guides for assistance, gain insights into past lives to overcome negative patterns and find healing, conduct psychic conversations to get your point across, and get answers to important questions through automatic writing. This inspiring guide, written by a professional clairvoyant healer, features the author's true life stories and countless ways to use the gift of clairvoyance to transform your life—and yourself.

978-0-7387-2723-3, 240 pp., 5 ³⁄₁₆ x 8 $14.95

You Are a Medium
Discover Your Natural Abilities to Communicate with the Other Side
SHERRIE DILLARD

Discovering your natural abilities to communicate with the other side is as simple as taking a unique quiz to determine your medium type. Once you know how your subtle abilities work, you can develop your skills with the simple exercises and techniques presented in *You Are a Medium*.

Everyone has the innate ability to communicate with those who have passed on. As you become more confident with your medium abilities, be prepared to make a breathtaking discovery: not only do our deceased loved ones help us from the other side—we also help them! Sharing inspiring case studies from her work with clients and students, Sherrie Dillard shows that when we succeed in learning our soul lessons, we become beacons of light to those in the beyond.

978-0-7387-3792-8, 288 pp., 6 x 9   **$16.99**

To order, call 1-877-NEW-WRLD
Prices subject to change without notice
Order at Llewellyn.com 24 hours a day, 7 days a week!